THE NEIGHBORHOOD OUTFIT

THE NEIGHBORHOOD OUTFIT

ORGANIZED CRIME IN CHICAGO HEIGHTS

Louis Corsino

UNIVERSITY OF ILLINOIS PRESS
Urbana, Chicago, and Springfield

∞ This book is printed on acid-free paper.

Library of Congress Cataloging-in-Publication Data
Corsino, Louis, 1948–
The neighborhood outfit: organized crime
in Chicago Heights / Louis Corsino.
pages cm
Includes bibliographical references and index.
ISBN 978-0-252-03871-6 (hardback)
ISBN 978-0-252-08029-6 (paper)
ISBN 978-0-252-09666-2 (ebook)
1. Organized crime—Illinois—Chicago Heights—History.
2. Italian Americans—Illinois—Chicago Heights—History.
3. Chicago Heights (Ill.)—History.
I. Title.
HV6795.C43C67 2014
364.10609773'1—dc23 2014018821

To

The Immigrants and Their Descendants in Chicago Heights

CONTENTS

PREFACE

This book has been some fifteen years in the making. Though in a more comprehensive sense, it has been brewing since I was a young child. Growing up in Chicago Heights, Illinois, I experienced what was in many ways a typical childhood. My father went to work each day; my mother stayed home; my grandparents lived down the block; my house was filled with the working-class status symbols so common during this era (linoleum floors inside the house, aluminum siding on the outside). I earned good grades in the public schools (though my older sisters always earned better grades); I went away to school (my sisters were not encouraged to do so) as a first-generation college student. This seemed like a pretty normal life for a second-generation Italian family in Chicago Heights, Illinois, during the 1950s and 1960s.

There were signs, however, that there was a world that lay underneath this mundane life—an underworld, so to speak. My father, Andy Corsino, worked for a large part of his life as a "route man" for a jukebox company in Chicago Heights—Co-Operative Music. This put him in touch with a cast of friends and associates who seemed, in retrospect, a bit unusual. Perhaps, the names should have been a giveaway—One-Armed Jimmy, Black George, Johnny Bum, among others. At the same time, on more than one occasion, my family and my family's circle of friends would have strikingly similar items of dress or household appliances. Years later, Martin Scorsese captured this experience brilliantly in an opening scene of *Goodfellas* when the mobsters hanging out at the cabstand were wearing the exact, same yellow sweaters that had presumably "fallen off of the truck." So many years after my own experiences in Chicago Heights, this scene struck a response cord. And I remember extended family get-togethers at my grandparents' house that would periodically become disrupted when Compare John (pronounced JO-wan) (or John Roberts aka Giovanni Roberto) made one of his visits to my grandparents' family basement. Roberts commanded great respect on the part of the adults and children. At that time, I had little idea of who Roberts was and why he was treated with this extreme deference. Still, I knew that when we took the family picture (which appears on the back cover), Roberts was to occupy the center position. I knew enough not to ask why.

Over time, I began to put the pieces together. I came to realize that my father (as well as other relatives and family friends) were "connected." For example, John Roberts was a leading organized crime head in Chicago Heights and was listed among the top Mafia leaders in the nation by the United States Treasury Department. Other family members and friends were variously at some point in time bootleggers, bagmen, and "muscle." I also realized that my father knew a great deal about the organized crime operations and would on occasion be called upon to carry out routine tasks for the "boys" of Chicago Heights or the Chicago Heights crew of the larger Chicago Outfit, not that my father was a part of the inner circle or took part in any of the violent activities. More so, he was a person who serviced the jukeboxes in the local taverns but who knew about and was friends with the Outfit guys who handled the slot machines in the backroom. Or he would be called up by one of the Outfit bosses to help load the slot machines on a truck in the middle of the night to avoid confiscation by a raid the next morning. Or he would be asked to dispose of incriminating evidence involving any number of organized crime activities perpetrated by the boys.

This more fully formed awareness of my family history came at a cost as I matured intellectually. It raised personal and academic questions as to how a person like my father could mesh himself into this criminal underworld. Characterizations of Outfit members as "thugs" or "goons" did not seem to capture the realities of my father's or most men's participation in organized crime. These were moral classifications, which though justified in a few instances, did not advance an understanding as to why Italians, in particular, dominated organized crime for the greater part of the century. Thus, I wondered whether it be correct to assume that Italians had a greater proportion of thugs and goons relative to other groups in the population and thus were better adapted to organized crime. By the same token, I did not feel comfortable with the explanation that the historical link between organized crime and Italians was simply the result of a "few bad apples." Again, such pronouncements seem also to be driven by moral concerns. Certainly, only a small proportion of Italians have participated in organized crime. But a link exists nevertheless and this link ran deeper and was more widespread than many Italians were willing to concede. My family and family friends stood witness to this. How then, I asked, could I make sense of this affinity without resorting to a search for some endemic, enduring stereotypical criminal motive that lay embedded in an Italian personality, culture, or legacy?

With my own familial experiences as a point of entrée and with my sociological knowledge in hand, I sought to answer this question with an examination of the boys of Chicago Heights. I drew upon a series of personal interviews, historical records, census manuscripts, and other available resources. The central thesis was to demonstrate how this organized crime operation grew out of the Italian enclave in this community and more specifically how it grew out of the cultural, political, and economic forces at work for the greater part of the last century. In examining these forces, social capital became the key conceptual tool that connected these more encompassing community processes and the ability of Italians to sustain a criminal operation for nearly the entire century. The following chapters detail this argument.

In undertaking such a study, I am keenly aware this analysis falls awkwardly between the popular first-person (in my case second-person) accounts of life in organized crime, on the one hand, and the academic, research-driven explanations on the other. As you read through the chapters, I believe you will find that the academic focus dominates. This was critical because the underlying roots of organized crime transcend the particular historical situation and particular historical actors. Specifically, if we are to understand contemporary organized crime groups, especially those developing out of African American and Latino communities (as they have in recent years in Chicago Heights), academic concepts and insights provide a firm basis for comparison and generalization. At the same time, this academic focus was essential because organized crime proceeds and sustains itself not on the basis of the sensational, headline grabbing activities, but on the more routine social relationships that link organized crime groups to the surrounding community. The first-person, blood-in-the streets narratives often bury these more sociological relevant processes. Indeed, *they can't shoot everyone* is a mantra that I cite throughout this study. Understanding the sociological significance of this phrase requires a more analytic perspective on the powers of organized crime.

Having said all this, my personal or familial experiences still play an important role. When possible, I have sought to add greater depth to the analysis by drawing upon these experiences. In particular, my father may not have been anything like a soldier or a "wiseguy," but he was on the inside. As a young man, he ran sugar to the bootleg operations throughout the area; for most of his working life, he was employed by the Co-Operative Music Company in Chicago Heights, which was the scene of numerous FBI stakeouts and a common meeting place for top Chicago Outfit leaders; later in his life, he partnered with Dino Valente and ran the Outfit jukebox business in Northwest Indiana and Calumet City. He did the latter until Valente ran afoul of Outfit leaders and was gunned down in Calumet City in 1978. Because of my father's long history with the Outfit, I took the opportunity to conduct a number of oral history interviews with him before he passed away in 1995. These interviews, along with twenty-five interviews of other Chicago Heights residents, proved invaluable in terms of providing specific details and background material on the Chicago Heights criminal operation. I have included such information in the following chapters when appropriate. At the same time, I have respected my father's wishes to not reveal certain information or at least not reveal specifics if he thought it might harm people still living or if it went against the still-dominant belief that you do not talk about Outfit business.

Of course, the personal and intellectual trajectory that resulted in this study would not have happened without the support of so many people. Luigi Corsino and Josephina Corsino (or Peppina), my grandparents, set the stage for this study by taking that perilous, immigrant voyage from Calabria to the United States at the turn of the last century. Many a day I would sit with my grandfather on the swing, under the grapevine, outside his home in Chicago Heights as he told stories of his experiences in Italy and the United States. At the time, I dutifully listened but my mind was probably more focused on baseball and the other things kids used to think about. Today, what would I give to have just one of those days back and to hear firsthand what a journey he and Peppina had experienced.

Of course, my father, Andy Corsino, and my mother, Natalie (or "Tillie") Corsino (nee Evoskis) were at the very center of my life and that of my sisters (Carolyn and Jo). As suggested, my father was the person who had the connections, who lived the life among the boys of Chicago Heights. And he provided the substantive detail through numerous conversations that allowed me to sort out the characters and relationships that lie at the foundation of this study. But much more than that, he was my father. I sometimes think that one of the prime motivations of this study, so many years after his death, is to keep his memory alive in my mind. The same could be said for my mother. She does not appear very much in the pages to follow because organized crime, especially then, was pretty much a man's world. And she was a Lithuanian woman from Spring Valley, Illinois. As such, she, and her family, did not have as great a role to play in the organized crime ventures of Chicago Heights. But if she does not have an obvious presence in this book, she is everywhere. If she did not contribute actual words toward this study, she nevertheless provided the love and care that ran through all our lives and which made any study, career, relationship worth pursuing.

Other family members were also of great help in putting this study together. The picture on the back cover is my acknowledgment to them for information they contributed to this study, but more so for the sense of community they have provided for all the years of growing up together. The picture includes my grandparents, mother and father, sisters, godfather, aunts, uncles, fictive kin, and a lot of cousins (and John Roberts). It does not include several cousins (Tommy Vilella and Joe Kuster) who were born shortly after this picture was taken around 1954. And it does not include the subsequent husbands and wives of my cousins who have also contributed as adults to the substantive material in this book and the general sense of *famiglia* that I have been privileged to experience. To all of these family members, I give my heartfelt appreciation.

There is one in-law, however, I would like to signal out. This is my brother-in-law Dominic (or Mac) Sesto. Born and raised in the East Side of Chicago Heights, Mac's contributions to this study can be seen everywhere. He allowed me to interview him a number of times, and I have had numerous informal conversations with him about the material in this book. He has supplied letters, documents, and pictures that in the context of this study have been priceless. He has introduced me to a collection of old-time, corner boys in Chicago Heights who at their weekly lunch in the Heights have been wonderful storytellers and sources of information. But Mac has done much more than provide access to information. He has been an inspiration for a great many people on how to live a principled and meaningful life.

At the risk of burying my personal appreciation so deep into this section, let me give special thanks to my wife Alison. Throughout the many hours I spent coding, writing, recoding, rewriting, she took care of the major share of the family issues while conducting a professional life of her own. In this, she was amazing and I am profoundly indebted. I am a lucky man, indeed. And I am also fortunate to have two lovely daughters, Mia and Andie, who make me feel both older and younger on an hour by hour basis. Daughters are a special gift.

Beyond these familial ties, I have been blessed with a collection of intellectual mentors and personal friends who have enriched my life and this study.

Gerald Platt, Professor Emeritus at the University of Massachusetts-Amherst, still to this day is an inspiration for his intellect, kindness, and boldness. If I could come close to matching him on any of these attributes, I would be honored. Joseph Sheley has for a very long time been a friend and colleague. As a colleague, he has encouraged this study from the beginning and provided some key insights. As a friend, he has provided just the right support and just the right amount of cold water in the face when I needed both. Roger Waldinger led a National Endowment for the Humanities seminar in which I participated in 1994 at the University of California, Los Angeles. It was a long time ago, but Roger's support for my study and sense that I had a story to tell has stuck with me through the years. His own ground-breaking research on immigration and entrepreneurship has served as a backdrop for much of this study. Dominic Candeloro, historian and fellow Chicago Heights native, has provided a wealth of information on the history of Italians in Chicago, and Chicago Heights in particular, and has provided access to information, opportunities for dialogue, and good cheer throughout this study. Robert "Mickey" Lombardo has also been an invaluable source of information and support. Lombardo's work on the Chicago Outfit and his comments on previous drafts have added greatly to the quality of this work. Finally, Matt Luzi and John Binder know more about organized crime in Chicago than just about anyone. Through the years, they have invited me along on jaunts through the city, visits to mob hangouts, and get-togethers with crime historians. I have learned a lot from their deep and fascinating knowledge of the Outfit.

The personal acknowledgments need to be supplemented with the gratitude I have for the help provided at a number of educational and cultural institutions. Along these lines, I would like to thank Concordia University, Chicago for providing funding for some very early papers on this topic. I am also indebted to North Central College for a number of summer grants and course releases that have made this study possible. In the course of my tenure at North Central, a number of students have assisted me in entering, coding, and analyzing the census data. These students have included: Kristine Lipowski, Adam Blackburn, Jennifer Dalesio, Nicole Asche, Jennifer Martin, Sherry Klinger, John Sienkiewicz, Alex Jansen, and Matthew Lamb. Also, Tom Gill, instructional media coordinator, has been of great service in helping me salvage and reproduce the images in this volume. In addition, I would like to give special thanks to the staff at the Chicago Heights Public Library, who have been unfailingly gracious in my multiple requests for information for microfiche copies of the *Chicago Heights Star* or for other documents in their special collections. Similarly, I am indebted to staff members at the Newberry

Library, the Chicago History Museum, and the National Archives, Great Lakes Region. Special thanks and appreciation are extended to the expert staff and professionals at the University of Illinois Press, which include Laurie Matheson, editor-in-chief, and Dawn Durante, Roger Cunningham, Jennifer Clark, and Dustin Hubbart. They have made this an especially gratifying personal and intellectual journey. Finally, let me acknowledge Karen Hallman who edited the manuscript. Like most authors, I thought I had a pretty good sense of style, grammar, and effective writing. However, after reviewing Karen's smart and detailed edits, I have come away with a new and insightful understanding of good writing. Whatever shortcomings remain in terms of grammar, style, and clarity are mine.

INTRODUCTION

You can't shoot everyone. At times, they tried. The Italians who dominated organized crime in Chicago have been variously portrayed as barbarians, thugs, and goons for the violent path they carved on the way to their notorious reign atop the vaunted criminal empire in the city. These labels were well earned. The Chicago Outfit and the Italians who were members did not shy away from viciousness. However, these "Stone Age"[1] characterizations fail to tell the whole, or even the most important, story of how Italians achieved such outstanding, though nefarious, success in this field. This success rested upon a set of more prosaic social networks and relations characterizing the Italian experience in Chicago. Narrating this more complete story, along with these exceptionally violent episodes, is the central theme in this work.

This study, then, attempts to draw a connection between the Chicago Outfit and Italians. In and of itself, this is not a popular, academic, or law enforcement revelation. For more than a century, perceptions of organized crime have been intimately intertwined with stereotypes of Italians or Italian Americans. Thus, as far back as 1888, a *Chicago Tribune* editorial argued for the existence of the Mafia in Chicago *because* of the large number of Sicilians who lived in the city.[2] More than a century later, Farrell and Case could contend that the assumption that situates organized crime as an "exclusive domain of Italians" is still very much alive as a result of a long history of federal investigations, current law enforcement practices, as well as mass media portrayals and social scientific perspectives.[3]

It is not difficult to find, therefore, a historical linkage between Italians and organized crime. The challenge, however, is to explain this linkage free from the abiding stereotypes and subtle prejudices that have often clouded these explanations. In other words, free from the essentialist accounts that are so often found within the general public, law enforcement agencies, and, more subtly, academic circles. Thus, the ties between Italians and organized crime have, with few notable exceptions, been depicted largely as a consequence of genetic makeup, modal personalities, constituent subcultures, or family legacy—that is, something ingrained in the Italian or the Italian way of life.[4] Such explanations leave much to be desired. They lurch awkwardly to overly broad characterizations of the Italian population and in the process pull most all Italians into the "Mafia nest."

Other explanations have attempted to correct for these personal and cultural biases by offering predominately structural arguments.[5] The Italian culture or community has been shown to have little to do with the emergence of organized crime. Instead, Italians are pushed into these criminal activities by blocked opportunities, queer ladders of mobility, ethnic succession processes, or social strains—factors that could impact any ethnic or minority group. As insightful as these later explanations have turned out to be, they still leave unanswered some of the most important questions. In particular, why did Italians, as opposed to other disadvantaged groups, come historically to dominate organized crime in the American context? Why did they achieve these unprecedented "criminal powers?"[6] From a structural perspective, are we led to the questionable conclusion that Italians were more structurally disadvantaged than other ethnic groups and, therefore, more disposed and motivated toward this criminal activity? Or must we conclude, with little empirical support, that because the massive immigration of Italians to America came after the Germans, the Irish, and the Jews had climbed all of the legitimate, semilegitimate, and illegitimate ladders of mobility, the Italians were forced by this structural positioning to reinvent organized crime at a much more sophisticated and ruthless level?

With these questions in mind, this study explores the emergence of the Italian Mafia in one particular setting. It examines a long-standing organizational component of the Chicago Outfit—namely, the Chicago Heights boys. The Chicago Heights operation will be examined from its beginning in the early 1900s to the heyday of Outfit activities in the post–World War II era. Along the way, I attempt to unravel the mix of social and cultural discriminations against Italians in the early part of the last century, the consequential group characteristics that emerged within the local Italian population, and the appropriation of these characteristics as social capital resources in the collective pursuit of social mobility.

Specifically, from the turn of the last century onward, the plight of the Chicago Heights Italians is depicted in terms of a confrontation with the discriminatory processes in mainstream society. As an unintended consequence, these processes promoted or enhanced the development of certain patterns within the Chicago Heights Italian communities—most distinctly, a vibrant ethnic enclave that generated close-knit social networks, a cluster of shared values and experiences, and an "Italian" identity. In turn, these group characteristics were turned into forms of social capital that Italians drew upon to achieve a social and economic advancement or in James Coleman's analytic terms "certain ends that in their absence would not be possible."[7] For some in Chicago Heights, this meant the development of fraternal organizations such as the Marchegiani Society or the Dante Club; for others, this led to the emergence of ethnic-based union organizing such as the Steel Workers Union or a more broad-based socialist response; for still others, these social capital resources led to the promotion of various ethnic enterprises such as neighborhood grocery stores or local taverns; and, for others, these resources were turned to the "dark side"[8] of these collective mobilization efforts—they were used to create a most successful and dominant branch of the Chicago Outfit—namely, the Chicago Heights boys.

By making this connection between Italians and organized crime, the aim is not to perpetuate the grossly exaggerated and damaging stereotypes that see Italians as prone to criminal or violent behavior. Indeed, an underlying assumption of this study is that no special theory, no special motive is required to understand an Italian (or any ethnic group) connection to organized crime. To put this differently, the same social forces that produced Italian grocery stores, Italian mutual-aid societies, and an Italian involvement in union-organizing activities also produced this Italian association with organized crime. To argue otherwise runs the risk of reverting back to the spurious theories of racial or social heredity that presumptively tied criminal behavior to essentialist attributes or predispositions. It would be akin to searching for special motives or unique cultural attributes for an Italian involvement in grocery stores, mutual-aid societies, or labor organizing—a grocery motive, a fraternal motive, or a labor motive—analytically comparable, in this sense, to a criminal motive. While most people today would reject such essentialist, stereotypical explanations, the tenacious connection between Italians and organized crime has been much more difficult to break. As such, the objective here is to depict an Italian tie to organized crime in its local, concrete, and, most importantly, contingent context.

Still, I do not want to explain away the presence of Italians in organized crime in a facile manner, as a result of a "few bad apples." Ralph Salerno, the esteemed crime-fighter, was on the right track when he suggested in 1969 that "the Italio-American community has been following the ostrich principle of putting its head in the sand and hoping the problem would go away." And he was citing an obvious truth when he went on to suggest that "these twenty million fine, decent people have failed to disassociate themselves from about 10,000 wrongdoers who enjoy a blending in with the 20 million."[9] Salerno, however, may have been sociologically shortsighted to argue that the general Italian population could so easily and effortlessly detach themselves from these "wrongdoers" in a simple act of will. The social conditions and ties between Outfit members and the Italian ethnic community ran much deeper and were more binding than this—just as the social conditions and ties between Italians and ethnic enterprises, mutual-aid societies, and labor unions ran much deeper.

So, by drawing upon interviews, government documents, census data, and secondary sources, this study will show how organized crime was embedded in the interaction between the Italian population and the larger Chicago Heights community. More than an alien conspiracy, an exotic association of antisocial personalities, a secret society or subculture, more than anything unique or uniquely Italian, the Chicago Heights boys will be examined as a product of the interactions between the structure of opportunities made available (and not made available) and the group characteristics of the local, Italian population. Revealing these relationships and situating Italians in these historically specific realities are the primary goals of this study.

The Personal Context

This study emerges out of a complex and overlapping mix of personal, community, and public interests and histories. My own family background, the development of Chicago Heights as an industrial community, and the abiding, public perception of Italians have conspired to shape this study. Each vantage point, on its own and in combination, provides insights and shortcomings in an attempt to understand the connections between Italians and organized crime. Therefore, before proceeding to locate this study within the larger community and public context, it would be useful to reveal the personal biases and perspectives that inform this inquiry. In not always recognizable ways, I am, though more properly my family, a part of the story being told.

I grew up in the largely blue collar, largely Italian suburb of Chicago Heights during the 1950s. My family first made it to the Heights nearly fifty years previously when my grandfather, Luigi Corsino, emigrated from Sambiase, Calabria, with his father, stepmother, two sisters, and brother. Luigi's path to

Chicago Heights, however, was anything but direct. Less than a year after arriving in the United States, Luigi's father died and he, along with his siblings, were placed by their stepmother in the Saint Vincent Orphanage and Asylum in Columbus, Ohio. Life in the orphanage was as one might expect—harsh, strict, and disciplined. Luigi did not take well to any of these. In particular, he was especially displeased by the institutional separation from his sisters whom he would only see from afar at the mandatory mass each morning. As such, Luigi exhibited the incorrigibility so often attributed to the delinquents and immigrants of that era. In return, the nuns who supervised the children made life especially difficult for Luigi with excessive punishments and restrictions. This prompted Luigi to plan his escape from the orphanage, with the goal of returning and taking custody of his younger brother and sisters. After several failed attempts, Luigi managed to scale the walls of the orphanage (and one would think that the nuns might have turned a blind eye to his escape efforts) and found his way into the rough-and-tumble Italian neighborhoods of Columbus. Several years later, Luigi managed to meet up with his brother, who had been shipped away from the orphanage on an "orphan train," and together they went to work in the coal mines of Ohio. The coal mines provided a salary, but the life of a coal miner was only marginally better than the depressed conditions of the Mezzogiorno back in Italy. This led Luigi to seek higher ground, so to speak, and he migrated to the rapidly industrializing city of Chicago Heights where Luigi came to stay with Angelina Sicalo, an aunt, in 1902.

Once in Chicago Heights, Luigi took a number of low-skilled jobs in the growing anti-immigrant labor market in the pre–World War I economy. However, when he married Josephina Pizzonia, as part of an arranged marriage in 1913 and soon had four children (including my father, Andy), Luigi had to look for a steadier, higher income. For several years, Luigi worked during the summer months on various railroad section gangs in the Badlands out west. Later he worked in a railroad scrap yard breaking rails with a sledgehammer and blowtorch. "Each day," Luigi used to say, "we would start with a mountain of rails so high you couldn't see the sun."

Luigi would have most likely continued in these low-paying jobs throughout his life. However, with the enactment of Prohibition in 1920, a new set of opportunities opened for Luigi and a number of other Italian immigrants in Chicago Heights. As the market for illegal liquor expanded, Luigi was approached by Dominic Roberto (aka Dominick Roberts), a *paesano,* a fellow countryman, from his hometown of Sambiase, and offered a job in one of the illegal stills set up on Fifteenth and Portland Avenues in Chicago Heights. Lured by the $75 a week salary and the *campanilismo* ties, Luigi accepted the offer and worked for the Chicago Heights Outfit for seven years making "whiskey." This continued until U.S. Treasury officers raided the still and arrested Luigi. Not long afterward, Luigi was sentenced for one month to the Woodstock, Illinois, jail.

Returning to Chicago Heights, Luigi spent the rest of his life working in a series of low-skilled construction and factory jobs. On occasion, his life would become more entangled with Outfit operations, especially when Al Capone made one of his many visits to Chicago Heights. Luigi's house was one of a number of places that Capone met with Dominic Roberto, Roberto's brother Giovanni Roberto (aka John Roberts), Jimmy Emery (aka Vincenzo Ammirati), and other Outfit leaders to discuss Outfit operations and simply to enjoy a respite from the pressures of running the illegal businesses. At other times, Luigi's house became another type of refuge. Thus, pursued by the police, Luigi's brother-in-law, Gregorio Pizzonia, a compatriot of Capone, once spent over six months hiding out in the house—with shades pulled down and sleeping in my father's bed—because he shot a man at a roadhouse in an argument over a woman. Fearing that Pizzonia would be arrested and possibly bring unwanted attention to the Chicago Heights operation, Capone used his ties with the produce industry in Michigan to set Pizzonia up with a new life in Lansing, Michigan, as a grocer. Joe Nicastro, a long-time resident of Chicago Heights, recalls the moving day.

> The guys knew they had to get him out of town, away from the police. Because they had made friends with people who ran Michigan Fruit, the guys arranged for him to go to Michigan. They also arranged for his girlfriend, Rose, to go too. I drove the women and Luigi up. In the other car, Al Capone, Jimmy Emery, and John Roberts all rode together. A chauffer drove Capone and the other guys. But I had trouble on the way up, the gas pedal stuck and I sped past Capone and the other car. When I got the car to stop, I jumped out and was afraid that Capone was angry. But he laughed and yelled, "What the hell is wrong with him. The kid must be crazy." We made it the rest of the way and got Pizzonia out of the Heights.[10]

Such situations provided their own challenges for Luigi and Josephina. However, my father, Andy, was of more immediate concern. Having quit high school after he turned sixteen, Andy held a series of temporary jobs for the next several years—as a rail-splitter in the local steel mills, as an ice cutter in the Lake Calumet Harbor, and as a runner with the Chicago Heights bootlegging operation. "I use to haul sugar at night," my father said, "sugar and moonshine cans. I was young, barely 20 years old, making good money, about $35 a week. They would pick us up at one or two in the morning and we'd go down these farm roads with these rattling cans. It was good. You worked three or four hours and then you were through for the day."

World War II brought a series of dramatic changes as my father was drafted in 1941 and spent four years in the service, including a two-year stint in Europe where he was awarded a Bronze Star for his combat service in Germany. Shortly before being shipped overseas, my father married Natalie Evoskis in 1941. Upon returning to Chicago Heights after the war, my father again took a variety of low-skilled jobs—applying hot tar to the back of roofing shingles for the Gold Seal Roofing Company, working on a sewer construction gang in nearby Park Forest, and tending bar at the Copa Cabana tavern in Chicago Heights. While at this last job, Andy came in daily contact with Mike Roberts (aka Michael Roberto), the younger brother of Dominic Roberto and John Roberts. Mike's job was to collect the money from the Outfit-run slot machines hidden away in a private room behind the bar. Dissatisfied with the pay and long hours bartending, Andy was encouraged by the younger Roberts to talk to Frank Laporte, the boss of Outfit operations in the southern suburbs, about working as a collector in the newly formed jukebox company, Co-Operative Music. My father met Laporte at his family grocery store in Chicago Heights and in large part because of my family's long-standing ties with the Robertos, he was offered the job as a route man for the jukebox company. "Dominic put in a good word for me and told Frankie I was honest and could be trusted. They knew I didn't go and shoot my mouth off all the time." My father worked for Co-Operative Music until 1974, when with permission from then–Chicago Heights Outfit boss Al Pilotto, he was allowed to set up his own small jukebox company in the nearby town of Calumet City.

These personal and work ties, then, provided the contours for a great deal of my own childhood experiences. For example, at least once each summer, I would fulfill the father-son ritual of spending a day at my father's place of work. Yet, unlike other boys who followed their father around in his office, my day consisted of riding in my father's Buick Electra through the nearby towns of Calumet City and Burnham visiting a variety of corner bars, strip joints, and gambling houses with such enticing names as the The Ball of Fire, The Play-House, and The Ron-da-voo. This job required my father to make fifteen or so stops each day to update first the 78 rpm and then later the 45 rpm disks, make minor repairs on the machine, and collect the weekly take in the jukeboxes—a few coins of which he would every so often slip to me under the table as a reward for my day of work.

The secretive tinge surrounding my family practices also extended to our consumer options. Thus, my family did most of its shopping at the department stores in downtown Chicago Heights—for example, Klines, Rau, and J. C. Penny. However, my family was not averse to shopping in the household basements of friends or extended family members. Here, we would be presented with ill-begotten items ranging from rib eye steaks, to fur stoles, to television sets, to sewing machines—all at bargain prices. And on occasion my father would venture to Fish Johnson's house in Miller, Indiana. With ties dating back to Al Capone and John Dillinger, Johnson had one of the biggest fencing operations in the Midwest.[11] His three-story house was filled with merchandise organized into different departments—shoes, suits, furs, tools, shirts, and the like. My father would visit Johnson's house several times each year, often bringing friends and sometimes policemen, who were willing to trade a measure of caution for items purchased at extremely reasonable prices. As my father said, "Yeah it was like a store. But it was all hot stuff. He had all kinds of stuff in there. But it was better than a department store. The prices were right."

My father also had a mysterious collection of friends and acquaintances who went by such names as One-Armed Jimmy, Tootsie, and Black Mike—so called because he had a fearsome reputation and once in a street fight bit off a piece of his assailant's nose. Friends such as these would periodically slip in and out of our family life bringing truckloads of goods and asking my father to store them in our basement or garage. On more than one occasion, in search of a baseball bat or glove, I would unknowingly stumble upon box after box of perfume, cigarettes, or sweaters. On some days, I would enter the garage and find an unknown car—most times belonging to Frank Laporte, John Roberts, or some other Outfit leader seeking to evade FBI surveillance.

At other times, my father would become more directly involved in Outfit activities. Thus, a knock on our backdoor in the middle of the night would arouse my father out of bed and he would be given a burlap bag full of guns or some such contraband. Sometimes my father would take the guns or other incriminating items to my grandfather's house, where they would be buried outside or melted down in the coal-burning furnace in the basement. Other times, he would drive to Calumet City and dispose of guns in the Little Calumet River just over the state line in Indiana. And every so often, my father would be called upon to spirit away illegal slot machines and other gambling devices when informants supplied Outfit bosses with tips about a police raid or crackdown.

To be sure, my father's job and contacts did not propel him or our family into the inner core of the Outfit. My father was not a "made man," wiseguy, soldier, or the like. As my father said, "I never wanted to go that far. Those were dangerous situations." Instead, my father, like so many others, moved in and out of Outfit business not on the basis of some mystical sense of membership or rituals, but on the more prosaic benefits and obligations that came attached to a network of friends and social relations that had been established over a lifetime, indeed over generations. These networks provided my father a job, knowledge of underworld goings on, access to tangible goods and services, and a connection to power.

This last point was brought to my attention in a most poignant fashion one summer night when I was still a teenager. On this evening, I was driving my cousin Stan home along Dixie Highway in Chicago Heights. The Santucci boys, kids we had known in high school, pulled alongside us at a stoplight. When the light turned green, we sped alongside each other until I pulled up and made the turn off Dixie Highway to bring Stan home. A few minutes after entering Stan's house, a rock the size of a softball came crashing through the kitchen door, spewing glass in all directions and barely missing Stan's two-year-old nephew. We ran outside, only to see the tailgates of the Santucci car pull away. Later that night when I told my father what had happened, he asked in an ominous manner if I wanted the Santucci boys "taken care of." I puzzled over what that meant, but did not ask. I also realized at that moment I was a few words, a nod of the head away from the systems of power and brute force that overlapped my father's more mundane life. I did not take him up on the offer. Nevertheless, as my father confided to me later, "It was good to be connected. If you wanted a favor done, everyone had power some place. If you weren't connected, then you were on the outside."

I approach, therefore, an intellectual understanding of the Chicago Heights Outfit with the insights and liabilities posed by this family history. This history provided my family with extensive knowledge, firsthand experiences, and direct connections to the Chicago Heights operations. And, in turn, this insider perspective made this study both feasible and personally compelling. However, I am mindful that these ties may create an undeserved partisanship, if not a romanticizing of organized crime. I would expect that given the multiple, and often unknown, layers of consciousness connecting me to this study, such biases are always near the surface. Accordingly, to the extent possible I approach the material in this study critically, with a skeptical eye regarding perspectives, beliefs, and data. At the same time, the relevant sociological literature on organized crime will serve here as a most useful vantage point for challenging these personal biases.

The Community Context

For personal reasons, then, this study focuses on the connection between Italians and organized crime in the Chicago Heights context. Beyond these personal interests, Chicago Heights draws our attention because of the long presence of Italians in the Heights and similarly the long history of organized crime in the city. Italians have constituted a sizeable percentage of city residents ever since the second wave of immigration ran its course in the period from 1890 to 1924.

Obviously, table I.1 should be examined with extreme caution. For a variety of reasons, the federal census used different methods for gathering information on the presence of nationality groups through the century. As such, the numbers in the table mix the immigration, ancestry, and ethnicity of Italians.[12] Still, looking beyond these operational and methodological problems, it seems

Table I.1 Italian presence in Chicago Heights, 1910–2010

Year	Foreign born[a]	Foreign stock[b]	Ancestry[c]	Total city population	Percentage Italian
1910	2,240	—	—	14,525	15.4
1920	2,396	—	—	19,653	12.2
1930	2,259	—	—	22,321	10.1
1940	1,905	—	—	22,461	8.4
1950	1,477	—	—	24,551	6.0
1960	—	3,572	—	34,331	10.4
1970	—	3,092	—	40,790	7.5
1980	—	—	5,914	37,026	16.0
1990	—	—	5,368	33,072	16.2
2000	—	—	3,757	32,776	11.5
2010	—	—	2,516	30,276	8.3

Sources: U.S. Bureau of the Census, *Census of Population and Housing, 1910–2010.*

[a]According to the U.S. Census, *foreign born* consists of those people born outside the United States and its territories, excluding the small number of those who although born in a foreign country are "native" citizens because their parents were American citizens.

[b]According to the U.S. Census, *foreign stock* consists of those persons born outside the United States *and* those persons who though born in the United States had at least one parent born outside the United States.

[c]According to the U.S. Census, *ancestry* consists of a self-identification whereby individuals report their nationality group, lineage, or the country in which the person or the person's parents or the person's ancestors were born before their arrival in the United States, regardless of the number of generations removed from their country of origin.

clear that in one form or another Italians have been a significant part of Chicago Heights's history for the entire century. Indeed, if in the critical period between 1910 and 1950, the census had measured "foreign stock" Italians, the presence of Italians in the city would have easily been three to four times the percentages in the table.

At the same time, the historical presence of organized crime in the city attracts our interest. For over a century, organized crime has had a foothold in the Heights. From the "slot machine trusts" in the early 1900s, to the takeover of the local stills by Al Capone in the 1920s and 1930s, to the prosecution of city officials for racketeering in the 1990s, organized crime has found a home in the social and political structures of the city. No less a figure than Eliot Ness cut his teeth in the crime-fighting field with an early exposure to the Chicago Heights bootlegger operation. Ness set up a field headquarters and worked as an undercover agent in Chicago Heights. According to Ness, the Chicago Heights operation was "the pickup depot for most of the illicit alcohol trade in the entire Middle West."[13] Schoenberg argued that in the 1920s, "conditions in Chicago Heights had become scandalous beyond bearing, even in Cook County."[14] And years later in 1991, federal authorities in their prosecution of Chicago Heights officials for extortion and racketeering described the Chicago Heights setting as an "'unholy alliance' of mobsters, politicians, and police."[15] Despite dramatic changes in city demographics, politics, and economic fortunes, organized crime in Chicago Heights has long presented itself as a topic for investigation.

Despite this presence, the Chicago Heights operation has never been given its nefarious due. Even though the Chicago Heights faction has, arguably, contributed more to the on-going vitality and commercial success of the Chicago Outfit than any other crew, it is the least researched, written about, and analyzed Outfit operation. Thus, Bergreen concludes, "to ignore Chicago Heights was to ignore the innermost circle of racketeering in Chicago and throughout the Midwest."[16] Matt Luzi, who most recently has written with fine detail on the Chicago Heights boys, subtitles his work "the forgotten crew of the Chicago Outfit."[17] With few exceptions, the story of the Chicago Heights gang has been relegated to several scattered references in the more encompassing works on the Chicago Outfit or brief mention in the few histories of Chicago Heights.[18] This is unfortunate, for Chicago Heights offers a well-defined, sociological case study, for "a modest scholarly effort to demonstrate the more sober realities" of organized crime.[19]

The Public Context

Whether located in Chicago Heights or elsewhere, the link between Italians, especially southern Italians, and organized crime has been a consistent theme among scholars, journalists, writers, government officials, filmmakers, and a large segment of the American public. Something about Italians—something about their genetic makeup, their personalities, their subculture, their family organization, or their immigrant status—has historically been viewed as "essentially" criminal. As Daniel Bell theorized more than half a century ago, "there is . . . in the American temper, a feeling that 'somewhere,' 'somebody' is pulling all the complicated strings to which this jumbled world dances."[20] In the field of crime, Bell suggested that the finger pointed quite squarely at Italians.

This finger pointing has often been instigated by a variety of government agencies, bodies, commissions, committees, and officials. Most infamously, the United States Immigration Commission of 1911, in their Dillingham Commission reports, conducted an exhaustive review of the foreign born and criminality. Perhaps foretelling its own conclusions, the commission began with a "dictionary of races" wherein southern Italians were defined, in part, as "given to brigandry and poverty."[21] Accordingly, it was not a major surprise when the commission concluded that Italians constituted the most criminalized segment of the society, especially with respect to crimes of violence and extortion. And such conclusions provided ample ammunition for those wanting to restrict the flow of Italian and other selected immigrant groups into the country. Thus, the Dillingham Commission provided a platform for a variety of citizens and groups attempting to protect the "real America" from the "bilge waters of foreign habits, vices, and influences."[22] Italians were condemned in particular. Though the commission found that prior conditions in Italy had a good deal to do with this Italian criminality, the commission could still argue for "the not unfounded belief that certain kinds of criminality are inherent in the Italian race."[23] At the same time, the commission concluded that the tendency to commit crimes was accompanied by "a seemingly inherent ability to avoid arrest and conviction."[24]

The Dillingham Commission study would lead over the next decade to a number of restrictive immigration policies with respect to disvalued immigrant groups, including the Italians. This study was followed in 1931 by the *Report on Lawlessness in Law Enforcement*, commonly known as the Wickersham Commission. This latter commission turned attention away from an exclusive focus on immigrants, per se, by also examining the laws and criminal practices enacted against immigrants. Organized crime was reconceived in terms of legal categories and systemic criminal justice issues rather than the particular groups engaged in organized crime activities. In so doing, the lawlessness of Italians moved beyond "somatic traits or germinal determiners"[25] to an investigation of the symbiotic adjustments of the Italian population to the larger urban, political, and ecological environments. As useful as this focus may have been, the findings and perspectives of the Wickersham report were essentially ignored.[26] When organized crime was next taken up again in a systematic way by the Kefauver Committee in the 1950s and the McClennan Committee in the 1960s, the focus was once again on the "who" not the "what." Italian lawlessness once again took center stage.[27]

This was dramatically reaffirmed by the 1967 President's Commission on Law Enforcement and Administration of Justice report, *The Challenge of Crime in a Free Society*. This report ignored much of its own evidence regarding the multiethnic character of organized crime and virtually defined organized crime as an Italian invention and preoccupation. In particular, organized crime was said to consist of a nationwide alliance of 24 Mafia families composed of Sicilians or people of Sicilian descent. One of the chief consultants to this government investigation, Donald Cressey, inexplicably changed the name of the criminal organization understudy from the more neutral *Confederation* to the obviously more Italian *Cosa Nostra* when he published his definitive work, *Theft of a Nation*, in 1969.[28] Even the major criminal justice control policy that emerged out of the work of the President's Commission, the Racketeer Influenced and Corrupt Organization Act (RICO), reportedly had, and continues to have, an Italian genealogy—in particular, the title of this legislation is tied to the classic 1931 film, *Little Caesar,* where the main character, Caesar Enrico Bandello (aka Rico), is a stereotyped Italian gangster. By implication, at least, this law was created to go after Italian mobsters.

Over the past century, this association between Italians and criminality has also found its way into the general public opinion.[29] Thus, the leading mass periodicals at the beginning of the century (for example, *Atlantic Monthly, Harper's, Scribner's, Saturday Evening Post, North American Review, McClure, Forum)* often maligned Italians for their propensity to engage in crime. Though some periodicals offered more balanced perspectives than others did, most all were highly skeptical of Italians and their capacities to assimilate. For example, Agnes Repplier in the *Atlantic Monthly* characterized Italians as dangerous, contemptible, and inferior. In another article from this publication, Arthur Sweeney ranked Italians at the bottom on a test for mental intelligence and concluded, "we have no place in this country for the man with the hoe ... guided by a mind scarcely superior to the ox whose brother he is." And sociologist Henry Pratt Fairchild in his widely read book *The Melting-Pot Mistake* opinioned that Italians, for a variety of cultural and heredity reasons, were ill-equipped to fully assimilate into American society. As Fairchild noted in his discussion of the Italian response to the Prohibition legislation, "To try to explain the theory of prohibition to a group of Italian workmen is very much like trying to explain to you, the reader, that in Siberia people walk on their ears. In other words, it sounds interesting, but it does not get over."[30]

Beginning in the 1930s, public opinion polling became a more scientific mechanism for gauging general beliefs toward Italians and criminality. While the polling results were less inflammatory, they conveyed similar, denigrating sentiments. Talese summarized these results. "In opinion polls reflecting native-born American preferences in new neighbors, Italians ranked near the bottom. They were seen as clannish, uncouth, instinctively criminal."[31] For example, a 1939 nationwide poll of adults revealed that Italians and Sicilians were thought to have "made the worst citizens." Indeed, Italians far outdistanced everybody else on this "worst citizen" measure, even besting America's other wartime enemies—the Germans and the Japanese.[32] More than forty years later, Italians were still viewed with considerable suspicion. A Louis Harris poll in 1972 revealed that, despite a great deal of evidence to the contrary, 78 percent of Americans believed there was a secret organization engaged in organized crime known as the Mafia operating in the country.[33] And in more recent times, a majority of the people in the American population still holds to the belief that "Italian-ness" and organized crime are joined. Thus, a 1990 national survey found that 74 percent of Americans believe that Italian Americans "are into a lot of the organized crime in this country."[34] And a 2001 national poll of teenagers by Zogby International revealed that 44 percent thought that "crime boss" was the most typical characteristic of Italian Americans.[35] In short, whether viewed in terms of mass circulation magazines or scientific polling techniques, the argument seems to be that where one finds Italians, one finds a high probability for an outbreak of a Mafia-style organization.

Overview

In his work *The Greatest Menace,* Bernstein suggests, "gangsters . . . surely tell us something about the communities from which they emerge."[36] What they tell us, however, is a matter of debate. Thus, the traditional popular and academic perspectives have held these gangsters came from an alien, social, and cultural milieu and that Italians, in particular, came predisposed or endowed with sociocultural characteristics that predicated a criminal involvement. As

Reynolds has argued, such explanations assumed, for all their insight that "the offender and the offended were from two different social worlds. Criminals had qualities which made them different from conventional folk."[37]

This study expands on Bernstein's suggestion and argues that gangsters also tell us something about the larger society that encircles these communities and, more to the point, the interaction between these two. I argue that in the Chicago Heights context social inequalities in this larger society may have spurred Italians to pursue a range of nontraditional options toward success, both legal and otherwise. These Italians were variously successful in these ventures because these social inequalities, in an unintended fashion, also produced (or prioritized) a set of social structural and cultural strategies that functioned as social resources for mobility. Specifically, processes of prejudice and discrimination helped formulate various mechanisms of social capital (for example, social networks, coethnic identities, structural holes) that local Italians could draw upon to create collective strategies aimed at overcoming these structural disadvantages—of which, organized crime was just one such collective effort.[38]

In this fashion, organized crime can be seen as a peculiar marriage of structural constraints and group characteristics.[39] But even further, a central argument of this study is that organized crime is also dependent on the development of social capital resources. Alone, neither structural factors (e.g., immigration status, poverty, residential segregation), nor group characteristics (e.g., cultural predispositions, kinship patterns, historical legacy) could explain the emergence of organized crime. The confluence or affinity of these structural and group conditions is not sufficient to account for organized crime unless they are joined by relevant social capital processes such as networks of social trust, community support or acquiesce, and access to clandestine information. Group characteristics, then, are not inevitable precursors, in the Italian case, of crime—dispositions that Italians hold in abeyance waiting to beguile or hoodwink an unsuspecting public. More properly, they are social resources that are made relevant when complex structural circumstances constrain more traditional strategies in pursuit of life goals. When viewed in this light, these social capital processes provide a powerful tool for understanding the differentiated responses of Italians to structural disadvantage and help explain, in a non-predisposing fashion, why Italians achieved a measure of success in the field of organized crime.

With this framework in mind, chapter 1 will begin this analysis by providing a historical overview of Chicago Heights and organized crime in the city. This examination suggests a rough connection between the two—namely, the rise, development, and decline of the Chicago Heights Outfit run parallel in many ways to the fortunes of the city. Chapter 2 focuses on the Italian population in Chicago Heights, specifically the existing structural and cultural constraints that made social mobility so difficult. Using census data, newspaper accounts, and interviews, I show how the occupational structure, patterns of residential housing, and cultural conflicts severely limited the life chances for most Italians in the city. Chapter 3 examines the collective mobilization strategies—labor organizing, mutual-aid societies, and ethnic entrepreneurship—Chicago Heights Italians pursued in response to the diminished opportunities for mobility—strategies made possible by a reservoir of social capital resources. Chapter 4 turns more directly toward organized crime. We identify the Chicago Heights boys and the mix of social capital processes, specifically the social closure and brokerage opportunities, that allowed this segment of the Chicago Outfit a near half century run as a highly profitable, successful criminal operation. Finally, we conclude with a more general discussion of the interrelationships between ethnicity, organized crime, and social capital, especially as it may apply to the contemporary context in Chicago Heights.

CHAPTER 1

CHICAGO HEIGHTS AND ORGANIZED CRIME

Chicago Heights was a twentieth-century city. The defining movements of the century—urbanization, industrialization, and immigration—tell much of the city's history and provide an understanding of the social conditions leading to the emergence of organized crime. With this in mind, we take a brief look back at these historical developments as they played themselves out in the Chicago Heights context. Following this, we trace the history of the vice operations in Chicago Heights from their beginning in the early 1900s, to their union with the Chicago Outfit in the 1920s, to their ascendance and decline throughout the remainder of the century.

Chicago Heights: A Brief History

Urbanization came late to Chicago Heights. When it did, however, it came on suddenly and powerfully. Originally the home to a number of Eastern Woodland Indian tribes, this pristine prairie land did not have its first white settlers until the 1830s. For the next several decades, the settlement, then known as Thorn Grove, grew slowly as Scotch-Irish and German immigrants, as well as pioneers from the southern states, displaced the few Pottawatomi Indians still remaining in the area.[1] Even when the village itself was invaded by the Joliet and Northern Indiana railroad line in 1853 and the Chicago & Eastern Illinois Railroad in 1869, it remained "primarily rural and peaceful."[2] Indeed, in 1884, Andreas characterized the area as a "happy rural village, contented, peaceful, and industrious."[3]

Yet, as the combined forces of capitalism and industry took hold, the village would hardly be left "to the sole enjoyment of its present limited population."[4] The crossing webs of rail lines, switching stations, and water tanks gave hints of a vastly different future for the area. While the population of the village stood just under 1,500 in 1895, by 1910, that number had increased to 14,525. And whereas not twenty years previous, one could stand downtown and view "nothing but a vast expanse of prairie in every direction, dotted here and there with a farm house,"[5] by 1910, residential neighborhoods, paved highways, street cars, and manufacturing plants dominated the area. "A hundred mammoth smokestacks rear their heads above 40 rumbling busy factories, while the hum of wheels and the grind of metal on metal rises all day long."[6] In such a short period, the "bliss of country life" had been replaced by a far more concentrated collection of industrial plots, residential developments, and commercial establishments. As Candeloro and Paul put it, Chicago Heights experienced the rapid transition from "sleepy village to industrial city."[7]

This increase in size and land use density was accompanied by a more diverse, residential population, at least in Eurocentric terms. Specifically, the long-time native, white settlers were now joined by an influx of immigrants from throughout Europe. And to a lesser extent, there was also a stream of African American residents from the rural south. Thus, by 1910, the city was more "foreign" and ethnically heterogeneous. Table 1.1 provides some indication of this new diversity. Immigrants or the children of immigrants—primarily from Italy, Russia, Germany, Austria, Greece, Hungary, and Sweden—were now added in large numbers to the mix of local residents.

In less than twenty years, then, the village of Thorn Grove (by this time, the name of the village had been officially changed to Bloom) had largely been reconstituted. In terms of the three-fold, classic definition of urbanization, it had undergone a nearly ten-fold increase in population size; it had become a compact, dense conglomeration of factories, businesses, and houses; and now there was a heterogeneous mix of residents with nearly three-quarters of the population foreign born or with at least one parent born in another country. Similar to other neighboring towns in the area, Chicago Heights had become an "instant city."[8]

This urbanization, however, did not proceed on its own. It was also a product of the rapid rise in industrialization and capitalism at the beginning of the twentieth century, especially in the booming Chicago metropolis. As the fastest growing big city in the nation, Chicago was soon becoming an obstacle to its

Table 1.1. Ethnic and native composition Chicago Heights and Illinois, 1910

Ethnic and native status	Chicago Heights Percentage	Number	Illinois Percentage	Number
Native white, native parentage	25.2	3,664	46.1	2,600,555
Native white, foreign parentage				
Austria	2.8	412	1.8	104,101
England	.7	95	.8	44,758
Germany	7.3	1,057	8.7	489,502
Ireland	1.2	168	2.9	160,879
Italy	6.8	984	.7	41,371
Russia	2.4	351	1.3	72,882
Sweden	1.8	265	1.7	94,830
All others	3.3	491	4.0	223,772
Subtotal	26.3	3,823	21.9	1,232,155
Native white, mixed parentage	5.8	848	8.7	491,692
Foreign born white				
Austria	6.4	923	2.9	163,020
England	.7	106	1.1	60,333
Germany	4.2	612	5.7	319,182
Greece	1.3	182	.2	10,030
Hungary	1.5	219	.7	39,857
Italy	15.4	2,240	1.3	72,160
Russia	7.0	1,013	2.6	149,016
Sweden	2.8	402	2.0	115,422
All others	2.5	380	4.8	273,390
Subtotal	41.8	6,077	21.3	1,202,560
Blacks	0.7	104	1.9	109,049
Other	<0.0		<0.0	2,580
Total	100.0	14,525	100.0	5,638,591

Source: Department of Commerce, Bureau of the Census, *Thirteenth Census of the United States 1910, Volume 2, Population: Reports by States, with Statistics for Counties, Cities, and Other Civil Divisions, Illinois.*

own growth. Industrial capacity in the central city was hampered by the lack of cheap land close to modes of transportation. At the same time, for much of the decades of the 1870s and 1880s, Chicago was the leading center of labor activism and radical, anticapitalist thought.[9] For such reasons, a number of investors turned to the nearby suburbs in search of cheap, undeveloped land—away from the Chicago tenements and radical political organizing efforts.

"All of these controversies and strikes that we have had here for some years . . . have prevented outsiders from coming in here and investing their capital," complained one Chicago contractor. "It has drawn the manufacturers away from the city, because they are afraid their men will get into trouble and get into strikes. . . . The result is, all around Chicago for forty or fifty miles, the smaller towns are getting these manufacturing plants."[10]

The Village of Bloom was one of these smaller towns and proved especially attractive, given that it was already served by the Joliet and Northern railroad and the Chicago & Eastern Illinois line. However, Bloom (as well as other suburban locations such as Waukegan, Elgin, Aurora, and Joliet) became an even more desirable site with the completion of the Chicago Outer Belt railroad line in 1887. Built by U.S. Steel, this line ran a huge circle around Chicago, crossing and connecting every rail line entering the main Chicago Terminal. Passing just south of the Bloom Village center, the Outer Belt gave the area tremendous rail access to markets and industrial sites both locally and within the nation as whole.

But as the *Chicago Heights Star* was to state years later, "Chicago Heights didn't get to be an industrial city by accident."[11] Nor was this growth simply a result of disembodied social and economic forces. This push toward an industrial community was driven by a group of investors (bank executives, real estate brokers, manufacturers, lawyers, and capitalists) who formed and were stockholders in the Chicago Heights Land Association. This association was one of the first to see the potential in the area for the establishment of a large industrial presence so geographically close, yet so socially and politically removed from Chicago. Engaged in the highly speculative but vastly profitable practice of land acquisition and town development, the association purchased 1,260 acres of land from a group of local promoters in 1891. Led principally by Charles Wacker, well-known Chicago developer, and Martin Kilgallen, the general manager and acclaimed "father of Chicago Heights," the association divided the land into industrial sites and four thousand residential lots. Over the next decade, Wacker and Kilgallen worked diligently to attract factories to the city under the exceedingly blunt advertising slogan, "Chicago Heights: The Men, the Land, the Money."[12] These efforts included convincing local leaders to incorporate as a village, which they did in 1892, and to change the name of the village to Chicago Heights—this latter to promote the connection to Chicago and to emphasize the healthy, flood-proof qualities of the area.[13] At the same time, Wacker and Kilgallen literally "set up shop" in the city and through a series of promotions and inducements in the forms of free water, free bricks, and favorable terminal transfer rates were able to attract a diverse collection of industrial plants—manufacturing everything from boxes, pianos, bricks, steel, pony wagons, chemicals, school supplies, cotton-baling machines, automobiles, mirrors, railroad cars, paint, horse collars, and zeppelins.[14]

The rise of Chicago Heights as an industrial center was impressive. By 1909, Chicago Heights had close to eighty industrial facilities. Again, this is particularly noteworthy given that the first major industrial plant, Inland Steel, did not agree to locate within the city boundaries until 1893. Chicago Heights's reputation as a blue-collar, industrial city was also impressive in terms of local labor force participation. Though the total population of the city was only 14,525, the city's industrial plants employed 4,444 people.[15] While these numbers are dwarfed in absolute terms by cities with larger populations, they nevertheless indicate the extent to which Chicago Heights had been transformed into an industrial city in such a short period. And if we leave aside the boosterism, we can understand why a common slogan in these early years proclaimed Chicago Heights "the best manufacturing city of its size in America."[16]

As suggested, the industrialization of Chicago Heights was accompanied by a strong immigration surge into the city. The availability of factory jobs, on the one hand, and the forces of chain migration, on the other, combined to transform the ethnic composition of the city. In 1910, foreign-born whites constituted 42 percent of the city's population.[17] What is particularly striking is the changing character of this immigrant population. Where previously the Scotch-Irish and Germany immigrants dominated the area and the local institutions, over 75 percent of this second wave of immigration came from Austria, Russia, Sweden, and Italy. And within these national boundaries, we find a complex mix of immigrants with Lithuanian, Polish, Jewish, Bohemian, and Slovakian ethnic and cultural ties. When the sizeable number of immigrants from Greece, Hungary, and Mexico and the beginnings of an African American presence are also accounted for, it is clear that Chicago Heights had become, if not a melting pot, then a culturally heterogeneous city.

In particular, the immigration of Italians to Chicago Heights was most pronounced and had the most long-term impact on the city. There were just a "handful of people" of Italian ancestry in Chicago Heights before 1890 (apparently a handful was too little to claim the existence of the Mafia, even for the *Chicago Tribune*).[18] However, by 1900, this number had increased to just over 300 and, as already indicated in table 1.1, at least 3,224 residents (native white with parentage from Italy plus foreign born from Italy) were of Italian ancestry by 1910—a ten-fold increase.[19] For Illinois cities over 10,000 people, Chicago Heights ranked only behind Chicago (72,846) in terms of the *absolute* number of residents with an Italian ancestry and well ahead of the next largest concentrations of Italians, Joliet (1,552) and Rockford (1,445). With respect to percentages, Chicago Heights was clearly the most Italian city in the state and one of the most Italian cities in the country.[20]

By the beginning of the second decade of the twentieth century, Chicago Heights was well on its way to becoming a city with a substantial Italian population and identity. Fueled by the dominant forces of urbanization, industrialization, and immigration, the development of Chicago Heights and an Italian presence went hand in hand. These forces, moreover, played a significant role in the daily lives of Italians once they came to reside in the city. Most significantly, choices about where to reside were largely molded by these social and economic processes. Upon entering Chicago Heights, Italians (and most other southern and eastern European, African American, and Mexican ethnic groups) were relegated to live in one of two sections of the city—namely, the East Side or the Hungry Hill areas. The East Side was located east of the Chicago & Eastern Illinois Railroad lines between Tenth and Twenty-first streets. The Hungry Hill (or the Hill) area was situated in the southeast section of Chicago Heights, with the dominant Italian presence along Twenty-first, Twenty-second, and Twenty-third streets—dubbed by locals as "Macaroni Boulevard."[21]

To suggest that Italians, or other ethnic groups, were relegated to live in these areas might be a bit harsh.[22] There were certainly elements of choice based on kinship ties, a sense of *campanilismo,* distance from employment, and the like. Yet, these choices were themselves heavily circumscribed. Specifically, as the population of Chicago Heights increased dramatically at the turn of the century, affordable housing was in short supply. And as the city population "spiked" in the years immediately proceeding World War I, the housing shortage led homeless workers to hound "the *Star* offices in search of lodging for their families."[23] Predictably, the costs of housing increased and new immigrants were forced to locate, whatever their preferences, in the most affordable housing located near the industrial plants on the east side of town.

At the same time, it may not stretch credibility to argue that the creation of these East Side ethnic enclaves was a part of the larger industrial plan of the Chicago Heights Land Association. Thus, the architects of this plan presumably were aware that building a residential community whose homes were intertwined within a maze of steel mills, chemical plants, and railroad switching yards would appeal only to those with the least amount of resources to live elsewhere. Somewhat benignly, these architects may have been aware that most immigrants needed to live close to work because of limited transportation options. More likely, they were oblivious to the housing needs of the immigrant population, especially if Goodspeed is correct in stating that "the policy of the land association has been to keep the factory district segregated from the residential part of the town."[24] Apparently, the extensive East Side housing planned by the Land Association was not counted among the "residential part" of the town. For whatever reasons, then, the creation of the densely populated, immigrant-rich East Side and Hungry Hill areas of Chicago Heights were predictable, if not intentional, outcomes of the larger industrial objectives of the planning association.

Finally, the character and dynamics of the immigration process itself contributed to these enclave developments. At least in the early years, the majority of Italian immigrants were single men. Even by 1910, more than 60 percent were men.[25] Many came to the city as classic "birds of passage" or immigrants "who would work until they either had earned enough money to bring their wives and families over to America or, if they were single, when they had earned enough to send for a pre-arranged wife."[26] And some, no doubt, came for the sense of adventure and roguishness that America offered. Whatever the precise reasons, residential accommodations were most likely secondary. As Vecoli suggests, a number of these Italian immigrants in Chicago Heights lived in "barracks-like boarding houses."[27] In the Hungry Hill area, it was not uncommon for as many as fourteen men to share accommodations on a round-the-clock basis such that while some were at work others slept in their beds.[28]

The 1920s started out much like the previous decade. The city's population continued to expand from 14,525 to 19,653; the number of industries increased from 80 to 103; and the number of industrial wage earners increased from 4,444 to 6,621.[29] And Italian immigration, after coming to a virtual standstill during World War I, experienced a postwar rush in the years immediately after the war.[30] Optimism about Chicago Heights ran so high that city planners envisioned the emergence of Chicago Heights as one of Illinois's largest municipalities.[31]

However, before the decade of the 1920s had run its course, the major social and demographic patterns established at the very beginning of the century changed dramatically. Population growth slowed, industrial development stagnated, and immigration, especially from southern Europe, came to a halt. A number of factors combined to bring about these changing fortunes. Thus, at the beginning of the decade, city fathers sought to moderate growth for fear that rapid change would destabilize the community and create a boom town with an inevitable decline.[32] At the same time, the national Immigration Acts of 1921 and 1924, and subsequent modifications, sharply curtailed the flow of immigrants into the country by establishing quotas for certain nationality groups, a good many of which were the southern and eastern European groups that had fueled the emergence of Chicago Heights over the past decade. And the Great Depression of 1929 set into motion a string of bank failures, factory closings, and job layoffs that continued until the beginning of World War II. Thus, between 1920 and 1930, the city population grew to 22,321—a 14 percent increase. However, between 1930 and 1940, the population increased to only 22,461—a less than 1 percent gain. In 1930, Chicago Heights vied with just a handful of Illinois communities (Melrose Park, Brookfield, and Chicago) for the highest rate of unemployment for cities over 10,000 people.[33] And it was estimated that anywhere from 30 to 60 percent of the city's residents were on relief during the height of the Depression.[34]

Though these social and economic misfortunes spread throughout Chicago Heights, the largely Italian East Side and Hungry Hill enclaves were especially hard hit. Thus, the *Chicago Heights Star* reported that "when the depression struck, the plight of our Italian neighbors was indeed a sad one. . . . The Italians, being mostly unskilled laborers, were the first to be effected and thrown out of employment . . . and with the exception of a comparative few have not returned to work since."[35] Italians also comprised the largest nationality group of those who applied for aid from the Chicago Heights Relief Association in 1932.[36] And these numbers might have been considerably higher if Italian Americans did not "abhor the government relief they have been receiving."[37] Or as Dominic Sesto, an East Side resident put it, "It was bad. People had to scrounge around to make ends meet—a nickel here, a dime there. Some of the people we knew were on relief. But most of us didn't. People just had too much pride."[38]

The fortunes of Chicago Heights improved dramatically as the United States prepared to enter World War II. As a manufacturing town, Chicago Heights benefited greatly from the national war effort. The steel plants, chemical companies, and glass works went back to full employment. Retail sales hit an all-time high and the city population increased to 24,551 in 1950. With eighty manufacturing plants and over 65 percent of the city's labor force employed in manufacturing, Chicago Heights rode the wave of the postwar boom. The city aggressively annexed a number of surrounding areas, attracted new industries, and witnessed a raft of new residential developments on the north side of town. As one study reported approvingly, "Chicago Heights is a small replica of Chicago in terms of population mix, industrial, economic and social development."[39]

In spite of this prosperity, a number of disturbing trends were beginning to surface. While this new quality housing was being built on the outskirts of the city, housing in the old East Side district was rapidly deteriorating. The number and substandard quality of these units led to the appointment of a special housing committee in 1949. In their report, the committee pointed to the blighted conditions in the East Side neighborhood and, at least indirectly, chastised the original town founders for the "close admixture of homes, businesses, and industry."[40]

Tied in with these housing problems, Chicago Heights experienced a new form of residential segregation. Where previously the East Side had been a mixture, however uncomfortable at times, of white ethnic groups, blacks, and Hispanics, the decades of the 1950s and 1960s saw the first stages in the substantial exodus of the white population to other parts of the city or neighboring villages. In particular, the Italians vacated the East Side and contributed to the isolation of blacks and Hispanics—a trend that was nearly complete by the end of the next decade. Thus, by 1980, the heart of the East Side Italian enclave had turned almost exclusively black, with a small Hispanic population. Close to 95 percent of the residents in the area were black and close to 5 percent were Hispanic.[41] In a more insidious manner, when Italians did rise to positions of power in the city government in the 1970s, a few among them sought to contain the black population on the East Side through a number of illegal practices, which included falsifying code violations, soliciting acts of vandalism, and hiring arsonists when blacks sought housing on the west side of town.[42]

Added to these problems, Chicago Heights was losing its manufacturing base. Thus, the city began to lose a good deal of its competitive advantage in the 1950s with the introduction of the interstate highway system, which made it less imperative for industrial plants to locate close to rail transportation. And with the emergence of a global economy in the 1970s, the city's mix of steel fabricators, chemical companies, and stamping plants was hit especially hard by more efficient regional and overseas competition. As early as 1963, Chicago Heights was one of the few cities in Illinois to see a *decline* in the number of people employed in manufacturing over the previous five-year period.[43] By 1970, the proportion of the city's labor force engaged in manufacturing had shrunk to just 37 percent, close to a 30 percent decrease in the span of two decades.[44] And though Chicago Heights reached its peak population at 40,900 in that year, the overall population has declined most every decade since then. Arguably, if Chicago Heights was on the leading edge of the new industrial society at the end of the 1800s, less than a century later, it was one of the first to suffer the eventual deindustrialization of the American economy.

In many ways, Chicago Heights stands today as it did at the beginning of the last century. In the late 1800s, it was a "sleepy village" in danger of being left behind by the rapidly advancing industrial and early capitalist society; in the late 1900s and beyond, it is a "gritty town" largely out of step with the postindustrial, global economy. If in the last century it was a town teeming with a young, displaced European immigrant population, today it is a city with a young, marginalized black and Hispanic population long excluded from sources of economic, political, and cultural power. And if in the past organized crime among Italians arose in response to the limited opportunities and subsequent creation of valuable social capital resources, there is reason to believe that similar processes may be at work as new forms of organized crime emerge within the African American and Latino populations in the city.[45] In this sense, a study of Chicago Heights may tell us a good deal about the connection between Italians and organized crime—in particular, the constraints and opportunities for success in the community context and how these forces generated these criminal enterprises. But this study may also shed light on contemporary organized crime groups and their own struggles to overcome the community processes that threaten survival and much needed social and economic advancement.

Organized Crime in Chicago Heights: A Brief History

Chicago Heights has been home to a number of well-known people—David Broder, Pulitzer Prize-winning columnist; Jim Bouton, New York Yankee star pitcher and author of the tradition breaking, first-person sport diary *Ball Four*; Eddie Condon, Chicago style jazz great; Sam Cooke, legendary crossover gospel, soul, and pop singer and writer. And there were others. But if you ask people who have heard about Chicago Heights what image comes to mind, there is an awfully good chance it would have something to do with organized crime. For years, this association has been imprinted in the public mind. For example,

> Chicago Heights has a remarkably sordid history. It long has had a reputation as a city where organized crime wielded heavy influence, and where gangland murders once were commonplace.[46]
>
> Prohibition, with its tremendous profit for outlaws and corrupt politicians, stamped the city of Chicago Heights with a criminal reputation that the respectable citizens of the community . . . feared would remain for all time.[47]
>
> For 70 years, dating back to Al Capone, this gritty blue collar suburbs 25 miles south of the Loop has been dogged by its reputation as a mob-town, where gangsters, politicians and police joined hands in an unholy alliance.[48]

So much for historical nuance. How did Chicago Heights acquire such a nefarious reputation? In the following, I provide a partial answer with a brief review of organized crime as it emerged in the first half of the century in Chicago Heights.

In broad strokes, the rise and decline of organized crime in the city roughly paralleled the rise and decline of Chicago Heights as an urban, industrial, and immigrant city. No doubt, some form of organized vice activities—gambling, in particular—was to be found in the local taverns and road houses prior to Chicago Heights's development as an industrial center. However, the emergence of an organized crime syndicate, or what city leaders termed the "slot machine trust," did not materialize until the early 1900s with the increasing flow of industrial jobs and immigrants into the city. Indeed, as early as 1906, just several years after incorporation as a city, political campaign debate was already centered on *reform* and the threats imposed by the emerging immigrant population. Candidates for the upcoming mayoral and aldermanic elections decried the proliferation of gambling, slot machines, and houses of prostitution in the red light district of the city. There were repeated calls over the next several years that all gambling in the local saloons be stopped and slot machines confiscated. An editorial in the *Chicago Heights Star* argued that the local "slot machine trust" had taken unfair advantage of "men who could ill afford to part with their money."[49] At the same time, local citizens blamed this slot machine trust for corrupting municipal officials. Charges that local officials received tribute for looking the other way on violations of the gambling statutes were commonly expressed in the local papers. In addition, bawdy houses of ill repute also came under attack as a number of saloon keepers were charged with harboring women and running houses of prostitution. Thus, in 1915, a candidate for mayor pledged to "crush the twenty-sixth street vice trust and send fifty or sixty vicious men who are now living from the earnings of unfortunate women to the bridewell, where they belong."[50]

The development of this vice trust, and especially the ill-famed reputation it brought to Chicago Heights, was disconcerting to the local business elite and the managing partners of the Chicago Heights Land Association. There was a fear that Chicago Heights would be perceived as a town overrun with gamblers, gang rule, and undesirables and that this would discourage industrial investment. Specifically, the local Chamber of Commerce and Manufacturers Association urged the city council to rid the city of these "organized robbers, organized gamblers, and organized practitioners of immorality." Failure to do so, threatened the chamber, would result in an appeal to the state's attorney office to clear the Heights of these criminals.[51]

Figure 1.1. At the beginning of the last century, the octopus was a common image for something alien, malevolent, and insidious. Here, it was used to characterize the evils of the slot-machine trust and by implication the alien character of the predominantly ethnic wards on the East Side of Chicago Heights. Courtesy of the Sun-Times Media, *South Town Star.*

These efforts, however, ultimately proved unsuccessful. For during the 1920s, Chicago Heights developed a nearly worldwide reputation for crime and vice operations. The *Chicago Tribune* dubbed Chicago Heights "the bad lands south of the city" and on the other side of the ocean the *Stockholm Daily News* wrote, "Hoodlums own city . . . raid in the worst community in the United States."[52] Eschewing such broad and hyperbolic characterizations, the *Chicago Heights Star,* nevertheless, bemoaned that in the world's eyes "Chicago Heights is simply Sodom and Gomorra over again, only more so."[53]

This reputation was not without merit. Over the decade of the 1920s, at least sixty-five murders were attributed directly to the battle for control of Chicago Heights's vice operations.[54] As such, Chicago Heights was said to be the city with the highest rate of slaying in the United States per capita.[55] Newspaper reports of bullet-ridden bodies shoved out of cars, found in roadside ditches, lying on sidewalks in front of their homes, or slumped dead in their parlor chairs became all too familiar to local readers. Closely tied to this violence was an illicit "alky" ring that arguably produced and distributed a greater share of illegal alcohol than any place in the country. Thus, in 1928, one federal officer, upon busting up one of the many illegal stills in the city said, "Chicago Heights is one huge distillery. There is nothing in the United States to equal it."[56] And as one might expect, the reputation of Chicago Heights as a lawless community resounded to local officials who were seen as complicit in letting local gangsters engage in unchecked violence, gambling, and the alcohol trade. During the decade, the mayor of Chicago Heights, the police chief, the former police chief, the postmaster, among others, were charged by a grand jury with conspiracy to violate prohibition and gambling laws.

Early on, this lawlessness was unstructured. The general conditions in Chicago Heights—the large immigrant population, the proximity to Chicago, the isolation of ethnic enclaves from the control of public officials—had created a fertile ground for the growth of a number of independent criminal entrepreneurs, especially with respect to gambling and prostitution. However, the production and distribution of illegal alcohol posed a more serious organizational challenge. Success in this market required, at minimum, clandestine production facilities, the importation of raw materials, the recruitment of skilled workers, a networked distribution system, protection from hijackers, and a retail presence. With the advent of Prohibition, then, we see a consolidation of organized crime activities in Chicago Heights. From Chicago, Johnny Torrio, then head of the embryonic Chicago Outfit, made an initial foray into Chicago Heights when he opened the Moonlight Café on Lincoln Highway in 1920.[57] And Lorenzo Juliano, who later was to ally himself with Al Capone, positioned himself as the "reputed bootlegger leader of the Chicago Heights district" through a string of alleged bombings and murders.[58]

However, one of the most successful organized crime operations during this time was headed by a local Chicago Heights man, Antonio Sanfilippo. An émigré from Sicily in 1904, Sanfilippo was a pharmacist who owned a drug store in the Hungry Hill area of the Heights. Sanfilippo used his Sicilian ethnic alliances to control the vote in the local Italian community and have himself elected as an alderman in the Chicago Heights city government in 1915. However, when Chicago Heights went to a commission form of government in 1921, in large part as an attempt to protect city officials from graft and corruption, Sanfilippo was defeated in a close election. Undaunted, Sanfilippo turned his personal skills and networks into the organization and control of a large number of "alky-cookers" in Chicago Heights.[59] Specifically, through fear, blackmail, friendship, and extortion, Sanfilippo organized not only the Italian but also many Polish and Slovakian homes into a highly efficient moonshine operation.[60] No doubt understating his leadership role, the *Chicago Heights Star* reported in 1924 that Sanfilippo was "according to street gossip . . . mixed up in the bootlegging business."[61]

Sanfilippo was assisted in his efforts by a number of fellow Sicilians, in particular Phil Piazza, Jim Lamberta, and Joe Martino. Together, these leaders attempted not as much to monopolize the actual vice operations on their own, though they did control a number of bootlegging and gambling houses, but to provide protection and connections for the variety of factions and illicit activities then taking place in Chicago Heights and the surrounding areas. Specifically, such patron-client relationships took the form of recruiting "still builders" and production sites, serving as a distribution network for the illegal hooch, and bribing police officers and public officials.[62] As one Chicago Heights leader reportedly told Eliot Ness, "we've got things pretty well fixed up around here with the cops and the prohibition boys. No use havin' no trouble."[63] In providing such services, the Chicago Heights organization was perhaps ahead of its time and served as a model for the Chicago Outfit. Even Torrio's entrée into the Chicago Heights market was presumably brokered with Sanfilippo's agreement to provide protection for Torrio's operation.[64]

These attempts at consolidation, however, did not proceed without considerable conflict and intrigue. Indeed, as the Sanfilippo organization became more powerful, it attracted both enemies and admirers. At one level, the independent alky-cookers and factions in Chicago Heights balked at having to pay tribute in return for protection, which often resulted, nevertheless, in raids by local officials.[65] At the same time, Piazza and Lamberta, chief lieutenants for Sanfilippo, were ambitious men who chafed at Sanfilippo's old-world tactics and power. And lurking on the outskirts of the Chicago Heights operation, Al Capone was coming to power and forging new alliances with three Chicago Heights associates—Dominic Roberto, Jimmy Emery, and Frank Laporte—who themselves were emerging as forces to be reckoned with in the Chicago Heights underworld. Whatever the combination of factors or characters involved, Sanfilippo paid the price with his life, for in 1924, he was found slumped in his car with four bullets in his head, all from behind. Police speculated that the men who shot Sanfilippo most likely were friends or associates of Sanfilippo. No one was ever charged with the murder. Nevertheless, Phil Piazza assumed control of the Chicago Heights operation.

The reign of Piazza as the "Italian boss of Chicago Heights" was short-lived.[66] Less than two months after narrowly escaping an attempt on his life, an attempt which resulted in the shotgun murder of Piazza lieutenant Lamberta, Piazza was himself gunned down outside his well-known gangster hangout (and subterranean alcohol production facility)—the Milano Café. Again, there were the usual suspects—local bootleggers angry at Piazza's heavy-handed street taxes and subordinates wishing to take over Piazza's lucrative operations. However, Piazza's death most likely came about as a result of the on-going "Beer Wars" that were twisting their ways simultaneously through the underworlds in both Chicago and Chicago Heights.[67]

In Chicago, Capone was now the undisputed head of the Chicago Outfit with the machinations surrounding the retirement of Johnny Torrio. Torrio's decision to give up the reigns of the Outfit came only after he was near-fatally wounded by Hymie Weiss and Bugs Moran—rivals of Torrio in control of bootlegging operations on the north side of Chicago. Weiss and Moran had engaged in this assassination attempt in response to the slaying of their partner and leader, Dion O'Banion. O'Banion's death was reportedly sanctioned by Torrio and Capone because O'Banion had sought increasing control and presence both in the south side Torrio-Capone organization and the west side operation run by the "Terrible Gennas"—six Sicilian brothers known for their murderous ways and iron-fisted control of the Taylor Street bootlegging operation. In further retaliation for O'Banion's murder, Weiss and Moran, with the aid of gunman Vincent Drucci, also engaged in a number of assassination attempts against Capone, but were unsuccessful. Undaunted, this north side trio had more success with the Genna brothers, for within a short time, two of the Genna brothers were murdered gangland style, another killed in a shoot out with police, and the remaining brothers gave up their Outfit business.[68] By the summer of 1925, when the smoke had cleared, almost literally, Capone, with the significant exception of the north side gang of Weiss, Moran, and Drucci, had assumed the control of the entire city. Capone was on his way to becoming the Big Fellow.

Less than thirty miles away, the Chicago Heights underworld was also undergoing a transformation. Piazza's reign as the head of the bootlegging ring had largely been a Sicilian operation. And in the early part of the century, the other large Southern Italian contingent in Chicago Heights, the Calabrese, were largely shut out from the spoils of these illegal operations. As such, Dominic Roberto and Jimmy Emery had by this time formed their own formidable Chicago Heights operation involved in bootlegging, gambling, and nighttime entertainment. As part of their crew, Roberto and Emery had also recruited Roberto's cousin, Frank Laporte. Together, these three Calabrian men created a tight-knit, loyal organization forged by kinship ties, a dislike for Piazza's harsh rule,[69] and a sense of *companilismo.* For example, Luigi Corsino, my grandfather, worked for Roberto and Emery making whiskey. However, this did not stop the Piazza clan from asking Luigi to make moonshine for their Sicilian organization. However, the lure of additional money was no match for the entrenched social and personal ties. As my father said, "he had offers with different people. The Piazza faction would ask him to come work for them. He could of if he wanted to, but he wouldn't do it. He came from the same hometown as Roberto and Laporte. The families went back a long time together."[70]

Yet, loyalty, in and of itself, would not be sufficient to topple Piazza and his organization. This would require muscle. And though Roberto, Emery, and Laporte were not adverse to using violence for personal gain, having already been suspected and charged by the Chicago Heights police with several murders,[71] they could not match the Piazza gang's collection of hired guns and resources. It was at this point that the developments in Chicago proved fortuitous for Roberto and his organization—and deadly for Piazza and his followers. As Piazza had risen to power, he had distanced himself from the Torrio-Capone organization and, perhaps, because of his Sicilian ties "had aligned himself firmly with the Gennas."[72] Thus, a number of high-ranking Genna operatives were frequent visitors to Piazza's Milano Café. However, when the Genna gang was decimated by the north side gang of Bugs Moran, Piazza lost an important ally. At the same time, as Capone gained more power, the lucrative Chicago Heights operation became appealing, especially given that the Heights operation had started out as a "Torrio-Capone suburb" and that Piazza had prospered "at Capone's sufferance."[73] What was required, however, was a connection, an organizational entrée into the Heights's collection of alky cookers, paid-off politicians, and community support. The Roberto-Emery-Laporte gang provided this crucial link.

Of course, this takeover of Chicago Heights would not come easy. Even with Lamberta and Piazza gone, there were still many in the Piazza gang who aspired to take control of the leaderless organization. So, over the next several years, with a lethal combination of Capone organizational firepower and Roberto knowledge and ruthlessness, the remaining leaders of the Piazza gang were systematically hunted down and killed. Besides Lamberta and Piazza, the following men, all with ties to the Piazza organization were slain: Joseph Catanda, Frank Camera, Joe Salvo, Giuseppe Nerone, Frank Capello, and Antonio Destefano Pelledrino. Indeed, this gang war was so methodical and predictable the *Chicago Tribune* took to keeping a scorecard and predicting precisely how many gangsters would meet their fate in this manner. Thus, in

1926, the *Tribune* would write, "the total toll in the battle for supremacy in the Chicago Heights liquor war is expected to take ten lives and thus far eight have died."[74] These predictions were chillingly accurate. In the next several days, the body of Joseph Termain, a former associate of Piazza, was found riddled with three bullets in his chest. And in 1928, old guard Piazza leader, Joe Martino, was gunned down in Chicago Heights almost immediately after being arrested by Eliot Ness and released on bail.

With Martino's death, the Capone-Roberto ascendance in Chicago Heights was nearly complete. While Capone continued to do battle both with his north side adversaries, resulting in the infamous Saint Valentine's Day Massacre in 1929, and with increased law enforcement efforts in Chicago and the Capone stronghold in Cicero, the Chicago Heights operation was wildly successful. Illegal booze, prostitution, and gambling had earned the Heights what local business leaders feared—the reputation as a "wide open town." And law enforcement officials, at least those outside the city, were also aware of the growing importance of Chicago Heights to the Chicago Outfit as a whole. Thus, James Deveroux, chief of the Cook County highway police, said,

> We have made fair progress in cleaning up Cicero. . . . But Chicago Heights has remained a sore spot. There are probably more than two dozen huge distilleries in the vicinity of that suburb. Their owners have been getting richer and tougher and have come to believe that they are entirely outside the law. We intend to show them differently.[75]

These statements may have constituted a part of the ritualistic bravado that law officers felt obliged to cite when talking about the Capone Outfit. Still, the Chicago Heights operation had become so outrageous that law enforcement officials had no option but to "show them differently." By the beginning of 1928, Dominic Roberto was no longer in day-to-day control of the Chicago Heights organization. He fled the country for fear of being arrested for a bootlegging operation. Upon his return, he ran afoul of conspiracy charges and lying under oath regarding his criminal past. Eventually, he was deported to Italy. Nevertheless, his successor, Jimmy Emery, took control of the Heights operation after being appointed to this position by Capone—a position that Binder and Luzi argue may have been symbolized in the figure 1.2.[76]

As a leader of the Chicago Heights operation, Emery may have exhibited his own bravado in 1928. A series of gangland murders had alerted U.S. Assistant District Attorney Daniel Anderson to the realization that the local police were woefully ineffective in controlling the bootlegging operation. However, these perceptions turned to moral and professional outrage when Leroy Gilbert,

Figure 1.2. This photo was taken in the backyard of Jimmy Emery's home in Chicago Heights in 1928. It includes a mix of Chicago and Chicago Heights Outfit leaders. Starting from the left in the front row: Frank Laporte, Vera Emery (Capone's goddaughter), Al Capone, Willie Henry, and Jimmy Emery. Starting from the left in the back row: Rocco DeGrazia, Louis "Little New York" Campagna, Claude "Screwy" Maddox, Nick Circella, and Sam Costello. Photo courtesy of Michael Roberts.

the chief of the police in nearby South Chicago Heights, was gunned down in his own home shortly before he was scheduled to appear before a grand jury regarding the arrest of two men who were caught ferrying illicit liquor through his South Chicago Heights community. The attack on Gilbert was especially gut wrenching for its frontal assault of a police officer and its brutality. As the *Chicago Daily News* reported, "As Gilbert sat in the parlor of his home two men crept to the windows, rested their shotguns on the sill and fired. Gilbert fell from his chair dead, the top of his head nearly blown off."[77]

In response, District Attorney Anderson, in cooperation with the Chicago Police Department, took the most unusual strategy of organizing a posse of over a hundred law enforcement officials for the purposes of conducting their own raid on Chicago Heights. Early in the morning of January 6, 1929, the posse sped into the city and split up—some officers were assigned to root out the known distilleries in the area, others to roost suspected criminals from their homes, and still others to commandeer the Chicago Heights police force, whose loyalty to these law enforcement efforts were in question. The immediate consequences of the raid were impressive. Some twenty men thought to have had a hand in the slaying of Police Chief Gilbert or who were involved in local vice operations were locked up in the Chicago Heights jail. And at the home of Oliver Ellis, a Capone associate, police officers found more than four hundred slot machines and incriminating evidence that would eventually lead to the arrest of Al Capone's brother, Ralph Capone. However, the long-term consequences for the Chicago Heights operation were negligible. Even the grand jury investigation of Capone's involvement with the Chicago Heights operation centered less on Chicago Heights and more on Capone and his knowledge of the St. Valentine's Day Massacre.[78]

Despite the raids, at the end of the 1920s, organized crime in Chicago Heights flourished. With the blessings and organizational resources of Capone, the Heights operation had achieved that rare joining of what Block has termed the power and enterprise syndicate.[79] That is, the Capone-Emery-Laporte gang had bludgeoned its way through both the extant legitimate and illegitimate power structures and brought an unprecedented centralization to the illegal enterprises associated with the alky business, gambling, and prostitution. For the time being, the control of the power syndicate and the enterprise syndicate were one. As such, the organization was able to extract enormous profits by providing protection and services for the criminal entrepreneurs who ran these illicit operations, but at the same time add substantially to these profits by extorting these same criminal entrepreneurs, such as Ellis, who had nowhere else to turn for help. William Roemer, legendary FBI organized crime agent, may have had the outlines of these syndicate processes in mind when he stated years later that "Chicago Heights has been the prototype of how the mob operates since the days of Al Capone."[80]

However, as Block argues, such centralization is highly contingent, for the power structures that graft themselves to these economic enterprises often rely on fragile alliances and ultimately resort to personal violence—a very unstable and fluid mechanism of control and domination. These forces of instability may have been at work as the Chicago Heights operation moved into the decade of the 1930s. This transformation began with the gradual demise of Capone and his influence in Chicago Heights. In the aftermath of the Saint Valentine's

Day Massacre, federal law enforcement efforts against Capone were enhanced and Capone was eventually convicted of the now-famous charge of income tax evasion. As Capone was sent to federal prison, the boys in Chicago Heights lost a chief benefactor and ally. Though the leaders in the Chicago Heights operation would retain close ties with Capone's successors such as Frank Nitti and Tony Accardo, these successors never had the intimate, personal and social ties that Capone had in Chicago Heights. As a result, the Chicago Heights operation, while always a critical enterprise and always a consistent stream of revenue for the Chicago Outfit, were never again a part of "the innermost circle of racketeering in Chicago and throughout the Midwest."[81]

At the same time, the Chicago Outfit, and the Chicago Heights operation in particular, were seriously undermined by the national repeal of Prohibition in 1933. Though the illegal stills continued to operate and produce "wildcat alcohol" well into the decade, the eventual legal sale and distribution of liquor cut into the black market profits of the Chicago Heights crew. The Heights operation responded by expanding its illegal activities to several old-line moneymakers such as gambling, strip joints, and prostitution. In particular, gambling in the form of dice games, punchboards, and pinball machines became more prominent as the Depression era progressed. Indeed, toward the end of the decade gambling became so prevalent that Chicago Heights police made open judgments about *which* gambling operations to raid. Thus, one police magistrate dismissed charges against eight "Negro" defendants following a raid on a dice game by declaring, "I could name at least sixteen places in town where there is gambling for fifty times the amount here."[82]

This transformation of the Chicago Heights operation did not always proceed in a nonviolent manner. Though the decade was relatively free from the gangland warfare of the 1920s, changes in the distribution of power and enterprise activities, predictably, produced opportunities and challenges that erupted into bloodshed. The most dramatic involved the daring, Saint Valentine's Day–like massacre of Sam Costello in 1938. Costello, a close associate of Capone and a former partner of Emery and Laporte, had become the leader of a rival, Sicilian-based bootlegging ring in Chicago Heights. With the end of Prohibition, bootlegging profits had dried up and Costello, police theorized, turned toward the lucrative, slot-machine racket in the surrounding communities.[83] This incursion into these gambling operations, however, incurred the enmity of the Emery-Laporte organization. As T. J. Sullivan, chief of the state department of criminal investigations, said at the time, "Racketeers fight more fiercely over controlling slots than they fought over beer and alcohol in Prohibition days. The revenue is tremendous."[84] In this vein, Costello's actions not only challenged Emery and Laporte's control in the area, but it threatened the profit base, especially given that the state district attorney, Thomas Courtney, was bringing new pressure to halt the slot machine traffic.[85] And in Chicago Heights itself, city voters had just overwhelmingly elected a mayor and city council pledged to eliminate gambling.

So, in a carefully planned and orchestrated attack, the Emery-Laporte organization staged a daytime raid on one of Costello's hangouts—a bakery on Butler Street in Chicago Heights. Dressed as hunters to disguise their appearance, three men walked into the bakery and one called out, "Hello, Sammie." When Costello approached to shake the man's hand, the killer opened fire and shot Costello. Several of Costello friends came running out from a backroom with guns. Bakery customers ran out of the building or jumped into nearby flour barrels to avoid being hit. When the shooting was over, Costello was mortally wounded and three Costello supporters were injured. The gunmen escaped. That night, in anticipation of an all-out gangland war, other Costello friends surrounded the local hospital to protect their injured comrades. This war, however, never materialized. With Costello now out of the picture, the Emery-Laporte crew had cemented its claim as the only "legitimate" Outfit operation in the area south of Chicago.

With this consolidation of power, the Chicago Heights operation would maintain this monopoly on vice activities in the southern suburbs of Chicago. This power was spread among three long-time Chicago Heights residents. First, Jimmy Emery retained control of the Chicago Heights organization for much of the 1930s and into the early 1940s. However, ill health and an interest in Outfit operations beyond Chicago Heights, especially thoroughbred racing, led Emery away from the day-to-day machinations of the Chicago Heights crew. As Emery gave up practical control, he was replaced by two powerful figures—Frankie Laporte and John Roberts. Laporte had been in line to assume a more powerful position based upon his long association with Emery, Dominic Roberto, and Capone. In particular, Laporte's appointment by Capone as "payroll master" in charge of locating and paying off public officials in the southern suburbs and his reputed toughness and willingness to do the dirty work of the Outfit gave him the connections and practical experience necessary to assume control of the operations in the area. At the same time, John Roberts—brother of since-deported Dominic Roberto—also had a long association with the Chicago Heights operation. Roberts began his career running "cat houses" and organizing gambling rings in Chicago Heights. Chicago Heights resident, Louie Patrizi, said, "he had his hand in most every card game in the area."[86] Arrested as a Chicago Heights "hoodlum suspect" by the Illinois State Attorney office in

1930, Roberts went on to handle the lucrative slot machine rackets in the area and become, as John Binder describes it, "one of the central figures in organized crime in Chicago's south suburbs."[87] Indeed, another insider recalled, "John was the boss. He was even bigger than Frankie. Frankie had the finesse, but John was the real guy. He was the one that carried all the weight."[88]

Whoever was in the top position, it was clear that Laporte and Roberts were at the center of the Chicago Heights Outfit during the boom times of the 1940s and 1950s. And after a period of retrenchment following the end of Prohibition, the boys expanded their base of operation both in terms of geography and products. First, while Chicago Heights remained a central place for criminal activities, it was eclipsed by a number of other nearby communities—none more infamous than Calumet City. An FBI report on gambling, prostitution, and bookie joint conditions in Chicago Heights in 1944 states, "There exists in Chicago Heights a syndicate which formerly controlled the operation of all these activities in and around the area. This organization is attempting to gain control of Calumet City to replace these activities which formerly took place in and around Chicago Heights."[89] This report may have underestimated the extent of illegal activities going on in both cities. Calumet City, in particular, had become *the* "syndicate town" for the Chicago Outfit. Though long a home for Outfit activities, in the 1940s, Calumet City achieved both local and national prominence for its mix of bars, strip joints, peep shows, and gambling houses along a two-block area in and around State Line Avenue. Here, Chicago Outfit leaders, national celebrities, and blue-collar workers mingled together in what *Life* magazine called "the busy Barbary Coast of Lake Michigan's booming industrial plain.[90] In particular, the Owl Club, owned jointly by Chicago Outfit leader Tony Accardo and Laporte, became one of the most infamous and profitable gambling and entertainment spots in the country. From the combination of slot machines, dice games, roulette wheels, punch cards, poker games, call girls, and liquor sales in the club, the Internal Revenue Service put the annual income of the Owl Club in excess of $2,000,000 in the late 1940s. And as my father told me, "At night these rooms were filled with so many people, you couldn't find parking for blocks. They used to make so much money, they'd take it home in suitcases each night."[91]

Second, while the Heights operation expanded its control into other geographic territories, it also developed or mined new sources of revenue. Thus, along with the stable of bookie joints, gambling dens, and prostitution rings, Laporte and Roberts led the organization into two especially lucrative ventures—labor racketeering and the vending machine industry. In the postwar years, especially in the booming industrial centers in and around Chicago

Heights, the infiltration of the construction trades proved especially profitable in terms of misappropriation of union funds and required kickbacks from employers and builders. Indeed, control of the unions was deemed so valuable that the Chicago Heights crew was loath to give it up even when their efforts to assume leadership positions in the unions proved legally unsuccessful. Thus, Al Pilotto, once a driver for Frank Laporte, was a long-time president of the International Hod Rod Carriers, Builders, and Common Laborers Local 5 Union in Chicago Heights. Though voted out of office in the early 1960s, Pilotto refused to go away. He still maintained an office in the union headquarters and in the opinion of some members ran the union and made the final decisions.[92] And perhaps, one of the most noxious union ventures involved the tactics employed in the American Federation of Labor and Congress of Industrial Organizations' American Guild of Variety Artists Midwest Division. Here, the boys ostensibly organized strippers, "B" girls, and exotic dancers in Outfit run locales for the purposes of improving working conditions and providing welfare benefits. Not surprisingly, the boys exploited their control of the American Guild of Variety Artists union to force dancers to engage in illegal barroom activities for fear of losing their jobs "or else."[93]

Along with this immersion into the local unions, the decades of the 1940s and 1950s saw the Heights operation move aggressively into the vending machine business, especially the jukebox industry. This movement into the jukebox business was an astute decision in its own right. As Segrave argues, the 1940s saw unprecedented growth in the industry as the popularity of jukeboxes spread across America and came to be associated with uniquely American, patriotic themes in the midst of World War II. At the same time, the industry provided special advantages for crime syndicates because it was a cash business, making it relatively easy to launder money gained in illegal ways.[94] However, the Chicago Heights operation dramatically increased its chances for success by "muscling" its way into various "stops" and by threatening competitors who sought to install boxes in the Outfit's territory. For example, the Chicago Heights based Co-Operative Music, owned by Laporte and Roberts, among others, controlled the area south of Chicago—including Chicago Heights, Calumet City, and surrounding villages. And as one worker for the company said,

> You never knew exactly who did what. But there was this one outfit from Blue Island that would not take "no" for an answer. It was run by some hard-headed Germans who would go to our stops and try to talk the owners into using their boxes.... One night some of the guys put a bomb in their place and burned the place down.[95]

With this monopoly, then, of gambling, prostitution, labor racketeering, and vending machines, the Chicago Heights operation was, indeed, at its height. However, the 1960s also proved to be the beginning of the end for the century-long run of organized crime's dominance in Chicago Heights. Increasing efforts on the part of law enforcement officials, changing mores, and untimely deaths undercut the boys' ease of operation and profits. Thus, the renewed attention placed on organized crime by the Kennedy administration at the national level and the tenacious enforcement efforts by Cook County Sheriff Richard Ogilvie at the local level closed down a number of gambling operations. The life of top crime leaders became a frantic game of avoiding being served subpoenas through trips out of town, elaborate disguises, and the constant switching of cars to avoid being followed by federal and local officials.[96] At the same time, the advent of a more sexually liberated society and increasing acceptance of "legitimate" gambling venues made the "sin strip" of Calumet City nearly obsolete. And in 1961, John Roberts passed away and Laporte, having suffered a heart attack, looked to sell off his illegal operations and go into semiretirement in California. When Laporte died in 1972, long-simmering struggles as to who would control the south suburbs rackets brought a series of mob hits and in-fighting. Eventually, Al Pilotto assumed control of the southern suburbs and pushed the illegal activities in the direction of greater involvement in racketeering and the "chop shop" operation. However, Pilotto, though a "capo" in the larger Chicago Outfit, barely survived an assassination attempt in 1981 and was sent to prison on a series of racketeering convictions in the following year. Pilotto was replaced by Albert Tocco who ran the Heights Outfit and specialized in running a chop shop operation where cars would be stolen and broken into component parts that then would be resold. Tocco, though with considerable in-fighting, became the top Chicago Heights crime boss until 1990 when he was convicted of a variety of racketeering, conspiracy, and extortion charges. Upon being indicted, Tocco fled the country and by so doing made the FBI's Ten Most Wanted List. A few months later, Tocco was arrested and sentenced to two hundred years in a federal prison.[97]

By this time, also, recruitment of workers into the Chicago Heights operation was extremely difficult. The general social and economic conditions that had made an association with organized crime a viable alternative for a number of Italians had diminished. Many Chicago Heights Italians had either achieved a measure of social mobility or had moved to other cities or nearby suburbs, effectively relinquishing much of what was left of their social capital. Lombardo's study of recruitment into the Chicago Outfit suggests that in 1987, the Chicago Heights crew consisted, excluding associates, of some twenty-five to thirty members, most though not all of Italian lineage. However, Lombardo adds that since then, the crew has declined further and quotes one informant who said, "I don't know if Chicago Heights exists anymore as a group because the last time I went out to the Heights, they didn't have it. It's just not there anymore. The old clubs that we were aware of just aren't there."[98] Nearly a hundred years since the origins of the slot machines trusts in the early 1900s, federal investigators declared the Chicago Heights Outfit "defunct" and Lombardo reports, "it is now difficult to locate organized crime figures in the Chicago Heights area."[99]

In a rough fashion, then, organized crime in Chicago Heights has paralleled the fortunes of the city and the fortunes of the Italian population, in particular. As the city grew and attracted more Italian residents, organized crime prospered. And as the city experienced declining fortunes and the Italian population was diluted, the presence of organized crime waned. Taken at this level, one may be drawn to the essentialist argument that there exists an "inner relationship" between Italians and organized crime. Critiquing such facile explanations, however, is the centerpiece of this study. By focusing on the Chicago Heights example, I attempt to show the more complex, more contingent relationship between Italians and organized crime. In the next chapter, I begin by examining the range of social, economic, and cultural conditions that presented obstacles to the social mobility aspirations of Italians in the Chicago Heights context.

CHAPTER 2

WERE THEY PUSHED?

Cultural, Political, and Economic Discrimination

Diego Gambetta, author of the widely praised *The Sicilian Mafia*, once asked in another work, "Were they pushed or did they jump?"[1] Gambetta was struggling with the general human predicament regarding social forces and individual choice. Are people pushed into behavior by the structure of opportunities available (or not available) or do they make rational choices based on perceived costs and benefits? No doubt both processes are at work and no doubt situations vary in terms of the degree of human agency. With these general questions in mind, this chapter begins with an examination of the larger cultural, political, and economic forces at work in Chicago Heights during the first half of the twentieth century. The central argument is that Italians in Chicago Heights were essentially pushed into a range of entrepreneurial mobilizations (e.g., mutual-aid societies, ethnic businesses, labor organizing, and, most significantly, organized crime) by a limited, restrictive access to the traditional routes toward mobility.

This line of reasoning essentially follows the classic work of Robert Merton and his discussion of big city political machines and the rackets, a perspective that so many years after its original formulation is still the touchstone for most explanations of organized crime.[2] In short, Merton argued that cultural and structural arrangements might create acute tensions whereby appropriate avenues for social mobility are blocked for disadvantaged groups. Under such circumstances, alternative types of organizational adjustments may emerge to meet these socially induced problems. These collective strategies can take a variety of forms—some legal, some not. Most significantly, Merton held that if we temporarily abandon our moral indignation regarding vice and criminal activities, organized crime can be viewed in analytic terms as one special instance of these alternative, organizational adjustments. It would be possible to see these illegal ventures not merely as "a means of self-aggrandizement for profit-hungry and power-hungry *individuals* but as an organized provision for *subgroups* otherwise excluded from or handicapped in the race for 'getting ahead.'"[3]

In the following, I paint a picture of the major structural and cultural disadvantages the Italians in Chicago Heights faced in their struggle to get ahead—the cultural, political, and economic situations many Italians were up against for much of the last century. In essence, I attempt to show how these forms of discrimination boxed most Italians into a spatial and social isolation in Chicago Heights. These exclusionary processes, as Merton argued, blocked the ascent of the mobility ladder. However, they also had the unintended consequences of transforming the prosaic features of the Italian culture and social structure into a rich supply of social capital.[4] Specifically, they enhanced the possibilities that Italians would turn to their *paesani* next door, their *cugini* on the next street over, their *amici* at the corner bar as resources for organizing a union, establishing ethnic businesses, recruiting members to mutual-aid societies, and for running a criminal organization. Structural and cultural disadvantages, on the one hand, and consequential social capital resources, on the other, are joined in an attempt to provide a more encompassing and integrated understanding as to how Italians may have been pushed, but also were able to leap into organized crime.

Cultural Opprobrium

A distaste for Italians seemed to emerge fairly early in the history of Chicago Heights. As immigration patterns led to a sizeable Italian presence in the city, nativistic sentiments were increasingly directed at a range of Italian habits and customs. These sentiments, often times mixed with more positive personal relationships, came from religious leaders, city officials, the local newspaper, business owners, teachers, and school children. They effected the Italian assimilation into the dominant American culture in a variety of institutional contexts.

Perhaps, the most far-reaching effects of this cultural discrimination occurred in the schools. Thus, it has been well documented elsewhere that southern Italians did not place a high value on formal education for their children, especially for females. And this pattern seems to have also been the case in Chicago Heights, for many parents restricted their children's education and many children quit school as soon as they were able. However, these negative attitudes to schooling were no doubt influenced by the less-than-positive reception many Italian children faced when they entered the alien, middle-class world of the classroom. For example, the Italian children were often separated from the other children or made to sit in the back row of the classroom so as not to disturb or mingle with their West Side counterparts. At the same time, students were routinely graded upon the difficult-to-master, middle-class standards of "cleanliness, attentiveness, appearance, deportment, initiative, and general health."[5] These were cultural standards that most Italian children would have trouble achieving and as a consequence would be penalized academically. In a setting, therefore, in which there were no Italian teachers, administrators, or school board members, the lower-class status and customs of the Italian children became a significant criteria for sifting and sorting opportunities for learning and mobility.

Not surprisingly, these traditional Italian customs became a source of embarrassment to the students. As Dominic Pandolfi, a long-time Chicago Heights resident, suggests, "the teachers were most concerned about these foreigners." These concerns translated into a disparagement of the Italian language, manner of dress, and foods. "For a long time," Pandolfi said, "we were embarrassed about it, eating squid, eel . . . and the kinds of stuff they (our Italian parents) eat."[6] Aldo DeAngelis, who rose to a position of prominence as an Illinois State senator, expressed similar feelings. "We always were ashamed to have anybody know we could speak another language. More importantly, we were ashamed of the fact that we were Italian. That was a bad thing."[7] At times, this discrimination turned more overt. "After school the teachers were very severe and very hostile towards Italians," Pandolfi said.[8] Other Italian residents suggested that fellow students were often the worst source of disparagement in the school. Nick Tieri said, "When I left Garfield School to go to Washington School, it was a bad situation. . . . I was called all kinds of names. But with English . . . You're a dago, a ginny, wop and everything."[9] Another resident, Theresa Giannetti, recalls, "When we went to school definitely there was a distinction between the kids from the East Side, the Hill and the West Side. . . . We were dagos to them."[10]

These cultural affronts were not confined to the schools. As Italians moved into the wider society, they faced disapproving attitudes on the part of the press, local social clubs, and religious leaders. For example, the perception that Italians were intimately tied to criminal activities was pervasive. The *Chi-*

cago Heights Star would routinely link Italians with criminality by publishing stories that read, for example, "Antonio Serirro, an Italian, is under arrest," "a manhunt is on for a Sicilian," or "another Italian is done away with." As Nick Tieri said, the general feeling was that "if you were Sicilian then, you belonged to their gang. That's the attitude . . . the people took."[11] Olivia Kowalski expressed similar sentiments, "they sort of connected everybody that was Italian with that (gangster) type of people."[12]

Italians faired little better in the civic associations and social clubs of the Chicago Heights community. The combination of Catholicism, foreign customs, and "rough-neck" reputation resulted in the exclusion of Italians from many of the civic-commercial organizations. Italian women were routinely denied acceptance into the most prestigious society groups and associations. At the same time, the local country clubs denied Italian membership, though Italian youth were allowed to work as caddies. Even when Italians participated in the myriad athletic and social clubs on the west side of town, cultural barriers set a higher standard for acceptance or inclusion. "We were second class citizens without a doubt," said Chicago Heights resident Nick Zaranti. "If you went out for athletics you had to really work trying to make a team because they wouldn't give you the playing time to prove yourself."[13]

The church community was another source of conflict. As Italian immigration accelerated at the beginning of the century, the Archdiocese of Chicago gave the local residents permission to establish a national parish in Chicago Heights. Thus, in 1905, St. Rocco was formed and the church was built on a gift of land from city leader Martin Kilgallen. Before this, however, St. Agnes, the "Irish Church" on the west side of town, largely ignored Italian (and Polish) participation. Staffed principally by Irish priests, St. Agnes proved *a bit* uncomfortable for many Italians who felt ill at ease with a clergy who did not understand their peculiar style of Catholicism, imbued as it was with a mixture of anticlericalism and mysticism. Rudolph Vecoli—who based a portion of his ground-breaking research, *Chicago's Italians Prior to World War I: A Study of Their Social and Economic Adjustment,* on the Italians in Chicago Heights—wrote more generally of the plight of Italians in the Catholic churches of the day.

> Those Italians who ventured into Irish or German churches found them as alien as Protestant chapels. The coldly, rational atmosphere, the discipline, the attentive congregation were foreign to the Italians who were used to behaving in church as they would in their own house. Nor did the poorly dressed, sometimes unwashed, Italians find a ready welcome in the churches

> of other nationalities. Often they were turned away or seated in the rear with Negroes. Sometimes they heard themselves denounced as "Dagos" from the pulpit and told that they were not wanted.[14]

The Protestant response to this "Italian problem," as it came to be called, was also exclusionary. However, a notable exception was the Presbyterian Church of Our Savior, which engaged in a concerted attempt to lure Italians away from their culture, or at least their Catholic faith, with the appointment of an Italian pastor in 1910. Our Savior provided a host of religious services, youth group activities, citizenship classes all devoted to not only enhancing the moral values of the Italian immigrants but also their assimilation into the American society. The efforts of this church were also advanced with the establishment of the Cosmopolitan Community Center (later to be named the Harold Colbert Jones Memorial Community Center)—a limited settlement house established jointly by the Presbyterian community and the Manufacturers Association of Chicago Heights. The goal of the center was to advance "the moral, intellectual and industrial development of the people of Chicago Heights."[15] This curious mix of moral and industrial development not withstanding, the center served immigrants from southern and eastern Europe, with a focus in the early years on the large Italian population. Particular attention was devoted to children. The center provided "clean sports," "wholesome recreation," and showers. In an era in which hot water was not always available in the homes on the East Side or Hill areas, the showers were most beneficial if not always appreciated by the children. However, the underlying goals of the center were not simply to physically cleanse these "dirty little urchins" but to "sow the seeds of a new self-respect and moral cleanness in these little fellows."[16] Indeed, these practices presented such an affront to the traditional Italian culture, a number of Italians forbade their children from participating in center activities. Father Bonnani of St. Rocco would often call Italian children into the rectory and warn them about the "brainwashing" activities of the center.

Chicago Heights Italians, then, felt the sting of this cultural opprobrium across diverse settings. Yet, the most basic cultural discrimination was ecological. In the early years, Italians were simply not supposed to be in certain places. This ecological exclusion sought to isolate Italians literally on "the other side of the tracks." As Nick Zaranti said, "The whole west part of town, starting from the railroad tracks, the CNI [*sic*] railroad tracks moving west. We hit the downtown area and then beyond that you couldn't even go . . . cause they just wouldn't allow you, think you would be stealing."[17] With only a slight change in the geographic barriers, Italian resident Art Marks tells the same story, "The

Italians were kind of looked down upon at the time. Being Italian wasn't easy in those days. You couldn't cross Chicago Road."[18]

Political Alienation

To be sure, Italians in Chicago Heights contributed to their own cultural reproach. For example, the "rough-neck" status of the Italian youth was well deserved. Delinquent and malicious activities were certainly not unknown. "Italian boys," as Chicago Heights civic leader Hap Bruno commented, "were inclined to be a little bit more on the loose."[19] And even within the Italian community, gangs from one street would often be in conflict with gangs from the next street over. These conflicts would periodically find their way into the schools making it most difficult for teachers and administrators.

Yet, when we turn to a discussion of power and politics, Italians seem to have less culpability in terms of their political alienation from the mainstream political processes. Voting totals in the predominately Italian sections of the city were often on a par or often not significantly below the totals for the west side of the city.[20] And however suspect the motivations, organizational leaders in these Italian districts created a political machine that resulted in significant political participation on the part of Italian residents. As a result, during the first several decades of the century, Italian involvement in local city government was in fact extensive. By 1910, for example, Italians dominated politics on the East Side and Hill areas. Italians regularly elected fellow Italians to aldermanic positions from these districts. Candeloro and Paul concluded that in these early years "Italians had a lock on Wards 3 and 4."[21]

This participation was a source of consternation to West Side civic leaders. Thus, as early as 1911, what the *Chicago Heights Star* termed "the better element of the city" called for the establishment of a commission form of government, where commissioners would be elected at large rather than from particular wards. Though phrased in terms of increased governmental efficiencies and reduced costs, there is little doubt that this new form of government was also aimed at reducing the machine-style politics found in the Italian wards of Chicago Heights. The first attempt to establish this commission form of government was defeated in 1915, despite having strong support from the *Chicago Heights Star* and other civic organizations. However, agitation for this new governmental form did not abate. In 1921, increased city corruption led to new efforts to raise the city government "from the slough of despond" into which it had fallen.[22] Opponents of this change argued that these reform efforts were motivated by the attempt to prevent the "foreign and colored vote" from having a say in local government affairs.[23] This time, fueled in part by the increasing hostility to this "foreign element" after World War I, the "at large" referendum passed with 56 percent of the vote.

The commission form of government proved a great success in attracting candidates to run for political office. However, it was disastrous for Italian politicians in the city. Previously, Italian representation in city government had generally exceeded their proportion of the city population. Yet, from 1921 to 1941, Chicago Heights had only two commissioners and no mayors of Italian descent. As Dominic Pandolfi lamented, "It was very sad because politics was downtown, other than Italian."[24] Paradoxically, as Chicago Heights became more Italian in terms of the proportion of residents of Italian descent, the ethnic representative of Italians in city government virtually ceased. Indeed, one of the Italian commissioners elected was Maurino Ricchiuto, who in 1935 won a closely contested race only after a recount gave him the necessary margin of victory and only after he publicly disavowed his connection to the directors of the Italian Voter's League. Ricchiuto was eventually elected as mayor (after anglicizing his name to Richton) in 1947, 1963, and 1967. The other Italian was Louis Ursitti, a storeowner from the Hill area. Ursitti had served a term as an alderman before the change over to commissioners and served a brief two-year term again after this change.

Handicapped in terms of their formal participation in Chicago Heights city politics, local Italians turned to other political options. In the 1930s and 1940s, a small number of Italians sought political office in local school board elections, state senate races, and township contests. Again, Italians met with limited success. In part, this lack of success prompted several local groups to organize for the purpose of increasing Italian political influence. Thus, the Italian Voters' League of Chicago Heights, led by M. A. Stella and Silvio Piacenti, sought to bring all voters of Italian extraction into the political process. As Piacenti said, "We hold the balance of power in Chicago Heights and there is no reason why we should not exercise it."[25]

The Italian Voters' League was well aware that their efforts to enact political change in the city would ultimately require the reinstatement of the aldermanic form of government, where proportionate representation would result in close to half of the elected aldermen coming from the East Side and Hill areas of the city. As such, they were one among a coalition of different groups and interests who formed the Citizens' Municipal Party. This party argued that there were "numerous qualified men and women in Chicago Heights who would welcome the opportunity to give honest and efficient public service."[26] However, the West Side opposition group, consisting of "dozens of business men, industrial executives, and members of civic bodies" countered that such a system would result in confusion, divisive factions, and a lack of city unity.[27] Having defeated a similar referendum in 1931, this opposition group expressed confidence that it could once again turn back this challenge. Such confidence was justified when in 1939, Chicago Heights citizens voted to keep the commission form of government in place. In so doing, the ethnic-based political machine as an alternative structure for mobility was effectively eliminated. As Wozny concludes, the election results were "a big blow to 'ethnic' politicians. Now, they had to campaign throughout the entire city, and not just in their own neighborhoods. If the East Side wanted representation, or if the Hill wanted representation they would have to form alliances and coalitions in order to beat out established candidates who had the backing of the non-ethnic population."[28] With few exceptions, these alliances succumbed to the strong ethnic loyalties that separated the Italians, the Poles, the Mexicans, the Hungarians, and the Blacks in these areas. For more than thirty years, these groups were systematically excluded from these political processes.

Economic Discrimination

During the early part of the twentieth century, the dominant cultural and political processes were heavily weighted against Italians in Chicago Heights. Routes to mobility were blocked as a powerful and obstinate majority on the waspish west side of town clashed with a less powerful but no less obstinate minority of the east side of town. Specifically, Italians lacked the cohesiveness and stability to mount a serious challenge to the "balance of power" in the community. At the same time, Italians were unwilling, at least in the short run, to give up their cultural practices (from eating eels, to religious fests, to bocce) in the face of challenges posed by a nativistic and, often times, hostile culture. Thus, for every taunt of "wop" or "dago," Italians countered with a "mangia cakes" (cake eaters) derision of the "westsiders."[29]

Yet, in the economic realm, this bravado was missing. Unwilling to give up their culture, many Italians gave up pieces of their health, dignity, and freedom by submitting to the harshest of working conditions in the industrial plants and shop floors. Seven-day work weeks, unsafe working conditions, despicable sanitary facilities were the common elements facing most Italian laborers. Hardly a week would pass without a newspaper report of a worker being crushed by a falling crane, maimed by a metal press, or scalded by molten led. One account of life inside a Chicago Heights factory leaves little room for interpretation.

> They worked under brutalizing conditions. . . . Every place was a place of heat, grime, dirt, dust, stench, harsh glares, overtime, piecework, pollution, no safety gadgets, sweat, etc. The workers were, as the Italians called them, "Bestie Da Soma," beasts of burden. Emphysema, stomach ailments, heart ailments were common.[30]

In a nearby plant in Steger, where many Chicago Heights Italians found work, conditions were not much better. Practicing a form of "industrial feudalism," factory owners instituted a requirement that all workers deposit a sum of money (not less than $50), which would then be reinvested by the company. Or workers were required to buy plots of land owned by the factory owner.[31] The paternalistic intent of these practices was to help the Italian workers develop an economic foothold in American society. However, the uneven and rapacious nature of these requirements was not lost on many Italians who worked in the factory. As one worker commented, "On the money deposited the workers receive three per cent while the padrone reinvesting it in his industry makes ten times that much. Those who require lots of ground have hardly finished paying for one, when if they wish to keep their jobs, they must buy another."[32]

As unsavory as these industrial jobs may have been, these were among the best options for the unskilled Italian immigrants. In fact, Italians often took full advantage of their *paesani* ties when one or another worker assumed the position of foreman or hiring agent in an industrial plant. To be in a position to hire fellow Italians provided exalted status for the few Italians able to secure such a relatively favorable position on the shop floor. Indeed, while other parts of the city named schools or parks after people with meritorious service in government or public affairs, the Hill area gave this honor to Guy Patrarca, a steel mill foreman who was instrumental in helping fellow Italians obtain low-skilled jobs in the plant.

These *paesani* hiring processes were also at work in one of the other "desirable" jobs—working on a railroad crew laying tracks. A crew foreman would often be besieged by family and friends to hire someone from their Italian hometown. It was in this manner that my grandfather, Luigi, obtained his railroad job. Once again, however, these jobs provided subsistence wages in return for brutal working conditions. Even by the standards of the time, work on these railroad gangs was severe with fourteen-hour days in the hot summer sun under the watchful eye of the gang boss, who though a *paesani* would be as overbearing and demanding as his non-Italian counterpart. At the end of the day, conditions were hardly much better. As my grandfather said, "Many times we had only stale bread and old sausage to eat. We slept each night on top of one another in cattle cars."

The lot of the Italian worker then was filled with desperation. For many, the lack of any definable skills put them in competition, and conflict, for the least desirable jobs—from rag picker, to street peddler, to field hands in the nearby onion farms. For many Italians who migrated to Chicago Heights, this was the price for a better way of life. Schiavo's characterization of the economic plight and motivation of Italians in Chicago applies equally well to Chicago Heights Italians. "He knew that his life in the new world would be one of sorrows, of sacrifices, of humiliations, of self-denials. But the desire to change his economic status was by far much stronger than any obstacle he was to overcome."[33]

Yet, this reciprocal exchange was not immediate or ensured. An examination of occupations and occupational mobility patterns for Italians reveals considerable "sacrifice" and considerably less "change in economic status." Table 2.1 presents the distribution of jobs across the occupational structure for Italian, adult males in Chicago Heights for 1910 and 1930. This distribution is presented alongside comparable data for other larger, industrial cities in the period from 1905 to 1915. The unmistakable conclusion is that Italians consistently started at the bottom of the ladder. Though the patterns and waves of Italian immigration differ somewhat from city to city, it is clear that Italians clump decidedly into the two last rungs of the occupational hierarchy—no city more so than in Chicago Heights in 1910.

Added to this, comparative data with respect to other immigrant groups at the time (e.g., Russians, Poles, Austro-Hungarians, Jews, and Irish) generally suggest that Italians ranked lower than these other groups in terms of occupational status. For example, with a singular exception, Perlmann's analysis of Providence, Rhode Island, concludes, "more than any other immigrant group . . . the Italian families were concentrated at the bottom of the economic order."[34] Logan's study of New York found that in 1920, "among new immigrant groups, Italians are remarkably concentrated in lower status occupations."[35] And Thernstrom's study of occupational mobility in Boston concludes that the Irish and the Italians "were conspicuously to the rear of the procession."[36]

By 1930, the economic plight of Chicago Heights Italians had improved (see table 2.1). Italians experienced a measure of economic success whereby the proportion of unskilled workers had declined and Italian workers, as a whole, had increased their presence in every occupational position except the high white-collar positions. Still, after years and decades of struggle, this ascent up the occupational ladder was slow. "It took a long time," said Chicago Heights resident Hap Bruno. Thus, as the Great Depression loomed on the horizon, over 70 percent of the male, Italian population was still located on the bottom two rungs of the occupational ladder.[37]

Table 2.1. Occupational ranking of Italian, adult males, Chicago Heights, 1910 and 1930, other cities, 1900–1915

Occupational Rank	Chicago Heights 1910[a]	Pittsburgh 1900[b]	New York 1905[c]	Providence 1915[d]	Boston 1910[e]	Chicago Heights 1930[f]
High white collar	1	0	2	5	2	6
Low white collar	4	2	18	13	10	10
Skilled	8	23	22	19	23	13
Semiskilled	5	3	16	23	NA	13
Unskilled	82	72	42	37	65	58
Total	100	100	100	97	100	100
Number	(1,420)	(507)	(1,015)	(863)	(132)	(1,613)

Note: All values are percentages.

Sources:

[a]Department of Commerce and Labor, Bureau of the Census, *Thirteenth Census of the United States: 1910 Population,* Chicago Heights manuscripts.

[b]John Bodnar, Roger Simon, and Michael Weber, *Lives of Their Own: Blacks, Italians and Poles in Pittsburgh, 1900–1960* (Urbana: University of Illinois Press, 1983), 64.

[c]Thomas Kessner, *The Golden Door: Italian and Jewish Immigrant Mobility in New York City, 1880–1915* (New York: Oxford Press, 1977), 52.

[d]Joel Perlmann, *Ethnic Differences: Schooling and Social Structure among the Irish, Italians, Jews and Blacks in an American City, 1880–1935* (Cambridge: Cambridge University Press, 1988), 86. The sample consisted of Italian immigrant fathers. The percentages do not total 100 percent because of rounding and the presence of an *unknown* category.

[e]Stephan Thernstrom, *The Other Bostonians: Poverty and Progress in the American Metropolis, 1880–1970* (Cambridge: Harvard University Press, 1973), 136. Thernstrom did not have a *semiskilled* category.

[f] Department of Commerce, Bureau of the Census, *Fifteenth Census of the United States: 1930 Population,* Chicago Heights manuscripts.

Low occupational standing does not prima facie constitute evidence for economic discrimination against Italians. The size of the immigrant population, the institutional completeness of the ethnic community, and the cultural values of the immigrant group are among the contributing factors to occupational mobility. Perhaps, the most self-evident explanation of occupational achievement includes the background characteristics and skills of the immigrant groups—and at the most basic level the ability to speak English and to read and write.[38] Such skills are difficult to measure, especially with historical data, for in most cases they exist along a continuum rather than in a dichotomous fashion. However, these foundational attributes stand as an acceptable proxy for skill levels more generally. Lacking such skills, occupational mobility would conceivably be much more difficult.

In the case at hand, therefore, how did Chicago Heights Italians fare in terms of these language and literacy skills? We return again to the limited but still useful data available in the 1910 and 1930 censuses. If English language ability and literacy are in fact essential for occupational mobility, then the first wave of Italians to Chicago Heights were at a distinct disadvantage.

Thus, in 1910, only 45 percent of adult Italians could speak English, which was significantly below the non-Italian, citywide average of nearly 78 percent. Only 33 percent of adult Italians were literate, compared to over 76 percent of the remaining adult population in Chicago Heights. The inability of a large segment of Italian men to speak English or to read and write would certainly limit their ability to rise to higher positions in the industrial plants where the simplest communication among plant workers and supervisors would be beyond their reach. One might reasonably suggest that this lack of skills played a role in driving Italians to "the bottom of the economic ladder."[39]

This settling of Italians near the bottom of the occupational hierarchy in Chicago Heights appears, then, at least economically justified in terms of their inferior skills, an example of what Becker has termed "effective discrimination."[40] Yet, this argument becomes more tenuous in the ensuing decades. While the economic status of Italians showed modest gains, the human capital skills of the Italian laborer were dramatically increasing. According to the 1930 census, over 92 percent of Italian adult males could speak English and

Table 2.2. Adult Italian literacy and English-speaking ability, Chicago Heights, 1910 and 1930

	1910	1930
Speak English		
Female	42.2	86.4
Male	46.1	92.1
Total	45.0	87.3
Literacy		
Female	36.2	77.3
Male	32.1	81.5
Total	32.7	80.0

Note: All values are percentages.

Sources: Department of Commerce and Labor, Bureau of the Census, *Thirteenth Census of the United States: 1910 Population* and *Fifteenth Census of the United States: 1930 Population*, Chicago Heights manuscripts.

86 percent of the adult Italian women—nearly double the percentages of both groups twenty years earlier. And like many other immigrant groups, the literacy rates climbed substantially such that in 1930, over 80 percent of adult Italians could read and write. The stereo-typical, Italian who spoke "broken English" was still to be found. However, this was in fact becoming the exception. As one Chicago Heights observer wrote, "many Italian-Americans speak the English language with such perfection that some of us Americans who are descendents of earlier settlers in this country are almost afraid to admit that we think we can speak English."[41] When these developments are coupled with the presumed cultural adjustments and workplace experiences acquired by these Italian immigrants in the period leading up to 1930, there is ample reason to expect, ceteris paribus, that Italian occupational mobility should have also increased substantially. That this did not happen leaves us to speculate about the existence of an abiding discrimination against the Italian worker, this time a "taste-based" discrimination motivated by an unjustified prejudice or low opinion on the part of employers toward the Italian population.[42]

This form of discrimination is difficult to prove. However, many of the Italian workers believed that such discrimination was present. Chicago Heights resident, Nick Tieri, said, "When you went to apply for a job as soon as you put down your name. What nationality are you? Italian? We have no use for you. . . . I've had that said to me several times."[43] Olivia Kowalski (nee Massacci) told a similar story, "I went to the Chicago College of Commerce for twenty four months. And when I sent out on interviews, and this is the truth, I had the ability. And I remember one man saying, 'Have you ever thought of changing your name?' He said, 'You would have less trouble getting a job.'"[44] Dominic Pandolfi was a Chicago Heights resident who received his teacher certificate and MA from the University of Chicago. When he initially applied for a teaching job at a Chicago Heights elementary school, he was told not to apply by the district superintendent who said bluntly, "I don't think they will accept you here."[45] And Jerry Colangelo, world-famous National Basketball Association and Major League Baseball owner and Chicago Heights native, was told by a fellow Italian, "Jerry if you're ever going to make it in life you're going to have to change your name. Colangelo is a name that will never make it. You're going to have to shorten it to Jerry Cole—or something like that."[46]

Spatial and Social Isolation

Carlo Pulcini did not make it to Chicago Heights from Italy until 1949. Still as a long-time member of the Marchegianna Society in the city, Pulcini had intimate familiarity with the "old timers" and second-generation Italians in the Heights. The stories these residents told were personal narratives of the different forms of discrimination outlined earlier. As Pulcini tells us, "At that time, the Italian immigrants were second class people . . . they were not more ignorant over the other nationalities but the other nationalities had the face to talk."[47] Pulcini leaves a lot of room for interpretation here, but he points to the lowly position of Italians compared to the other nationalities. Italians were not alone in suffering this discrimination. The other immigrant groups from southern and eastern Europe faced similar challenges. And the Blacks and Mexicans from the south, southwest, and Mexico were, in the words of Ramon Garcia, welcomed for their labor, "but not their language, customs, and their culture."[48] In the early part of the century, however, the Italians posed the biggest threat for they dramatically outnumbered these other groups in Chicago Heights—and this threat was made all the more menacing and exotic by extreme forms of spatial and social isolation.

As suggested, a collection of cultural, political, and economic forces were at work in the beginning of the twentieth century, the effect of which was to erect a spatial barrier between Chicago Heights Italians (as well as other immigrant groups) and the more established residents of the city. Again, the raw census data may prove useful in documenting this segregation. The period from 1910 to 1930 saw an overall increase in the Italian presence in Chicago Heights. Though the number of foreign-born Italians remained virtually the same (see table I.1), second-generation Italians swelled the ranks of Italian residents. Thus, by 1930, people of Italian ancestry (or the "foreign stock") constituted over 25 percent of the Chicago Heights population. Of particular importance was the residential concentration of these Italian residents. The East Side and the Hill areas (primarily Wards 3, 4, and 5) contained 97.3 percent of the Italian population in 1910, and 88.1 percent in 1930. Admittedly, the Italian population made small inroads on the west side of the city over this twenty-year period. However, even this modest dispersion may be deceiving. An examination of Italian residents in these wards reveals that the majority of these westsiders were actually located on the margins or boundaries of these wards, often in the then rural or unincorporated areas of the city.

More-refined measures of residential segregation include the index of dissimilarity and the isolation index. The former gives evidence of the degree to which minority and majority groups in a city are evenly spread out in residential neighborhoods; the latter measures the average probability based on residential location that a member of a particular group will interact with another member of that group—in our specific case, the probabilities that an Italian living in Chicago Heights would interact with other Italians in the city and thus be "isolated" from other residents. Both measures range between 0.000 and

1.00, the higher the coefficient in both cases, the greater degree of residential segregation and isolation, respectively. Using the 1910 and 1930 censuses and basing the calculations on city wards, we derived both indices for foreign stock Italians in Chicago Heights over against native whites of native parentage, this latter grouping a rough approximation of the more-established residents in the city or those farthest removed historically from their immigrant roots.

Looking first at 1910, the indices suggest a substantial residential separation. The index of dissimilarity was 0.682, with indices above 0.60 generally considered to be high; the isolation index was 0.430, with indices above 0.30 considered high. Both indices place Chicago Heights Italians among the most segregated and isolated of any *Italian* community when compared with Italian populations in other American cities—a finding that is particularly noteworthy given that Italians were generally the most residentially segregated and isolated of any ethnic group in American cities in 1910.[49] Twenty years later, the majority of European ethnic groups saw a decline in residential segregation and isolation.[50] This was not the case for Chicago Heights Italians. The dissimilarity index stood at 0.775 and the isolation index at 0.460—both indices higher than in 1910.[51]

As indicative as these numbers might be, it is difficult to separate the extent to which Chicago Heights Italians "jumped" into these housing patterns because of the "institutional completeness" of the Italian neighborhoods or the desire to associate with fellow Italians, customs, or folkways as opposed to the extent to which these Italians were "pushed" into these neighborhoods because of the cultural, political, and economic restrictions identified previously. To be sure, both factors were at work. The voluntary character of this residential segregation can be gleaned, in part, from the value that many Italian residents placed on the sense of community and close ties found in the neighborhood. Though perhaps a bit nostalgic and overstated, one local history concluded, "There was no desire to assimilate into other areas of Chicago Heights because people really enjoyed living in the Hill neighborhood."[52] And even when this segregation began to dissipate many years later, the cultural preferences for living among fellow Italians were still strong. Thus, at least some Italians were dismayed that people would choose to move away from the East Side and buy houses in the non-Italian section on the north side of town. As Nick Zaranti said, "Everybody would make fun of the Italians who bought these homes. We called it Suckerville. Far away from your friends and family in Suckerville."[53]

Yet, we should be cautious about attributing these patterns of segregation primarily to these individual or cultural preferences, for such preferences may have developed or been fortified by a long-standing belief among Italians that the native population harbored a strong prejudice against them. As Lieberson speculates, "it is often hard to know whether choice of one's own group for neighbors is a response to real or anticipated trouble with outsiders, and hence whether such 'voluntary choices' are themselves the products of outside forces."[54] Such speculations seem to have some basis in reality if the comments of one worker in a neighboring steel town were representative. "It is bad enough to work with Dagoes," complained this worker, "I wouldn't think of living next to them."[55] From the other side of the fence, Hap Bruno said, "If you moved somewhere, my God, they were afraid of you. They didn't know what the hell kind of person you were."[56]

As pernicious and pervasive as this spatial isolation turned out to be, it should not simply be assumed that this ushered in an abiding social isolation. Though separated geographically, it is conceivable that a number of Chicago Heights Italians enjoyed close, trusting relationships with their West Side, non-Italian neighbors. Anecdotal evidence suggests some of this. For example, Maurino Ricchiuto based his political career on the support he garnered "from friends and conscientious voters on *both sides of the city*."[57] The West Side's Donovan Savings and Loan firm was a favorite of Italians from the East Side.[58] Along these lines, Theresa Giannetti expressed a good deal of animosity toward Mr. Giannini, a fellow resident on the Hill, "We called (him) the villain," she said. "He was the mortgage lender . . . a loan shark. He would foreclose on people. . . . Now if my mother would have had the mortgage with the Donovan agency, she never would have lost the home. He never took a home back, no."[59]

Yet, these close cross-town ties and sentiments were most likely the exception. Our review of the cultural, political, and economic institutions argues that the majority of Chicago Heights Italians experienced a "lack of contact or of sustained interaction with individuals and institutions that represent mainstream society."[60] Churches, sports teams, political organizations, schools, and social clubs were separated spatially and socially by a restrictive series of rules and practices. "A good example of exclusion is furnished by those who dance," Devatenos writes, "public dances were never a success in Chicago Heights, because certain groups always managed to start rows at these dances. As a result, those who wanted to enjoy peaceful dancing have organized to hold private dances to the exclusion of the 'rough-necks.'"[61]

This lack of sustained interaction is also pointed to, at least indirectly, by a series of articles published in the *Chicago Heights Star* in 1936. The series, focusing on "our Italian neighbors," clearly approaches the nearby Italian culture and social structure from the perspective of "the other," a distant, immigrant group different in some fundamental way from the dominant mainstream society. Though located just a few blocks east of the downtown district, the Italian neighborhood undergoes an ethnographic analysis whereby we are told about the Italian desire for "large families," the line of goods that are carried in the local stores, and the fact that "several medical men" have established their practices in the downtown business district. With an anthropological wonder, one article explains to the West Side audience that "whether the family is large or small, the majority of Italians always bake their own bread themselves."[62] Taken all together, these articles demonstrate just how distant and exotic the Italian community was to the mainstream society in Chicago Heights.

Though difficult to document, another indication of this social isolation is the dearth of friendship networks that crossed the railroad tracks. For example, Devatenos suggests that exclusion among boys and their gangs was commonplace. Boys from the East Side or the Hill would not allow boys from the West Side (who were called "sissies") to mix with their gangs; this exclusion was reciprocated by the West Side boys who refused to let the "ruffs" become one of them.[63] A review of the Society pages in the *Chicago Heights Star* reveals a string of wedding announcements, society luncheons, card games, get-togethers, and book clubs as examples of the informal socializing that took place in the city. Seldom did the list of bridesmaids, luncheon attendees, or card players suggest sociability between the members of the Italian community and the mainstream society. It was rare to find an Italian surname among the luncheon or book reading groups. Bridesmaids or ushers tended to be either all Italian or all non-Italian depending on the side of the tracks where the wedding took place. And West Side card players favored bridge and East Side card players pinochle.

Another imperfect but useful measure for revealing the absence of friendship networks between Italians and the mainstream society is the application for citizenship filed by Italian residents of Chicago Heights. Between 1907 and 1930, 593 Italians filed formal naturalization petitions. As a part of this application process, the applicant had to submit the names (and addresses and occupations) of two witnesses who were citizens, who in turn had to file affidavits testifying that "he has personal knowledge that the said petitioner is a person of good moral character." Since the immigrant had to reside in the United States at least five years before submitting the final application and given that many Italian immigrants often waited longer, it is conceivable that close personal ties could have developed between immigrants and the more established residents of Chicago Heights, close enough at least for the Italian immigrant to seek the support and good name of these West Side residents in this all important matter.

This did not happen in the vast majority of cases. As limited as this archival data may be, it still gives strong indication that Chicago Heights Italians had few personal ties with residents on the West Side of town. Thus, if each of the 593 Italians had to select two witnesses, there were 1,186 opportunities to select a witness who had "personal knowledge" of the applicants' moral character. After accounting for missing data and witnesses who lived outside of Chicago Heights, the actual number of Chicago Heights citizens listed on these forms totaled 1,140. Of these individuals, over 90 percent were fellow residents of the East Side or Hill areas (again, primarily Wards 3, 4, and 5). One might expect most of these witnesses were relatives of the applicant. However, the overwhelming majority were friends, fellow workers, business agents, or local saloonkeepers. Or to put it another way, only in rare circumstances did an Italian applicant for naturalization reach across the tracks for assistance in securing a favorable citizenship decision. These contacts were for the most part not available.

In the early part of the twentieth century, then, Chicago Heights Italians were boxed into a restrictive geographic and social space. The industrial plants to the east, the landfills to the south, the unincorporated area to the north, the Chicago & Eastern Illinois Railroad tracks to the west geographically isolated Italians "from the mainstream of Chicago Heights life."[64] This spatial segregation, in turn, deepened the incipient social separation of the Italian community from the dominant social institutions and social relations of the city. Italian residents congregated in different churches, attended different schools, worked in different industries, joined different political and social clubs, and made different neighbors and friends. This isolation was so powerful and institutionalized the traditional routes to mobility seemed beyond the grasp of all but a few privileged Italians. As Alba suggests more generally, by the end of the 1930s, Italian Americans seemed doomed "to a perpetual position of inferiority and separateness in American society."[65]

Social Isolation and Social Capital

Social isolation extracts a heavy cost for individuals in their pursuit of social mobility. Specifically, social isolation from mainstream society disadvantages certain groups because it distances individuals from a set of beneficial, social relations. In turn, individuals are systematically excluded from informal job networks, experience a restricted geographic awareness and set of involvements, and suffer a susceptibility to prejudice and stereotypes—in short, encounter a general and pervasive vulnerability to the social and economic ills of a society.[66] We saw this at work in the Chicago Heights context. The opportunity for Italian residents to develop these beneficial ties with West Side pastors, schoolteachers, middle-class businessmen, community leaders, or neighbors was made most difficult by the persistent patterns of cultural, political, and economic discrimination.

If it was difficult to acquire this social capital in the "mainstream of Chicago Heights life," most Italian residents were nevertheless awash in these beneficial relations and networks within their own neighborhoods. The common lives of these residents—whether this involved getting a job, buying a home, starting a family, dealing with illness or death, providing for public safety, and so on—were approached as much as community events as they were individual decisions. Building a home, for example, was often a neighborhood project. "Friends gathered and spent what little spare time they had to help build the home. The women got together and prepared meals for all the workers."[67]

Economic exchanges were also embedded in the extant social relations in the community. As one Chicago Heights resident put it, shopkeepers at times "gave away the store" to needy customers in the neighborhood by extending credit or simply not charging them the full price for merchandise. Specifically, Candeloro tells us of Rosie May Mancini, who would "somehow forget to record the full amount in her book" when a customer was unable to come up with the cash for a purchase.[68] Along the same lines, Joe Nicastro said, "My family use to deliver milk in the neighborhood. When things got real bad, my mother use to say 'Oh, don't collect this time.' She would just give it away."[69] Dominic Prancrazio, another Chicago Heights merchant, told a similar story, "I lose a lot of money . . . I gave too much credit."[70] And my grandmother, Josephina, use to send one of her children and later her grandchildren to Ripani's, a small Italian grocery store on Wentworth Avenue, for bread, sausage, or, unbeknown to us, a live chicken wrapped none too securely in a burlap sack. We never exchanged money for these groceries or unyielding chickens. My grandmother would settle up with the Ripanis at a later date. In ways, therefore, reminiscent of Coleman's description of "effective norms," these exchanges suggest an obligation on the part of merchants to forego immediate self-interests in service of the stability and cohesiveness of the larger Italian community.[71] This honoring of the public good stood as a powerful source of social capital for both the merchants and residents conjointly.

Weddings were yet another opportunity to draw on the social capital in the community. Since many residents did not have the resources to stage a wedding reception, neighbors would customarily contribute anything from live chickens, to bottles of wine, to homemade cookies and desserts for the feast. "It was a community event," Ida Marks said.[72] At the reception itself, guests would line up and hand the bride and groom the *buste* or the envelope containing a cash gift to help pay for the reception and to provide "a tidy little profit for the new couple."[73] These economic exchanges were most always based on an unmistakable obligation to return these gifts and favors in kind when the need arose for others. These Italian residents took Coleman's notion of "outstanding credit slips" quite literally, for as Candeloro writes "close records were kept of these gifts for further reference when the time would come for reciprocation."[74]

In the early part of the past century then, the social capital opportunities for Chicago Heights Italians were quite mixed—a wide-ranging exclusion from these opportunities in the mainstream society, an in-depth immersion into community and neighborhood ties on the East Side and Hill areas. In short, one reservoir was almost empty, the other overflowing. These two reservoirs of social capital have often been connected in theoretical terms. Thus, more linear explanations view the diminished opportunities and social connections of immigrant groups in the wider society as a consequence, first and foremost, of the cultural preferences and social structures within these immigrant communities. That is, as the Italian community emphasized intense, inward-directed community relations this was at the expense of social contacts and participation in the mainstream society. Thus, Banfield characterizes the traditional, Italian culture as inherently antithetical to the common good. The "amoral familism" of the southern Italian culture stood in the way of more far-reaching ties outside the community, indeed outside one's extended family.[75] Glazer and Moynihan, for all their insights, pointed to the "tight little Italian neighborhood" as an inhibiting factor for Italians in developing beneficial relationships in the society as a whole. The "old weight of the South Italian culture" prevented Italians from moving more rapidly into the higher status positions in American society.[76] Discrimination in the wider society notwithstanding, Italians failed to advance in economic and social terms because enduring beliefs and associations stubbornly misdirected available social capital resources.

More recent explanations also see a relationship between these two reserves of social capital. However, instead of viewing local community values and associations as the principal barriers to a sustained contact in the larger society, these explanations depict these values and associations as emergent responses to the discrimination and lack of contacts outside the community. Common sentiments, a collective identity, and coethnic ties are made relevant or are born out of a shared adversity rather than being the "fragmentary elements of the ancestral culture transplanted to the American city."[77] Portes and Sensenbrenner's concept of "bounded solidarity" is most relevant here. Immigrant groups, especially peasants from Southern Italy, cluster together in residential neighborhoods, invest a sense of trust in fellow ethnics, and develop a common identity not mechanically out of a cultural predisposition to "clannishness" or "secretiveness" but often because these groups "had to accept definitions of their own identity based on host-society stereotypes."[78] The social isolation and exclusion from the dominant society created the conditions for an emergent culture and social structure and a wealth of social capital. In the next chapter, we will examine how Chicago Heights Italians parlayed this wealth into a range of collective mobilizations aimed at increasing their portion of the American pie.

CHAPTER 3

DID THEY JUMP?

Labor Organizations, Mutual-Aid Societies, and Ethnic Businesses

For the greater part of the last century, Chicago Heights Italians found themselves on the wrong end of the cultural, political, and economic hierarchy in the city. This position made it extremely difficult for Italians to make recognizable gains in social mobility for themselves or their families. A wide-ranging institutional discrimination, the boom and bust character of the economy, and the cultural preferences of the Italian population conspired to place the majority of Italians on an uncertain path toward a better life. In the face of such challenges, Chicago Heights Italians gathered together their local social capital resources. They built houses together, extended credit to one another, took care of neighbors who were sick, assisted their fellow countrymen in staging celebratory events and rites of passage.

Over and above these more prosaic activities, some members of the community drew on these social capital resources in a more intentional manner. Thus, a small but outspoken few talked politics with their fellow Italians and on the basis of these ethnic alliances recruited workers into a union and socialist challenge to the discriminations in the local factories and churches. Others formed an array of social clubs and mutual-aid societies bent not only on socializing with their old country townsmen, but also on using these ties to advance their own personal ambitions and to provide a source of monetary and social support should their *paesani* encounter unexpected hardships. And still others established ethnic businesses in the form of grocery stores, bakeries, barber shops, taverns, construction companies, and restaurants. The close ethnic ties in the community gave these Italian entrepreneurs a special advantage in terms of servicing the special consumer needs of the Italian population and promoting a high degree of customer loyalty. In all, each of the collective mobilizations above was fueled by the social capital in the community. Each aimed at an enhanced social mobility. Each generated success stories. But each also came up against obstacles that limited their appeal in the Italian community. In the following pages, we take a brief look at each of these collective responses.

Labor Organizations

Coming face to face with the disparaging environment in the industrial plants, foundries, and rail yards of Chicago Heights, Italian workers drew on their associations in the neighborhoods to agitate for better wages and working conditions. Local barbershops appeared to be one place where men came together to discuss politics and read the popular socialist papers such as *Il Martello* and *La Parola dei Socialisti.* At least among friends, many railed against the low wages, the unsafe working conditions, and the lack of job security confronting the unskilled workers. As one resident put it, workers were at the mercy of bosses. "In those days," said Frank Corradetti," if you made one mistake, you didn't have a job."[1]

Many of these discussions never moved beyond the relative safety of the barbershop, corner tavern, or local pinochle game. At times, however, these complaints resulted in direct action, some of which were confrontational. For example, in 1908, ten Italians were arrested in Chicago Heights because they attacked a streetcar motorman who ran his streetcar through a parade of Italians who were celebrating the anniversary of the unification of Italy.[2] Several years later in 1911, a group of 250 Italian construction workers (predominantly from Chicago Heights) struck the Illinois Central Railroad for higher wages in nearby Matteson. When their requests were denied, these workers "caused considerable disturbance" among the other laborers and attacked a railroad official.[3]

In the early years, these protests were pushed forward by a dedicated group of socialist sympathizers within the Italian population. "While few in number," Vecoli offers, "the socialists were quite vociferous."[4] Umberto La Morticella, a Chicago Heights resident, raises the number and the vociferousness, "Chicago Heights had a goodly number of socialists and anarchists."[5] Very early on, these socialists drew up their friendships and family ties and formed the *Co-operativa di consumo di Chicago Heights* in 1911. Though this co-operative eventually became more of a social and recreational institution in the city, its origins were steeped in socialist goals and actions. One of the fundamental principles of the organization was to "constitute a restraint upon the unfair jacking up of profits and prices by retailers." It sought to provide such service "firmly rooted in the spirit and practice of 'Cooperatism.'"[6] By most accounts, it was quite successful. "A large portion of people who lived on the East Side," said Nick Zaranti, "were members of the Co-op."[7] And at various times throughout the next several decades, the co-operative was used by union members for routine business or was the meeting site for striking workers and socialist sympathizers.

The enmity of the socialists, however, was not only directed against the unfair practices of retailers and commercial establishments. It was also forwarded against St. Rocco Parish, the Catholic church in the Hill area. In no uncertain terms, the Italian socialists voiced their anticlerical position against the Catholic priests and hierarchy. "We believe that it is our right and our duty to tell our credulous countrymen to distrust these blood-suckers, to unyoke themselves from their religious ideas. We say to the people: If there is a God, Heaven will certainly be a reward for those honest men who work and suffer, without the need of buying it, maintaining priest in laziness."[8]

The church, as one might suppose, responded with its own might against these "antagonistic forces."[9] Italian socialists were branded as murderous anarchists.[10] Father Dunne, chancellor of the Chicago Archdiocese, asked, "Is it unreasonable to suppose that Chicago is the headquarters of a gang of assassins determined to rid the world of us, and is it improbable that they have already planned to commit some heinous crime here?"[11] So palpable was this fear, Father Pasquale Renzullo, pastor at St. Rocco, requested permission from Chicago Heights officials to carry a gun upon receiving a friendly warning from a parishioner that "the socialists intend to make an attempt upon your life."[12] Giuseppe Bertelli, a leading socialist organizer and editor of *La Parola*, took Father Renzullo to task for requesting a gun permit. "Christ did not carry a gun, but turned his cheek to be slapped," Bertelli added. "We wish to alleviate Italian suffering and oppression. We do not fight priests, but fight their policies. We don't need to use the stiletto and the gun."[13]

The socialist agenda, however, went well beyond these critiques of particular merchants and priests. At times working with the mainstream union movement and at other times in opposition, a core group of Italian radicals in Chicago Heights made a concerted effort to offer a socialist response to the exploitation of the Italian working class. As Nick Zaranti said, "the Italians organized a lot of unions in those days, in the early days."[14] For example, Chicago Heights Italians played critical roles in organizing local chapters of the Brick Tile and Terra Cotta Workers and the Steel Workers Union. Italians, though by no means all with a socialist bent, dominated the Hod Carriers and Building Laborers Union, where for a number of years, the top positions in the union were regularly passed back and forth between Italians from the East Side and Hill areas. And the Barber's Union, in particular, benefited from the organizing skills and local community ties of Joseph Giganti, a Chicago Heights native and barber who went on to become a socialist organizer not only in the Heights but in the greater Chicago, Midwest, and national arena as a whole.[15]

As elsewhere, one of the chief strategies of these socialist organizers was to play on the on-going ties among Italians and "establish a firm foothold in the ethnic community."[16] With this in mind, the local socialist leaders, with the assistance of the International Workers of the World (or the IWW), sponsored an organizing meeting headed by Carlo Tresca, editor of *Il Martello* and one of the country's most pronounced anarchists. According to Umberto La Morticella, "many people came with the intent to be at the meeting."[17] However, in the very patriotic times surrounding World War I, the socialist agenda elicited considerable opposition. Thus, the *Chicago Heights Star* labeled the IWW agenda as pure propaganda and sarcastically retranslated the organization's initialism to the pejorative "I Won't Work."[18] More directly, the meeting was "nipped in the bud" by the strategic placement of police officers at the entrance of the meeting hall.[19] "The City Hall became aware of the meeting, and so dispatched four policemen to this meeting place," said La Morticella. "In order to get into the hall one had to pass between the policemen. One of the cops was Italian; he knew every resident of the Hill by his first name. The confirmed radicals and myself . . . didn't give a damn about the police, and went right through. Many people . . . cowered at the sight of the police."[20] The efforts of city hall had a chilling effect on the meeting and held down attendance. Beyond this, the ensuing protest of the socialist organizers resulted in a number of arrests, including that of Chicago Heights resident Dominick Mormile, who along with several other leaders, was charged with violation of the Espionage Act and taken to Chicago to appear before federal authorities.

These organizing efforts, then, faced formidable challenges given the powerful combination of antiunion forces both outside and within the local Italian community. On the outside, the Sacco and Vanzetti arrest and trial had a disparaging effect on labor militants, especially Italian immigrants. More broadly, the Red Scare and anti-Bolshevism tactics after World War I marginalized and demonized most any union organizing efforts, especially among immigrant populations. For example, in 1922, the Manufacturing Association of Chicago Heights considered a proposal to create a state police organization as a response to the increasing sophistication of the "modern criminal." Yet, the operating definition of this modern criminal was expanded to fit the perceived threat of these union, socialist organizers. Thus, a chief argument in favor of establishing a state police organization was the role this force would play in controlling the IWW. Fearing the Wobblies and their ability to "bore from within," the Manufacturing Association was told that these labor organizers "gave little trouble" where a state police organization had been put into place.[21]

At the same time, large manufacturers devised ingenious strategies to undermine allegiances to the local community and to dilute union strength. Cohen describes, more generally, the dramatic change in management ideology among Chicago industrialists during this time. She points to the contest between management and community leaders for the loyalty of the industrial labor force. Employing a variety of strategies, management hoped to "secure employees' loyalty to the company by reforming the way they related to both peers and superiors."[22] These strategies included a wage incentive system, promises of an eight-hour day, a range of industry-run social and recreational opportunities, and the "democratization" of plant government through the establishment of worker councils and employee representation plans.

These manipulative strategies were certainly on the minds of the industrialists in Chicago Heights. Again in the 1922 meeting of the Chicago Heights Manufacturing Association, Harvey Ellerd, manager of the industrial relations department of Armour & Co., made a call for these more "Intelligent Labor Policies." He told the assembled Chicago Heights industrialists that the aim of these policies was to establish "pleasant relations" between workers and the companies, in large part, by teaching workers "not to follow irresponsible outside leaders."[23] The clear message was that the Italian population in Chicago Heights needed to be managed and it was best to do so by severing the militant organizing elements from the more "loyal Italians"[24] and severing the Italian population, more generally, from its ethnic moorings.

The Inland Steel plant in Chicago Heights provides one example of these attempts at undercutting and reshaping the local ethnic community ties. Located strategically between the East Side and Hill sections of Chicago Heights, Inland styled itself as a leader in improving the way of life of its workers. It was one of the first in the Chicago area to offer an eight-hour day, a pension plan, and a Christmas bonus. It sought to improve and formalize relations between workers and supervisors by retraining foremen according to the emerging field of industrial relations. A set of rules was established instructing foremen to "control your anger, always hear the other side."[25] Outside the plant, company baseball teams, picnics, singing choirs, and motion picture screenings lured workers into new patterns of association and loyalties.

To be sure, these company practices provided immediate benefits for at least a segment of the local workforce. However, these benefits did relatively little for the long-term, collective interests of the Inland workers. Thus, the Inland pension plan was riddled with so many contingencies and uncertainties weighted in management's favor that the prospects for actually collecting the pension at a reasonable retirement age was much in doubt. As Dominic Pandolfi said, "No, it's a sad thing how they were beaten out of their pensions. The people who worked in the Steel Mills, Inland Steel."[26] The prospects for promotion often pitted one Italian against another in a demeaning competition for a favorable position within the factory. As Umberto La Morticella said, "The Inland Steel bosses were great practicioners of nepotism. . . . Those workers who went to the boss's house and dug his garden, painted his house, cleared out his basement, had his wife help the boss' in doing house cleaning."[27] The eight-hour day, while eventually instituted, was proposed and pulled back a number of times because of management fears that it would decrease the competitiveness of Inland relative to other companies in the area. And when a nationwide steel strike was called in 1919, Inland was quick to abandon its local workforce and sent out recruiters to the South and Southwest to find replacements for striking workers. In 1922, Inland workers engaged in a wildcat walkout in the Chicago Heights plant over the refusal of Inland officials to negotiate a six-cent-an-hour raise. Apparently, the injunction to "always hear the other side" did not extend to the top levels of management. When asked to comment on the walkout, Inland officially denied the strike. "It's a lie, a damned lie," an officer declared. "There's not a breath of truth in the whole thing. We haven't a strike in any department. Things are running smoothly."[28] More generally, Kornblum concludes that these progressive labor policies in South Chicago did not appreciably change the work lives of the local residents. "Immigrant workers and many less skilled native Americans were unlikely to benefit from these programs."[29]

For a number of reasons, then, union organizing activity declined in subsequent years. As Candeloro concludes, "Surprisingly, oral history sources uniformly testify to the absence of labor radicalism and violence in this rather rough industrial town even in the depressed 1930s."[30] Nick Tieri said there were "no clashes of any kind" regarding union workers.[31] The socialist presence largely disappeared. Having been vilified as disloyal, as assassins, and as un-American, these socialists were increasingly cut off from their base of support among Italians in Chicago Heights. At the same time, the restrictions on immigration from Italy, which began to take effect during the 1920s, undercut the fresh supply of socialist advocates, primarily from the Marche and

Abruzzi regions, which had fueled much of the socialist fervor in the past. As such, there developed a general indifference, if not hostility, toward unions among Chicago Heights Italians. Olivia Kowalski (nee Biaselli) gives some indication of this when she said, "I don't believe in unions. I don't know why. . . . It's against my grain."[32] Frank Corradetti characterized the beliefs of Italian residents more generally by adding, "There was a good deal of anti-union sentiment within the Italian community."[33] And many Italians took exception to the costs associated with joining a union. Dominic Sesto said, "My father worked at Inland Steel, was a member of the CIO. However, it was tough to recruit Italians into the union. They didn't want to pay dues to the union and make their pay check even smaller. And there was a fear that if you joined the union, you would be one of the first to be fired when they laid off workers."[34] Finally, Alphonse Leone expressed a more general frustration in believing that unions could serve as an effective collective response in achieving economic mobility. "All I see is a battle between union and management . . . they're the ones getting the advantages, not the working man."[35]

Social Clubs and Mutual-Aid Societies

In the residentially segregated and socially isolated Italian neighborhoods of Chicago Heights, labor organizing efforts overlapped and competed with other nontraditional avenues for social mobility. Precisely, from the beginning of the century onward, Chicago Heights Italians banded together in formal associations that were part mutual benefit societies, part political organizations, and large part social clubs. As Nick Zaranti said, "Well into the 20s and 30s, especially on the East Side and Hungry Hill . . . they had different athletic clubs or social clubs, just about every other block had some club."[36] These groups varied from the breakfast clubs and sewing gatherings such as the Silver Tavern group, the Dozenettes, or the Fifth Avenue Men's Club to the more formal, ethnic associations such as the Chicago Heights Dante Club, the Christopher Columbus Society, the Sons of Italy Lodge, the Progressive Hunters' Club, the Unione Siciliana, the Italian Voters' League, the Marchegianna Society, Club Lavoratori, the Italian Citizens Club of Chicago Heights, the American Calabrese Social Club, the Amasenese Lodge, the Aquila Abruzzi Society, the Sambia Sese Club, the Society Garibaldini, to name just some of these groups.

These formal associations, with memberships ranging from several dozen to three hundred, had a mix of sociability, philanthropic, and mobility goals.[37] For example, at one end of the spectrum, we find the Christopher Columbus Society where a common tradition was to stroll door-to-door tasting each other's homemade wine at the end of the wine-making season. Though this sounds particularly inviting, even today, this social activity was not directly tied to doing good deeds or promoting social advancement. Still, the trust and reciprocity developed in these informal encounters would on occasion have direct benefits for an individual's well being. "I remember my father," said Dominic Sesto, "would go around collecting money for one of the guys who was about to be deported. He didn't have the money to get a lawyer so they all threw in some money—I don't know half a buck or a dollar—to see if they could help him out."[38]

Other mutual aid associations were more intentional in their efforts to mine social relations in an attempt to "get by" or in the words of de Souza Briggs "cope with the everyday challenges that life presents."[39] That is, they self-consciously used their ethnic loyalties to provide some minimal protection and support for the day-to-day struggles Italian immigrants faced in the Chicago Heights environment. For example, the more focused ethnic, mutual aid societies (such as the Italo-American Union, the Marchegianna Society, and the Amasenese Lodge) offered health insurance and death benefits to *paesani*. Specifically, they hired a local doctor, Renato Rosini, to minister to the medical needs of club members. And they, like so many other associations, offered a range of insurance plans and options, backed not as much by the well-funded coffers of the organization but by a sense of fraternity and a commitment to help one's fellow Italian (or provincial) brothers and sisters.

Not surprisingly, a segment of the Italian population was not content to simply manage their way through these daily struggles. Instead, they sought to develop relationships in the myriad associations and groups in the pursuit of social recognition, new business contacts, jobs, and political support. These formal associations provided a rich source of social contacts and shared norms to "get ahead" or "to change or improve . . . life circumstances."[40] The Marchegianna Society was one of the most prominent mutual benefit societies in Chicago Heights. As Candeloro writes, "Fish fries on Friday, family dances on Saturday, and dramatic performances on Sunday right there in the neighborhood helped keep the Marchegiani in close touch with one another."[41] Being in close touch, in turn, made it possible for the members of this society to expect a strategic advantage when they applied for a job or promotion at the local steel plant or foundry. For example, Alberto Spina, president of the Marchegianna Society for fifteen years, held an influential management position at the American Manganese Steel Company and "began a chain of employment that made the large steel company a virtual Marchegianna institution."[42] More generally, in recounting the long history of the Marchegianna Society, Chicago

Heights resident Anthony Scariano pointed to the importance of these embedded social relationships for social mobility. "The Society," Scariano said, "is there to take care of its own who have fallen on hard times, but it is also an important network for Italian businessmen and politicians who are willing to give a leg up to one of their own."[43]

The Dante Club was another prominent formal association. With an eye toward the more encompassing goal of assimilation into the dominant West Side culture, it was dedicated to the "welfare of not only the East Side but of the entire city."[44] The route to these assimilation goals was also strategic, involving the promotion of "social intercourse" not only among fellow Italians but also across the social and geographic boundaries that separated the East Side and Hill from the more established Chicago Heights society.[45] Thus, organizational initiatives sought to downplay traditional Italian programming, such as Italian language classes for children, in favor of the patriotic and civil activities likely to garner the attention and approval of the mainstream society. As such, meetings had to be conducted in English, not Italian. And most meetings centered on an "Americanization" theme or presentation that was often followed by a social hour where the Italian members could exchange information with one another and with the "business and political elite of Chicago Heights"—from judges, to corporate officers, to Chicago Heights city officials.[46] In this manner, the Dante Club served as a useful stepping-stone for the mobility aspirations of a small but prominent collection of Italian leaders, including Italian aldermen and city employees, as well as future commissioners, mayors, and public officials.

While these fraternal associations may have advanced the mobility of a number of Italians, these avenues of success were limited. Once again, social and economic forces both inside and outside the community circumscribed these associations as a collective strategy for social advancement. From within, there were limitations due to the social class composition within the Italian enclave. Specifically, the most prominent and successful mutual aid societies in Chicago Heights—for example, the Dante Club and the Marchegianna Society—were predominantly middle class institutions, or more properly institutions with middle-class aspirations. They espoused middle-class values, planned middle-class events, and sought middle-class, Italian residents. As such, they appealed to a significant but segmented portion of the local Italian population.

Along these lines, a rough but revealing indicator of the middle-class character of these organizations, at least compared to other Italians, is the occupational status of its members, specifically its officers. Table 3.1 provides some clues as to the high proportion of middle-class members in the Marchegianna Society. Following upon this, a principal goal of the society, along with its social and mutual-aid functions, was to "increase the interest of members in American life."[47] Americanization was the agreed-on path to middle-class status. Similarly, a list of the Dante Club officials shows a disproportionate share of lawyers, managers, proprietors, and city officials—disproportionate, given the largely unskilled and semiskilled character of the Italian population in Chicago Heights more generally. Hap Bruno, Dante Club president in the 1930s, said the club was "mainly businessmen in town and some of the professional men—like lawyers and a few CPA's."[48] Minstrel shows, minuets, and learned lectures were among the most favored activities of the Dante Club. In contrast, the Unione Siciliana (later, the Italo Union) with its more southern Italian roots, was decidedly working class in its membership and officers. Programming was more lowbrow, as large parades, spaghetti-eating contests, and greased-pole climbing were staples of the organization.[49]

There is reason to believe that these middle-class, mutual-aid society leaders were correct in their reading of the mobility ladder. Though it took decades

Table 3.1. Italian mutual-aid society membership and occupational status, circa 1935

Dante Club Member (occupation)	Marchegianna Society Member (occupation)	Unione Siciliana/Italo-American Member (occupation)
Nick Augustino (clerk)	Frank Bruti (proprietor)	Antonio Battaglia (chauffer)
Nick Berardinelli (fireman)	Remo Cioe (director)	Nicola Biasello (laborer)
Peter Biaselli (salesman)	Fred De Marco (clerk)	Antonio Biondo (laborer)
Mario Bruno (bookkeeper)	Joe Green (laborer)	Joseph Bova (laborer)
John Costabile (policeman)	Umberto Lisciani (manager)	Luino Battista Casso (mason)
Mike Costabile (lawyer)	Hugo Long (physician)	Sam Lobue (laborer)
Joe Debarberri (salesman)	Mike Mandella (laquerer)	Guisepue Pagoria (laborer)
Frank D'Andrea (retired)	Sam Matz (laborer)	Alfonso Prisco (laborer)
Charles Grupp (policeman)	Joe Natale (laborer)	Joseph Sinopoli (proprietor)
Emil Iaccabucci (proprietor)	Maurino Richton (lawyer)	Alfredo Spanda (laborer)
Nicholas Monacelli (electrician)	Albert Spina (superintendent)	Joe Spata (laborer)
Ray Palanca (manager)	Ettore Mascitti (press operator)	
Silvio Piacenti (lawyer)		
Joe Piacenti (manager)		
Joseph Tintari (contractor)		
Louis Ursitti (proprietor)		
John Mancini (justice of the peace)		
Pasquale Luongo (proprietor)		

Sources: This is a partial list of mutual-aid society officers gathered from a review of available information, including articles and obituaries from the *Chicago Heights Star;* Marchegianna Society, Casa Italia Cultural Center Files; and personal interviews.

and arguably the loyalty tests inspired by the challenges of World War II, the adoption of the American themes of patriotism and individualism served many Italians well in their quest for a middle-class lifestyle. However, in the troubling times before this mass ascent up the ladder, there was considerable resistance on the part of most Italians in Chicago Heights to these attempts to wean them away from their Italian (or provincial) identities. Having encountered these exclusionary processes in the churches, schools, and workplaces, many first- and second-generation Italians often found themselves at odds with the middle-class ambitions and programming of these organizations. In this sense, Vecoli's characterization of Italian, mutual-aid society leaders as men out of step with their fellow countrymen—as men "who founded societies not out of a sense of fraternity but to satisfy their ambition and vanity"—may be overly harsh but helps explain nevertheless the indigenous limitations of these mutual-aid societies.[50]

At the same time, these mutual-aid societies were beset by challenges emanating in the larger society. Thus, the Great Depression placed enormous burdens on the financial resources of these local organizations as they sought to provide benefits to the many Italian workers who were now unemployed. "Under the pressure of the depression," Cohen writes, "many workers began to have trouble keeping up insurance payments, which in no time threatened the stability of fraternal organizations."[51] In a related sense, these fraternal organizations were dealt another blow with the growth of government-run, New Deal programs. Social Security and a variety of more immediate relief measures ended up being a more reliable source of support than the "nickel-a-week" insurance benefits provided by the mutual aid societies. And the large steel mills and factories in Chicago Heights contested the ethnic loyalties and these self-governing associations by offering a series of sick pay, death insurance, and pension benefits. Though it is most difficult to assess the extent to which factory workers took advantage of these employers' insurance plans, it is safe to say that even a modest transfer of dues and investments from the ethnic association to these company plans would jeopardize the financial stability of these ethnic mutual-aid societies.

The combination of internal and external forces, then, took their toll on the Italian mutual-aid societies of Chicago Heights. By the 1940s and 1950s, most had disbanded or had become primarily social clubs with little social capital payoffs in terms of mobility. Thus, the Dante Club ceased operations during the 1940s, and the Christopher Columbus Society did so in the following decade. The American Calabrese Social Club ceased operations after World War II. The Italo-American Union had long since ceded most of its efforts to the national organization. The Progressive Hunters' Club continued to attract a small group of Italian men, but club activities were more centered on high-stake poker games in the backrooms of bars than advancing oneself socially—and, certainly, there was little "progressive hunting" to speak of. Finally, memberships in the Marchegianna Society and the Amaseno Lodge fluctuated throughout the decades, but these organizations—though able to sustain their philanthropic, mutual-aid, and festival roles for the greater part of the century—were much more limited and circumscribed than in the past.

Ethnic Businesses

Labor-organizing and mutual-benefit societies provided, then, alternative avenues for social mobility. Both involved collective mobilizations in an obvious sense. Labor organizers both in their rhetoric and actions argued that the achievement of union goals within the Chicago Heights context would require a strong communal solidarity. And bringing workers to this point would begin with an appeal to ethnic ties but would eventually transcend ethnicity and become organized around a class consciousness. The failed efforts of the IWW and the Socialists in Chicago Heights speak to the difficulties in pulling this off. Similarly, the charters of mutual-aid societies were inherently communal, "fostering . . . among the members closer personal acquaintance and friendly spirit and mutual cooperation."[52] Social networks and common identities would be intentionally structured, and as a result, members would be provided a collective step up the mobility ladder. And there were some obvious successes. However, these fraternal organizations were hampered by the social class divisions and segmentations within the community. As Bodnar concludes more generally, "the fact that class antagonisms separated ethnic aggregations is indisputable."[53]

Yet, a third mobilization, though in a less intentional fashion, was also highly dependent on the social capital developed in the ethnic enclave. Specifically, a vast body of literature has pointed to the peculiar social and economic status of various ethnic (and in particular immigrant) groups who though blocked from traditional opportunities for mobility strike out on their own business ventures aided by the ethnic and class relationships they have developed along the way.[54] Irving Light's seminal work has extended this "disadvantage thesis" by arguing that the social capital resources so essential to the success of the ethnic entrepreneur may derive not only from the cultural and structural traditions carried from the past (for example, the sense of *campanilismo*), but also very much from the reactive cultural practices that emerge in the present setting.[55] For example, the "bounded solidarity" referred to in the previous chapter takes shape because ethnic groups in a restrictive, isolating environment attach themselves more strongly to one another and develop a stronger collective identity *because* they have found themselves in a restrictive, isolating milieu. In so doing, some ethnic groups may find that they have considerable social capital resources to draw on (for example, a ready supply of cheap labor, no interest borrowing privileges, a built in customer loyalty) in their pursuit of business success.

These processes seemed to be at work with a breed of Italian entrepreneurs in Chicago Heights during the first half of the last century. Plagued as they were by the cultural and structural obstacles to mobility, a hearty collection of tavern owners, merchants, shoemakers, and the like drew on their embedded ties in the community to advance their economic and social prospects. For example, Vito Chementi opened a tavern on the East Side only after he was able to secure a loan, interest free, from a fellow Italian countryman. "Without that money," said Chementi, "I don't open the place. No bank would give it to me."[56] Pat Pancrazio said her father, Dominic Pancrazio, was only able to keep his local grocery store open for twenty-five years because "the people in the neighborhood knew my father, knew he would treat them fairly, extend them credit if they needed it."[57] And a review of Italian entrepreneurs in Chicago Heights reveals that the vast majority employed their wives, children, and brother-in-laws as sources of cheap labor in these businesses. Indeed, a young, attractive daughter of a saloonkeeper was valued not only for her labor, but also as a more immediate social capital resource. "Whoever had a daughter would have her serve in his saloon to attract the young men."[58]

Perhaps, most important to the success of these entrepreneurs was the unwitting creation of protected markets. That is, these small business owners could appeal to the cultural preferences of the local Italians—indeed, many times to the old country, regional preferences—in ways that larger, non-Italian stores could not. Being a part of the community, these entrepreneurs could offer the haircut with the appropriate conversation, the suit with the right Italian cut, and the bread with the appropriate crustiness to qualify as authentic. As such, many Italians extended an extreme form of customer loyalty, over and above market differentials, to their fellow coethnic entrepreneurs. Italians "shopped at their own 'mom and pop' stores on the Hill and bought from the horse drawn vegetable cart, milk wagon, and ice wagon that clopped down the cobblestone streets."[59] Though chain stores, such as A & P, were increasingly becoming a part of the Chicago Heights market, most East Side and Hill residents continued to shop at their neighborhood store where personal and social relations weighed more heavily than the new mass-produced and even cheaper items in the larger, nonethnic stores. As Cohen argues, "gradually over the 1920s, workers came to share more in the new consumer goods, but in their own stores, in their own neighborhoods, and in their own way."[60] For example, Santi Cipriani owned a grocery store in Chicago Heights. He would often carry imported items and specialty meats not available in the larger stores. His daughter, Jacqueline Rush, said Cipriani would often shop with the customers to be sure they bought the items they actually needed. "People would come in with recipes, and he would tell them how to do things."[61]

For the better part of the century, therefore, Italian entrepreneurs dotted the ethnic neighborhoods of Chicago Heights. Thus, at the beginning of the twentieth century when the population of the city totaled less than a thousand Italians, there were already more than a half dozen saloonkeepers, an equal number of grocers, as well as a small number of barbers, bakers, and brewers. In the following decades as the Italian population increased, the number and range of self-employed Italian entrepreneurs also grew. Thus, 5.5 percent of Italian adult males were self-employed in 1910, the comparable figure was 6.7 percent in 1930.[62] Table 3.2 provides additional information on the range of self-employment among Italians.

These numbers shed some light on the varied attempts of Italian entrepreneurs to achieve a measure of economic mobility. They include barbers, bakers,

Table 3.2. Self-employment, Italian adult males, Chicago Heights, 1910 and 1930

	1910		1930	
Type of self-employment	Percentage	Number	Percentage	Number
Barber	10.9	9	6.4	9
Shoemaker	—	—	6.4	9
Tailor	2.5	2	3.6	5
Fruit vendor/peddler	—	—	2.9	4
Teamster/express	7.3	6	1.4	2
Merchant (liquor, saloon, restaurant)	24.4	20	—	—
Merchant (grocery, fruit)	26.8	22	17.1	24
Merchant (general, druggist, bakery, etc.)	15.9	13	35.7	50
Building and contractor	1.2	1	12.9	18
Skilled trade (electrician, bricklayer, etc.)	8.5	7	5.0	7
Other	2.5	2	8.6	12
Total	100	82	100	140

Sources: The Department of Commerce and Labor, Bureau of the Census, *Thirteenth Census of the United States: 1910 Population* and *Fifteenth Census of the United States: 1930 Population,* Chicago Heights manuscripts.

tailors, lawyers, construction employers, gas station owners, florists, mandolin players, painters, plumbers, and peddlers—including, the "muscatel man" and his exhortations "Hey Muscatel" or "Hey Bananno," which were a common part of the street scene in Chicago Heights for a number of years. The majority of Italian entrepreneurs, however, were merchants of one type or another, over two-thirds in 1910, over half in 1930. Due in large part to the spatial and social isolation of the East Side and Hill areas, corner stores, restaurants, and taverns filled a critical need for many residents—specifically, they were within walking distance, catered to the cultural preferences of the Italian population, and were attuned to the social and economic rhythms of the neighborhood more generally.

From the perspective of the entrepreneurs, these local shops also made a good deal of sense. The economic and social threshold for embarking on such ventures was within reach for most Italians despite their limited set of work skills. Thus, it took relatively little professional training—compared, for instance, to becoming a barber, tailor, or shoemaker—to run a successful business. The saloon or tavern business was a prime example. "Human capital . . . was not important for becoming a saloonkeeper," as Rothbart suggests. "The skills that were important were social skills, which were as accessible to a poor, unschooled immigrant as to anyone else."[63] At the same time, the small financial capital to labor ratio for most businesses also kept the barriers to self-employment relatively low. As such, we see a flood of corner grocery stores in the area, nearly one, and sometimes two if we add in the Polish stores, on every block. As Dominic Pancrazio remembers, "The East Side had more businesses than the West Side. We had a lot of businesses."[64] And Devatenos could slyly comment in 1924 that "there are a few things which are in a way peculiar to Chicago Heights. For example in Chicago Heights we find an overabundance of 'soft-drink' parlors, over seventy-five of them."[65]

To be sure, these businesses provided a steady path to success for a segment of the Italian community. For example, Gaetano D'Amico began with a neighborhood grocery in the Hill area and while still working at Inland Steel set up a macaroni production plant that employed over a hundred people.[66] Provino Mosca opened up a restaurant on Halsted Street in the 1930s. This led to a lifetime success for Provino and his family and eventually a move to New Orleans where Provino established the still popular Mosca's Restaurant on the West Bank. Another restaurant, Savoia's, began as a grocery store on Seventeenth street in Chicago Heights. Gus Bamonti turned it into a neighborhood tavern, with no-interest loans from Italian neighbors, to take advantage of all the factory workers who passed by on their way back and forth every day.

As an incentive to stop in, Bamonti offered free sandwiches. These became so popular Bamonti eventually transformed his tavern into a restaurant, which has survived in one form or another to the present day.

Yet entrepreneurship by definition is an extremely risky form of commerce, made all the more so in the 1930s by the overwhelming presence of the Great Depression. And *ethnic* entrepreneurship is even more problematic. As Boissevain, et al. argue, "competition is . . . often structured into an ethnic entrepreneur's situation."[67] Precisely, as immigrants with roughly the same set of skills and the same economic situations enter into an ethnic enclave, they often follow the path of others and open similar types of businesses. This creates an intensive, internal competition, especially as other ethnic groups (the Poles, in particular, in Chicago Heights) began to offer similar services. In the limited market of Chicago Heights, there was simply not enough buying power to support the number of grocery stores, bakeries, and general stores that emerged in the community. And even for the businesses that did survive, with groceries being the best example, many had extremely small profit margins. "Daily profits were more likely to be measured in pennies rather than dollars."[68]

Saloons and taverns, however, provide a different story. They enjoyed tremendous advantages in the heavily male-dominated, factory worker culture of Chicago Heights. As Abadinsky argues, saloons played a critical role in the adjustment processes of the immigrant to the urban environment.[69] Workers gravitated toward taverns not only for drinks but also for a variety of social and recreational services. Italians, in particular, made good use of bars to congregate and learn about work opportunities, play bocce, and gamble in the backroom. In characterizing Chicago saloons, Duis suggests that "the Italian saloon survived primarily because it provided certain services in the neighborhood. Customers seemed to flock to the places simply to pass the time and visit."[70] In so doing, local Italians provided a steady stream of profits for the Italian tavern entrepreneur. While still risky, this niche proved attractive to those Italian entrepreneurs wishing to avoid the drudgeries of factory work and wishing to find a more immediate path to economic mobility. Thus, some of the most successful Italian businessmen in Chicago Heights were those who were proprietors of local saloons and taverns, the type of men who in Duis' words "turned to the liquor business to seek their fortune."[71] Just some of these men include: John Cappeti, Andrew Lobue, Frank Pasente, Dominic Pandolfi, Tony Long, Pete Cassaza, Sam Ugna, Joe Zagone, Rocco Castabello, Mike Rich, Leo Vellino, and Pasquale Luongo. And if fortune, per se, was not in the cards, a good many of these men, nevertheless, moved ahead of other local Italians in the quest for recognition and mobility. For example, Dominic Pandolfi was appointed to the Board of Directors of the Commercial Bank of Chicago Heights; Pasquale Luongo became a leader of the Dante Club; and at various points in time, Pete Cassaza, Tony Long, and Joe Zagone were elected as aldermen before the city changed to the at-large commission form of government.

Yet, these men had cause to worry. The undercurrents of the temperance movement, which were being felt in Chicago Heights even before the turn of the century, were rising to the surface. With such a sordid reputation, Chicago Heights was one of the first communities to elicit a call from the local churches and civic leaders for the control and hoped-for elimination of the city's saloons. Thus, in 1897, the local clergy was able to collect seven hundred signatures protesting the location of a beer garden within the village limits. As the *Chicago Heights Star* reported, "the temperance people of Chicago Heights are greatly incensed over (this) recent action."[72] For the next decade, temperance advocates kept up their assault on the saloon business. In 1907, W. H. Freeman, editor of the *Chicago Heights Signal*, argued in front of a large gathering of residents hosted by the Municipal League that,

> I have no hesitancy in saying . . . one saloon for every 133 people is too many for Chicago Heights. . . . It is a well-known fact that people who think; that people who read newspapers; that people who go to the library, when they seek homes look for a prohibition district. Why? It must be because they regard the influence of the saloon as pernicious.[73]

Pernicious or not, saloons on the East Side and Hill areas were so embedded into the economic and social hierarchies of these communities, these calls for reform had little immediate, practical consequences for the Italian saloon owner. Indeed, a review of the 1914 City Directory for Chicago Heights suggests an increase in the number of saloons operated by Italian entrepreneurs (at least twenty-seven), as well as the presence of several breweries employing a number of local Italians.[74]

The Prohibition movement, however, was relentless. With the ratification of the Eighteenth Amendment in 1919, a sizeable element of Italian entrepreneurs and workers in Chicago Heights were now officially without a place of employment. In anticipation of this legislation, some saloonkeepers adjusted by opening up "soft drink" parlors, tobacco shops, or candy stores. Others sought to squeeze themselves into the already crowded field of grocers, bakers, and restaurant owners. A sizeable element went underground or backroom, both literally or figuratively.[75] All of these options posed unique challenges. And even when these entrepreneurs overcame these challenges, the profits from these ventures were far less than those obtained by running a legal saloon. Starting in the 1920s and continuing well into the 1930s, the saloon as an entrepreneurial avenue for success was no longer available, except as a "queer ladder of mobility."

Prohibition and organized crime, therefore, are linked historically. This connection, however, takes different, complex forms. With respect to the Chicago Outfit, in particular, Prohibition has often been blamed for encouraging the development of organized crime because it created an illegal market for alcohol that only those willing to violate the law could satisfy. As Gus Russo concluded, "Windy City 'speakeasies' popped up on every corner. Breweries operated in plain sight, with a least twenty-nine in Chicago alone. Countless more were established in suburbs such as Joliet, Cicero, Waukegan, and Niles."[76] He could have included Chicago Heights. But more than providing an illegal market, Prohibition, in a very practical sense, eliminated a legal market. Moral arguments aside, the effective elimination of any small business—a barber shop, a bakery, a butcher shop—would decrease the mobility opportunities for any newcomer attempting to climb a ladder to success. However, the effective elimination of the local tavern for Italians was especially damaging for this was a "bootstrap" operation where "even the poorest among the recent immigrants could realize the dream of rapid social mobility."[77]

Prohibition, therefore, had social capital consequences for both Italian immigrants and saloon owners. For immigrants, the local saloon was often a conduit to the larger society—to the jobs, banks, and governmental offices.[78] Without this connection, "the intermediary between the individual workers and the larger society" was lost for many of these workers.[79] For the saloon owner, this meant giving up his business or, more than likely, finding entrepreneurial ways to continue to operate his saloon. In particular, the saloon owner had to move beyond the close neighborhood ties and petty vice operations found in most local bars. Instead, entrepreneurial success meant developing relationships and agreements with *organized* criminals—those who had more systematic connections to corrupt city officials, underworld suppliers, and an even more dangerous and unpredictable conglomeration of competitors. In essence, Prohibition, though in conjunction with other factors, pushed a number of saloon owners, though many had already taken the first step, into the organized crime arena. In the Chicago Heights context, it took awhile and a good deal of bloodshed for these relationships to be worked out. However, the Jimmy Emery, Dominic Roberto, and Frank Laporte (Emery was a tavern owner himself) triumvirate seized upon the plight of these tavern owners and "promised the alky-cookers and Italians of Chicago Heights a better deal; little or no tribute, and guaranteed protection from the police."[80]

Conclusion

Make no mistake; most Italians in Chicago Heights labored in routine jobs. But also make no mistake, most saw no or only marginal gains in social mobility in their lifetimes. They worked hard and took comfort in knowing that they had adjusted to their new surroundings. But dramatic or even tangible gains in economic security or social status were not readily visible. The move upward was not inevitable or ensured, at least from the vantage point of most Italians who lived in the decade of the 1920s and 1930s. Nativism, restrictive cultural and structural barriers, and the vicissitudes of the Great Depression were in fact daily reminders of the challenges to a more secure future for the immigrants or their children. As Foner and Alba tell us for southern Italians more generally, "the climb up was often slow and gradual rather than a matter of giant leaps forward, and some of the second generation suffered painful setbacks and difficulties along the way."[81]

This long, slow climb was not to everyone's liking. An entrepreneurial class emerged within the Chicago Heights context and this class produced a coterie of labor organizers, mutual-aid society officials, and ethnic entrepreneurs. These different types of leaders, though with quite different agendas and goals, were similar in a number of respects. In structural terms, there was considerable cross over or simultaneous participation in one or another organization. As Haller suggests, "For many ambitious men, the worlds were tied together because in their own lifetimes they moved easily from one area to another or else held positions in two or more simultaneously."[82] That is, fraternal leaders often played a prominent role in unions; ethnic entrepreneurs were well represented in fraternal organizations; and union leaders often emerged from the stock of ethnic-run businesses.

At the same time, there were baseline similarities along *strategic* lines. Specifically, these varied attempts to speed up the processes of mobility were alike because they were all heavily dependent on social capital resources drawn from two different reserves. At one level, entrepreneurs, labor organizers, and mutual-aid society leaders called on the existing ethnic attachments and networks in the community—the indigenous social capital produced in large measure by the social isolation of the Italians in Chicago Heights—as starting points for building these individual and collective efforts. Yet, at another level, each of these mobilization efforts was advanced, in a halting and not always successful manner, by strategic attempts to stretch beyond these closed ties to individuals and groups outside these limited circles—to outside union organizers, to the business and political elite of Chicago Heights, to the more organized criminal elements in Chicago.

Finally, on a pragmatic level, each of these collective responses produced individual success stories. But each collective response had a limited applicability due to structural and cultural constraints within the Italian enclave. Thus, only so many ethnic businesses can emerge before the market for barbershops, taverns, and grocery stores becomes saturated. Mutual-aid societies faced an uphill battle in assimilating immigrants to middle-class values because the vast majority of lower-class immigrants had provincial values that were resistant to these efforts. Unions were confronted by the extraordinary efforts of industrial management and business associations to sever Italians from their community associations or, failing that, labeling union leaders as disloyal, anti-American, or criminal. When these internal dynamics were paired with the larger currents running through the society (from the Red Scare, to World War I, to the Great Depression, to Prohibition, to the New Deal) it becomes clear why most Italians were hesitant about committing themselves to one or another of these collective strategies for success, even though many continued to taste "America in the raw," as Umberto La Morticella said.[83] And it becomes a bit clearer why organized crime, which had the virtue and the dishonor of cutting through many of these hesitancies, appealed to a significant segment of the Italian population in Chicago Heights.

CHAPTER 4

YOU CAN'T SHOOT EVERYONE

The Italians of Chicago Heights, then, were a practical lot. Faced with the struggle to survive in a disparaging cultural, political, and economic environment, this population drew heavily on their social capital resources to maintain or enhance their social standing. As such, Italians became union organizers, club politicians, and entrepreneurs. And several local Italians took different routes and parlayed their unique individual skills in the fields of sports, entertainment, and medicine.[1] However, a most wide-ranging, albeit notorious, response was an association with organized crime. To be sure, this foray into illegal activity did not involve all Chicago Heights Italians in some culturally programmed fashion. Still, this connection with organized crime was embedded in the Chicago Heights community in more than a parasitic manner. Indeed, as Candeloro writes, "One observer has suggested that bootleggers were major employers of runners, sugar buyers, and plumbers (to construct stills), and that the industry brought a measure of prosperity to the community during the Prohibition Years."[2] During its heyday, then, the practice of organized crime—though often overlapping with the efforts of labor organizations, mutual-benefit societies, and ethnic entrepreneurs—was yet another avenue for Italians to respond with "creative reinvention"[3] to the gap that existed between their disadvantaged situation and their individual aspirations for success.

Determining more precisely which Chicago Heights Italians became part of this criminal element is difficult. The secretive nature of organized crime did not lend itself to membership lists or public disclosure. Even in the wide-open town of Chicago Heights, gang members were generally circumspect about acknowledging their criminal associations. At the same time, the Chicago Heights boys were far less formal than other criminal organizations were in initiating members through rituals, ceremonies, or "made man" mythologies. The lines defining who was and who was not a member of the Chicago Heights crew were historically more fluid and based on the social ties one carried through a lifetime, even across generations. As one informant offered, "an individual only has to be a 'good guy' with a 'good heart' to get on the payroll."[4] And similar to other criminal organizations, there were vastly different levels of involvement and association—from Frank Laporte who had a hand in running the illegal enterprises for nearly forty years, to the widow Concetta Gasbarro who let the Capone boys use her basement to make bootleg booze in return for help in supporting her seven children.[5] Closer to home, my great uncle, grandfather, godfather, confirmation father, and father all played different roles in the illegal operations through the years. Some were minor, some more substantial. Still, it would be difficult to say with any certainty whether we should include any of these relatives as a part of the Chicago Heights criminal organization.

With these cautions in mind and as suggested previously, the best indicator of organized crime membership flows out of Block's critical distinction between enterprise and power syndicates.[6] The *enterprise syndicate* refers to those people who provided, in retail fashion, the illicit products and services such as bootlegging, prostitution, and gambling. They were the bookies, rumrunners, and "can house" proprietors. *Power syndicates,* on the other hand, were concerned with those activities organized around the enforcement and control of the organized crime operations such as protecting these operations from the encroachment of other criminal groups, managing favorable relations with law enforcement officials, or mediating disputes within the organization. In a few cases, these two syndicates are joined—that is, the illegal operations are operated, controlled, and protected by the same group of people. This was the case in Chicago Heights in the latter half of the 1920s shortly after the Roberto-Emery-Laporte–led gang vanquished the rival Sicilian faction. However, this distinction between enterprise and power syndicates is still useful, for it allows us to separate out those who provided the illegal services—for example, the Concetta Gasbarros, the moonshiners, and the craps game operators—from those organized crime figures who controlled, directed, and were more deeply involved in Chicago Heights criminal activities. This latter group will be of most concern here.

Yet, even focusing on this core group presents problems. Over a fifty-year span from 1920 to 1970, there was a good deal of personnel change in the group as people moved away, were sent to prison, deported, or died of natural or unnatural causes. And as suggested, the secretive nature of the organization has always posed a problem for reporters, crime commissions, and law enforcement officials in identifying organized crime members. But the bravado of the Chicago Heights crew works in our favor in this situation. Thus, it was not uncommon for the boys to not only gather for celebrations and get-togethers in the Heights but to publicize these gatherings. Most famously, Nick Neroni, a labor leader and syndicate member, would periodically hold a picnic for organized crime leaders at his farm on the outskirts of the Hill area. In 1925, Neroni put an announcement in the *Chicago Heights Signal* that stated that the Bloom Township Italian Republican Club would have its picnic in July and participants would include Phil Piazza, Dominic Roberto, Charles Costello, and Jimmy Emery, among others.[7] Several years later, Neroni would again host a get-together. The exact date and occasion for the picnic are unknown. However, Luzi's exhaustive study of a group picture taken at this later get-together (see figure 4.1) places the photo sometime in 1927 and, most importantly, Luzi argues that it represents a celebration of the end to the gang wars in Chicago Heights (as spoken of in chapter 1) and a symbol of the unification of the Chicago Heights criminal organization.[8] Luzi's argument is convincing. At the same time, the picture freezes at one point in time the power syndicate of the Chicago Heights criminal enterprise or "the entire power structure of the Chicago Heights faction of the Capone gang from the 1920s . . . the cornerstone of organized crime in Chicago Heights."[9]

The men in the picture, then, provide a starting point for a more detailed look at the people who constituted the boys of Chicago Heights. The first question is who are these boys, these men? Again, thanks to Luzi's research, we are able to identify with confidence all but one of the men pictured.[10] These identifications reveal a mix of criminal histories and legal entanglements.[11] The criminal machinations of Frank Laporte, Dominic Roberto, Jimmy Emery, and John Roberts have been detailed previously. Joe Guzzino, who went on to become the man in charge of gambling in Calumet City, was an enforcer who was implicated in the 1926 slaying of Jim Lamberta, Sicilian gang leader. Nick Neroni was the business agent and the organization's man in the Local 5, International Hod Carriers, Builders, and Common Laborers Union. James Strangis was an alky runner. Because he was suspected of pilfering the bootleg liquor, he was shot and set ablaze in the stolen booze as a not too subtle warning to others.[12] Sam Laporte was a grocer and reported bootlegger who died in a gunfight over an argument about an unpaid grocery bill. Charlie Costello was an associate of slain gang leader Phillip Piazza, and was described as be-

Figure 4.1. The boys of Chicago Heights gathering to celebrate the unification of the Chicago Heights operation at Nick Naroni's farm in 1927. Starting from the left in front row: Luigi Angellotti, Anthony Scibi, George Zeranti, Nick Costello, John Nicastro, Frank Laporte, Jim Dipeso. Starting from the left in the middle row: Jim Strangis, Tony Costello, John Roberts, Sam Costello, Pete Zeranti, Dominic Roberto, Charlie Costello, Charlie Presto, Jimmy Emery, Sam Geraci, Nick DiGiovanni. Starting from the left in the back row: Mike Roberts, Jim Roberts, Sabastiano Zeranti, Sam Laporte, J. Pulia, Joe Arrigo, John Perry, Nick Naroni, Joe Guzzino, Sam DiGiovanni, John Piazza, Unknown, William Wilchinski, Tony Srebalus. Courtesy of Matt Luzi, Personal Collection.

ing "long an outstanding figure in the turbulent affairs of Chicago Heights."[13] Costello's brothers, Sam and Tony, were arrested in a 1929 federal raid in Chicago Heights and were grouped in a category that the chief prosecutor labeled as "killers, bootleggers, and racketeers."[14] Sam Costello, a close associate of Al Capone, was eventually killed in the infamous bakery shooting described previously, and Nick, his brother, was wounded in the gun battle. Another clan was led by Pete Zeranti who eventually became part owner and overseer of outfit run businesses such as Co-Operative Music.[15] Along with his brothers, George and Curly, Pete was arrested and released in the 1929 federal raid in Chicago Heights, as was Nick DiGiovanni.[16] Sam DiGiovanni was another "old-timer" who was the leader of the Sicilian operation in Chicago Heights and had a hand in illegal operations well into the 1950s.[17] Sam Geraci was also described as "an old-time prohibition bootlegger and hoodlum."[18] Joe Arrigo was hired by Chicago Outfit boss Johnny Torrio to run the Outfit's first foray into Chicago Heights, the Moonlight Café.[19] John Perry, along with Jim Dipeso and Bill Willis, was indicted by a federal grand jury in 1929 for operating a brewery and still.[20] Later, Perry was to become the head of the boys' gambling operations in Calumet City during the 1930s and 1940s.[21] Charlie Presto owned a local tavern that had a notorious reputation as a hangout for Outfit members. Tony Srebalus was a former alderman and brewery agent. He was accused of "shaking down" Greek coffee houses in Chicago Heights in return for the nonenforcement of gambling laws.[22] Finally, Mike Roberts and John Nicastro were involved in Outfit operations, Roberts as a money collector for illegal slot machines, Nicastro, among other duties, as a "bagman" transporting money to since-deported Dominic Roberto in Italy.

Strictly speaking, neither this photo nor the criminal histories provide definitive proof of a criminal organization in Chicago Heights or that these men made up the power syndicate of this organization. However, photos such as these have traditionally been used in a court of law to argue for organized criminal conspiracy.[23] And numerous accounts attest to a degree of hierarchy in the Chicago Heights operation. At the same time, Luzi argues that Dominic Roberto's central position in the photo, as well as the strategic positions of other men, provides a rough approximation of the relative degree of power in the organization.[24] And my father's long-time association with people in the Outfit lends even more credence to the hierarchical concentration of power represented in this photo. "Dominic (Roberto) was at the top. He was way up there. He was a lieutenant with the Capone organization. Jimmy Emery and John (Roberts) were up there too. At that time, Frankie (Laporte) wasn't big, that came later. The others, they took orders from Dominic."[25]

With a similar caution, one could argue that other men could have been included in this picture because they played an important role in the Chicago Heights criminal operations. For example, the 1929 federal raid in Chicago Heights and subsequent indictment identifies eighty-one defendants who "unlawfully, willfully, knowingly, and feloniously conspire, combine, confederate and agree together, and with divers other persons to the said grand jury unknown, to commit divers offenses against the United States."[26] And based on newspaper and other accounts, names such as Mike Picchi, a feared enforcer; Phil Bacino, a Calumet City syndicate leader; and Frances Curry, a slot-machine king in Joliet might have found a place standing or sitting in one of these rows. So, this picture may best be seen as a convenience sample, so to speak, of the criminal power structure in Chicago Heights at the beginning of its ascendance. Though a convenience sample, it is an awfully good sample of the most important players in the Chicago Heights operation. As such, it will provide a window for understanding how individuals simultaneously jumped toward and were pushed into organized crime.

Economic, Cultural, and Symbolic Capital

As Chicago Heights emerged from a sleepy village into a thriving industrial center, it attracted ambitious men and women with a keen interest in maximizing their economic success. Charles Wacker, Chicago developer; Phillip Dee Block, Inland Steel Founder; and even Louis Sullivan, famed architect, were among those who profited as Chicago Heights prospered. So too, the Chicago Heights boys were most concerned with increasing their allotment of economic capital. The majority of these men, arriving from the poverty-stricken Mezzogiorno at the beginning of the century, experienced extreme hardships—poor housing, poor health, diminished opportunities—with little to no accumulated wealth. As Joe Nicastro said, "John Roberts, he came over on the bottom of the boat from Italy. When he got here, he had lice all over his body and his clothes. My grandmother had to put the clothes in lye to get rid of all the lice."[27] An account of Frank Laporte's early life has it that "He came to the United States from Italy with his parents when he was very young. He was the oldest of eight children and the family was very poor, so that he was forced to go to work in a Chicago Heights steel mill at a very early age."[28] Louie Patrizi, a long-time Chicago Heights resident, recalls Dominic Roberto's early struggles, "When he came here he went to work at Calumet Steel. He had nothing."[29] Though social recognition and political power were always welcomed, material gain was the most immediate concern.

Yet, obtaining economic wealth or even a sustainable income in a legitimate manner was beyond the grasp of most Outfit members. Though some did end up owning businesses—for example, Jim Dipeso became a successful restaurant owner, Charlie Presto a local tavern owner, Sam Costello an East Side bakery owner—these were the exceptions. Their immigrant background in the increasingly anti-immigrant climate and their lack of formal schooling placed most of these men on the lower rungs of the American labor force. Equally, if not more importantly, this quest for economic mobility was made most difficult by the highly stratified and concentrated character of economic resources in Chicago Heights. A small segment of developers and industrialists had a tight hold on wealth and property. Thus, most residential and commercial property in Chicago Heights was still under the control of the Chicago Heights Land Association. The association owned roughly half of all the land in Chicago Heights and nearly all of the property on the East Side and the Hill areas where Italian homes and businesses were largely concentrated. As such, there was little economic competition, as this small-town oligarchy controlled the prospects for buying or renting a home or starting or prospering in a business. In fact, the local Italian parish, St. Rocco, was only made possible at the behest of the Land Association and their willingness to donate the available land.

At the same time, the manufacturing engine that allowed Chicago Heights to prosper and experience dramatic growth was largely concentrated in the hands of a finite number of people and businesses. For example, in 1919, four manufacturers (Inland Steel, American Manganese Steel Company, Calumet Steel, and Victor Chemical) employed more than one-third of all the workers.[30] In turn, these industrial concerns, primarily through the Chicago Heights Manufacturing Association and the Chicago Heights Chamber of Commerce, used their economic dominance to keep wages at the lowest levels possible. Thus, a study commissioned by the chamber in 1927 could boast that "Illinois Labor Laws are favorable to industry. The minimum age limit is 14 years with no minimum wage established."[31] With no minimum wage, the common laborer in the manufacturing industry, where most of the boys first found work, was paid between forty and fifty-five cents per hour, with Italians generally toward the lower end of this range.[32] Given the brutalizing environment found in many factories and this subsistence wage, it is not hard to imagine how the lure of organized crime would have played on the minds of Outfit members.

If this direct route to economic resources was highly problematic, then, perhaps, economic success could be purchased with the appropriate mix of cultural capital. That is, the possession of the proper cultural signals could serve as a resource to buy into the economic circles and status groups that controlled the flow of wealth, income, and recognition in society. We saw this, in part, with several of the mutual-benefit societies and ethnic group associations (for example, the Dante Club). Their attempt to adopt the civic-minded worldview of city officials and industry leaders—for example, to trade in the spaghetti-eating contests for patriotic displays—were signals that these men wanted to be let into the dominant economic and social class culture of Chicago Heights. Put another way, these men sought to demonstrate that they had the right mix of middle-class aspirations and the appropriate distance from the lower-class, Italian culture to be accepted in these more esteemed cultural circles.

These cultural investments eventually bought a measure of acceptance and inclusion for a select group of Italian residents in Chicago Heights. However, the boys were sorely lacking in their ability to exchange cultural capital for a more privileged position in society—this on several different levels. First, there were significant differences between elites and these Outfit members in terms of core values or worldviews. Thus, a review of editorials in the *Chicago Heights Star* from 1920 to 1929 gives some indication of the proper values that stood as markers for cultural inclusion. Specifically, elites placed a heavy emphasis on being a "good citizen" of the town, which in large measure equated to the possession of a progressive, probusiness mentality and a community, citywide perspective. These values were best captured in the elite theme that Chicago Heights would prosper with "a unified civic interest that will prevent diversified interests from checking the progress of the city."[33]

On this measure, the boys were at a distinct disadvantage. The self-interest of these leaders barely extended to their own old-country *paesani,* let alone to the many other groups that would be included in this call for a "unified civic interest." The provincial character of these men was certainly made explicit with the decade-long battle they carried on with *fellow* Italian immigrants, mostly Sicilian, for the control of Chicago Heights. Indeed, the power of the Chicago Heights crew as an organization rested on this closed, highly exclusionary set of values.

At the same time, there was also a significant cultural capital divide between the dominant elite groups and outfit members with respect to the "high cultural" forms of participation. For the elite, West Side groups, this consisted of an eclectic mix of bridge clubs, theater recitals, Shakespeare club luncheons, exclusive business associations, and European study tours. A circular sent out by Charles Wacker on behalf of the Chicago Heights Land Association boasted that "the city was home to the Rotary, Lions and Kiwanis clubs; a progressive Women's club; a Country and Golf Club."[34] For their part, the boys could not hope to participate in these highbrow status groups. Their southern Italian upbringing, lack of formal education, and traditional attitude toward women created a cultural gap that they had little ability to close. Efforts to bridge this gap were stylistically painful. One West Side resident recalls the awkward presence of Outfit members on a local golf course, "I remember caddying for Ralph Capone, Al Capone's brother. . . . It was at Burnham Woods Country Club, and the Capones owned it. They had one man walking down the fairway with a sub-machine gun, and one walking down the other side with a sub-machine gun."[35]

This mixture of submachine guns and golfing aside, most of the boys spent their leisure time in the local roadhouses, pool halls, nightclubs, and fraternal clubs. They played poker rather than bridge, the horses rather than golf, craps rather than the stock market. These gambling activities did not constitute a pathway to cultural acceptance by the local elite; they were "not included in the roster of *virtuous* games of chance" (italics added).[36] This cultural divide was made exceedingly clear in a *Chicago Heights Star* editorial that imperiously argued, "A professional crap game is worthy of a setting where the stench of manure and filth is so revolting as to drive decent persons to the open."[37]

The boys were also set apart from the elite circles by their lack of symbolic capital—or the ability to use symbolic identifications and practices as a resource to bring a sense of honor, respect, or legitimacy to their activities. On an individual level, the self-denigrating nicknames assigned to Outfit members—for example, Johnny Bum, Black Sam, Barrelhouse, the Shooter—did little to entice proper deference on the part of the general public or the West Side elites.[38] On a collective level, the criminal pasts of these men also posed obvious challenges in any attempt to integrate into this dominant elite group. For several decades, the slot-machine trust had been a black mark on the reputation of the community and a perceived impediment to attracting new business ventures and industries. As such, city leaders put forth a considerable public relations effort to overcome the reputation of Chicago Heights as a "wide-open" town. They engaged in a consistent and public campaign to denigrate "the ungoverned actions of a vulturous few."[39]

For their part, Chicago Heights Outfit leaders sought to deflect attention away from these criminal labels and buy back a measure of respect in the community. These attempts, however, often resulted in very crude symbolic practices. Thus, while West Side community leaders were able to symbolically distance themselves from their vested, material interests through such grandiose, philanthropic efforts as funding the Jones Community Center, donating land for the construction of St. Rocco Church, or providing welfare relief during the Great Depression, Outfit leaders were woefully inept in this symbolic game of philanthropy and distinction. As Candeloro tells us, "Many residents remember Capone's frequent visits to the city, especially his Robin-Hood-like performance at a 1931 baptismal reception in Mt. Carmel School Hall. As 'well-wishers' filed past, Capone peeled off one-, five-, ten-, and twenty-dollar bills from stacks on the front table."[40] Bergreen provides a somewhat similar picture suggesting that Capone "rode through the main streets of the little city, throwing silver dollars from the window of his Cadillac."[41] Overall, Outfit members had little economic, cultural, and symbolic capital to purchase a high standing in the community. What capital they did possess was, essentially, dead currency.

Social Capital—Brokerage and Closure

At this point, it may be useful to summarize the main arguments. Upon their arrival in Chicago Heights, Italian immigrants were confronted with a hostile mix of cultural, political, and economic discrimination. This discrimination contributed to a spatial and social isolation of Italians in the East Side and Hill areas of Chicago Heights. This isolation made it exceedingly difficult for most Italians to acquire the range of bridging social capital resources that would result in better schools, better jobs, better housing. However, what this social isolation did provide was the regeneration and intensification of extant social ties and associations—it enhanced the already strong bonding social capital resources that characterized this largely immigrant group. Drawing on these social ties and obligations, a segment of the Italian population engaged in more nontraditional routes to social mobility—these routes included organizing labor unions, forming mutual benefit societies, and creating ethnic businesses.

Yet, another avenue for social mobility involved the illegal activities associated with organized crime. While these illegal operations existed from the beginning of Chicago Heights's incorporation as a city in the early 1900s, the 1920s saw a dramatic increase in the size and scope of these operations as Prohibition created a tremendous black market opportunity for illegal liquor. Exhibiting a strong entrepreneurial sense and a willingness to use violence to accomplish their goals, a select group of Italian residents in Chicago Heights allied themselves with Al Capone to gain control of the illegal liquor, gambling, and prostitution trades in the Heights.

Having arrived at this point, we are still left to consider why this collection of Italian criminals was able to create a criminal organization—specifically, why the boys were able to dominate the local vice operations and maintain this dominance through the years, indeed over decades. In part, this domination was a result of *hierarchical relations.* As patriarchal or patrimonial leaders, Dominic Roberto, Jimmy Emery, Frank Laporte, and John Roberts were able to extract a measure of authority based on coercion. This willingness to exert power and engage in violence was always present and at times flared into the open. But as Max Weber argued, the sheer appropriation of power by physical force contains inherent uncertainties, the most vexing being that the use of coercion is often viewed as illegitimate and elicits opposition.[42] The internecine battles within Chicago Heights, especially between the Calabrese and Sicilian factions, attest to the fragile character of these hierarchical ties.

Another explanation for the Outfit's viability involved *market relations*. In this view, the Outfit's success was less a result of coercive domination per se but more a consequence of a wide number of symmetrical exchanges that profited the criminal organization and its customers, broadly conceived. In Weber's terms, these exchanges can be defined as "a compromise of interests on the part of the parties in the course of which goods or other advantages are passed as reciprocal advantages."[43] In more prosaic terms, the Outfit prospered because its illicit products or services (illegal liquor, gambling, prostitution, protection, and the like) were uniquely aligned with the needs and preferences of customers, suppliers, and competitors. This resulted in a supply and demand dynamic that bound Outfit members to people in the larger community in a mutually beneficial relationship.

Yet, the boys related to those both within and outside the organization in a more robust fashion than simply as power wielders and economic exchange partners. Specifically, these individuals were simultaneously embedded in a host of *social relations* and networks. The frequency, intensity, and quality of these networks generated a bountiful supply of social capital in running an efficient, albeit criminal, organization. An analysis of social capital, therefore, becomes critical to understanding the longevity and dominance of the Outfit in the Chicago Heights context. Having said this, the Outfit was not a social club, a philanthropic organization, or a social service agency intent on nurturing positive relations or good deeds in the community. The rich social capital resources that emerged were a by-product of the activities and social forces that had little to do with the intentions of Outfit members.[44] Still, without an understanding of the ways the boys were embedded in the social networks in the Chicago Heights community, we are left with a distorted picture of Outfit members—either as vultures preying on those with less power below them or as savvy businessmen who were particularly adroit in matching the supply and demand calculus of illegal markets. Standing alone, neither of these caricatures captures the more-substantive relations of Outfit members. And both can be understood more fully by positioning members within their relevant social relations and networks.

To dig even a bit deeper, these network ties can themselves be separated along the lines of Burt's critical formulation of brokerage and closure.[45] Brokerage refers to a structural positioning between different clusters of otherwise unconnected or marginally connected people or groups. Burt called these "structural holes" and argued that these types of social relationships provide access to a wealth of nonredundant, network resources in the form of diverse ideas, adaptive flexibility, or strategic opportunities not generally available to the clusters "on opposite sides of a hole."[46] These structural advantages, in turn, advance the probability that individuals or groups will be able to achieve their desired ends (control, prestige, profit, and such) over and above what they would have achieved without these connections. Hence, these types of social relationships constitute a unique collection of social capital resources. Specifically, with these social capital resources in hand, an individual who stands near the hole in a social structure is at a higher risk of success.

This probability of success, however, would be seriously compromised without the social capital that accrues from closure. Occupying a structural hole provides one with a "vision advantage" or the possibility of envisioning ideas, adaptations, and strategies that would be harder to come by within the social confines of a closed, highly redundant network. Yet, standing in this hole is risky for there is little of the built-up trust and familiarity that more likely characterizes closed networks. Without these mutually supportive ties and trusting relationships, uncertainty increases and coordination and communication decreases. Or put another way, the rich, detailed, and readily available information essential to the effective coordination and communication goes wanting. The vision advantage is dampened as the management task of bridging the structural hole becomes burdened with inefficiencies and risks.

As such, Burt argues that the advantages of social capital are maximized when this tension between brokerage and closure is resolved, when there is an effective trade-off between the two. This is most likely to occur in "structurally autonomous" groups—that is, where the extent of network closure is high and select members of the group bridge the structural holes beyond their own network.[47] In such cases, brokerage provides access to diverse perspectives, information, and opportunities and closure, on the other hand, to the most effective and efficient social mechanisms of trust and control. As Burt argues, "Brokerage is about coordinating people between whom it would be valuable, but risky, to trust. Closure is about making it safe to trust. The key to creating value is to put the two together, building closure around valuable bridge relations."[48] Putting the two together was arguably why the boys of Chicago Heights were so successful for such an extended period of time.

We will examine these processes in more detail. We begin with a discussion of closure and the social capital generated within the Chicago Heights context—specifically, the advantages that accrue to people when they know each other and can, presumably, be trusted, especially in those contexts that are highly unpredictable and contingent. We then turn to a discussion of brokerage within this same context and the social capital advantages this provided in terms of expanding the vision, the "good ideas," and the adaptive capacity of the Chicago Heights criminal operation.

The Boys of Chicago Heights: Brokerage and Closure

Evidence for closure and social capital is especially difficult to come by in cases involving archival studies. Direct access to the preferences and behaviors of social actors is limited by the availability of relevant data. Nevertheless, in the case at hand, the presence of closure among the Chicago Heights boys can reasonably be argued on a number of grounds. First, the Naroni Grove photograph itself provides some indication of these strong bonds. Naroni's dog notwithstanding, simply wandering onto the farm or into the picture was not permitted. This was a highly restrictive event that required strong, intimate ties.

Second, the similarities in the personal and social positions of the men suggest a common worldview or outlook. Table 4.1 shows the heavy reliance on fellow Italians in the organization, indeed the reliance on immigrants from southern Italy. This southern Italian heritage can be distilled even further. Eight of the men have strong ties to Sambiase, a tiny village in Calabria.[49] Another eight men were born in Caccamo, Sicily, or had a large number of relatives or friends from the town.[50] At the same time, a majority of these men were unskilled workers, many employed initially as laborers in the local steel mills. These common experiences do not automatically translate into strong ties, let alone social capital effects. Still, Portes's notion of "bounded solidarity" suggests that people thrown into a common situation may "learn to identify with each other and support each other's initiatives."[51] These processes may be in play here. Broadly speaking, the literature on homophily concludes unmistakably that "similarity breeds connection."[52]

Third, geographic proximity is also an indirect measure of closure. People are more likely to develop contacts and have close ties with people who share a social space. If this is a reasonable conclusion, then the boys of Chicago Heights occupied a fertile ground, so to speak, for the emergence of these ties. As Figure 4.2 indicates, these members actually lived next door or down the street from each other for at least a part of their lives. Twenty-eight of the members lived within a mile radius of one another or at most a fifteen-minute walk.[53] A matter of a few city blocks separated the majority of the men. This neighborhood proximity provided ample opportunity for the boys to get together casually at

Table 4.1. Personal and social characteristics Chicago Heights boys

Name	Ethnicity	Age (1927)	Immigration (Year)	Birth Place	Occupation (~1920)
Luigi Angellotti	Italian	38	Y (1906)	Acquaviva, Picena	Laborer
Joe Arrigo	Italian	56	Y (1891)	Italy	Fruit peddler
Charles Costello	Italian	37	Y (1899)	Caccamo, Sicily	Laborer
Nick Costello	Italian	21	N	Chicago Heights	Merchant
Sam Costello	Italian	33	N	Louisiana	Merchant
Tony Costello	Italian	25	N	Louisiana	Merchant
Jim Dipeso	Italian	54	Y (1892)	Italy	Teamster
Nick DiGiovanni	Italian	27	Y (1924)	Palazzo Adriano	Baker
Sam DiGiovanni	Italian	36	Y (1911)	Palazzo Adriano	Merchant
Jimmy Emery	Italian	35	Y (1912)	Cosenza, Calabria	Painter
Sam Geraci	Italian	40	Y (1913)	Caccamo, Sicily	Laborer
Joe Guzzino	Italian	32	N	Louisiana	Laborer
Frank Laporte	Italian	27	Y (1913)	Sambiase, Calabria	Laborer
Sam Laporte	Italian	50	Y (1905)	Sambiase, Calabria	Laborer
Nick Naroni	Italian	41	Y (1906)	Acquaviva, Picena	Laborer
John Nicastro	Italian	25	N	Chicago Heights	Laborer
John Perry	Italian	32	Y (1905)	Cosenza, Sicily	Express man
John Piazza	Italian	43	Y (1900)	Caccamo, Sicily	Teamster
Charlie Presto	Italian	NA	NA	NA	Tavern owner
J. Pulia	Italian	NA	NA	NA	NA
Dominic Roberto	Italian	31	Y (1913)	Sambiase, Calabria	Laborer
Jim Roberto	Italian	43	Y (1907)	Sambiase, Calabria	NA
John Roberts	Italian	26	Y (1920)	Sambiase, Calabria	Laborer
Mike Roberts	Italian	33	Y (1903)	Sambiase, Calabria	Laborer
Tony Srebalus	Lithuanian	38	Y (1890)	Russia	Brewery agent
Jim Strangis	Italian	33	Y (NA)	Sambiase, Calabria	Laborer
William Wilchinski	Polish	32	N	Chicago	Deputy sheriff
George Zeranti	Italian	23	N	Chicago Heights	Laborer
Pete Zeranti	Italian	42	Y (1898)	Caccamo, Sicily	Barber
Sebastiano Zeranti	Italian	40	Y (1909)	Caccamo, Sicily	Laborer

Sources: "Naturalization Petitions for the United States District and Circuit Courts, Northern District of Illinois and Immigration and Naturalization Service District 9, 1907–1954, Chicago Heights"; Department of Commerce, Bureau of the Census, *Fourteenth Census of the United States: 1920 Population, Chicago Heights manuscripts;* U.S. Department of Justice, Federal Bureau of Investigation, Subject: Frank La Porte; U.S. World War I Draft Registration Cards, 1917–1918; *Chicago Heights Star; Chicago Heights City Directory, 1923–1925.*

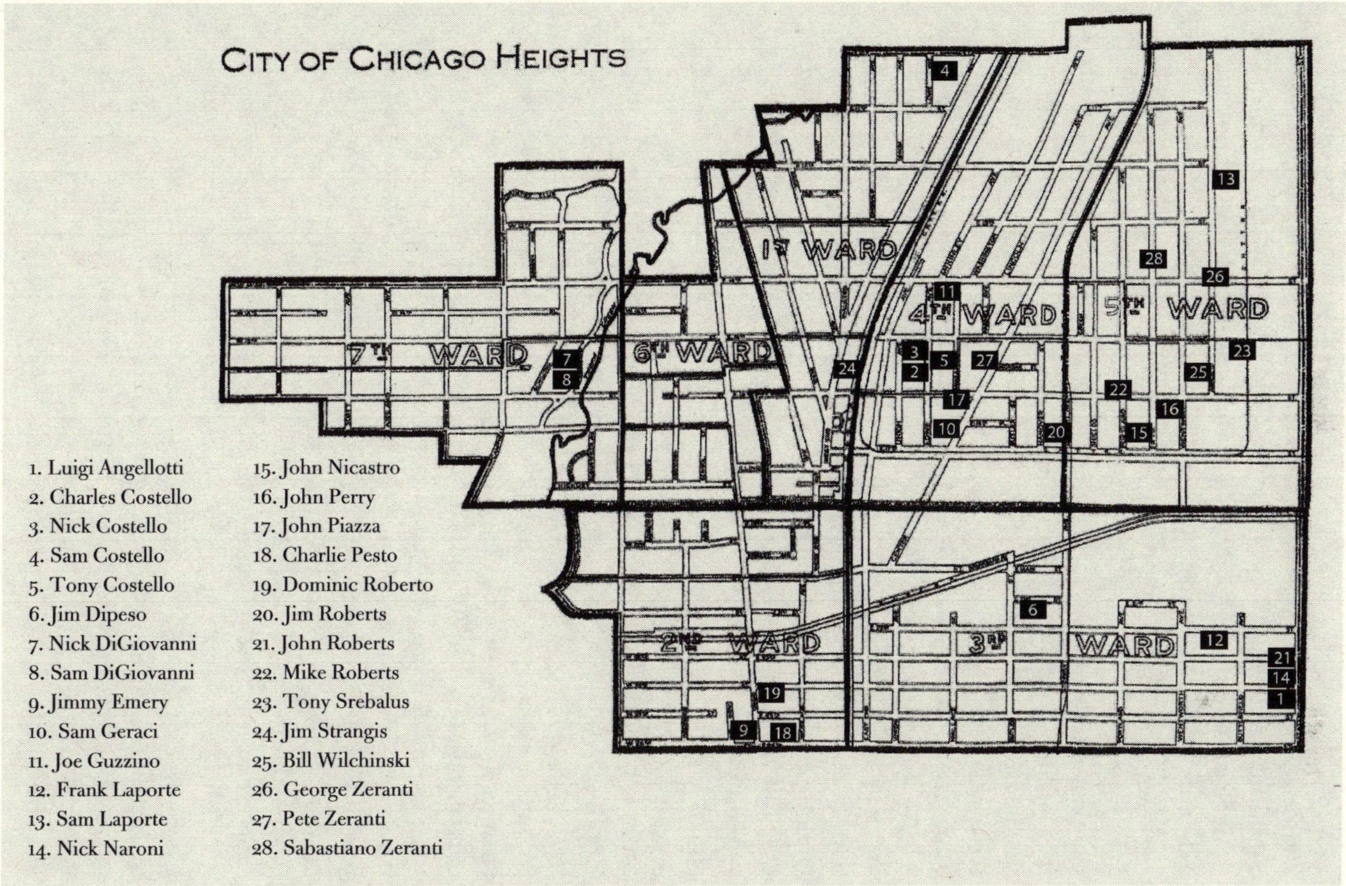

Figure 4.2. Residential Locations of "Boys" of Chicago Heights, 1920s. Modified Map, Board of Election Commissioners, 1922. Courtesy of Newberry Library.

each other's houses or in a more public setting such as Charlie Presto's tavern, Pete Zeranti's barbershop, or Naroni's farm, all of which these men did with considerable frequency.

As revealing as these measures of closure may be, the most self-evident indicator of closed networks involves a more direct analysis of relational variables or more simply the ties between the social actors. The assumption is that networks that have a collection of redundant, overlapping ties will exhibit more closure, which means more trust, which means more social capital. With these assumptions in hand, what evidence is there for such a closed network among the Chicago Heights Outfit members? Perhaps not at all surprising, the evidence for closure is considerable. Figure 4.3 details a range of friendship, kinship, occupational, and residential ties among the thirty men.[54] Some members were isolates and their position in the Outfit was more functional. For example, Wilchinski was a local police officer who was on the Outfit's payroll. And Arrigo was brought in by Johnny Torrio to run the Chicago Outfit's prostitution houses in Chicago Heights and therefore did not have extensive ties to the men in the Heights. Beyond these men, however, we find a tight-knit collection of Outfit members bound together not simply by their criminal interests but because they were variously brothers, cousins, in-laws, sons, and friends of one another. This network did have fractures, most prominently between the Calabrese group led by Dominic Roberts and his brother John Roberts and the Sicilian group led by Sam Costello and Pete Zeranti, with Jimmy Emery as a broker. Still, due to the similarity in backgrounds, the geographic closeness, and the kinship and friendship bonds, this group of men knew each other, knew each other's families and backgrounds, and saw each other nearly every day. The social ties ran deep. As such, these men were able to keep a watchful eye on one another from various vantage points and, thereby, decrease the "risks that would otherwise inhibit trust."[55] Some thirty-odd years later, an FBI informant could still claim that of all the Chicago Outfit crews, the Chicago Heights members were the "tightest group in the Chicago area."[56]

Closed networks, however, tend toward inertia. They can be incredibly supportive and enriching but poor vehicles for social advancement or mobility. Many of the mutual-aid societies we looked at earlier may be so characterized because closure may have been impervious to new ideas, new relationships. As such, the social capital generated by closed networks is put to its greatest advantage when it is coupled with the social capital that accrues through brokerage. In such situations, trust and vision are joined. Effective management and control is put in the service of opportunity and entrepreneurship. Social capital is more completely transformed into live currency that can buy more advantage.

This was the formula that proved so successful for the Chicago Heights boys. To be sure, the closed networks found in the local Italian culture contributed to the nefarious success of the Outfit. This was especially the case in the pre-Outfit days or when the slot-machine trust primarily serviced fellow immigrants on the East Side and the Hill sections. However, the unprecedented success of the Chicago Heights operations did not take place until the likes of Dominic Roberto and others saw the opportunities presented in spanning their connections to the "opposite sides" of the hole. These structural holes were numerous, for the abiding segregation and separation of the Italian population created an array of opportunities for brokerage. Broadly conceived, however, the most advantageous holes found the close-knit, social capital–rich Italian community on one side; the ravenous Chicago-based Capone–led Outfit on another; and the collection of "legitimate" local politicians, businessmen, and law enforcement officials on the third. Nestled among these social networks, the Chicago Heights boys found truth in Burt's maxim that "individuals with networks rich in structural holes are the individuals who know about, have a hand in, and exercise control over, more rewarding opportunities."[57]

These opportunities did not present themselves equally to every boy in the Chicago Heights operation. Some of these members were either so young or so deeply entrenched in the local Italian community they could not see the brokerage opportunities. This advantage fell, instead, to a few select individuals. Specifically, over the fifty-year period from 1920 to 1970, Jimmy Emery, Dominic Roberto, John Roberts, and Frank Laporte assumed top positions in the Chicago Heights Outfit along with a most prominent role in the upper echelon of the Chicago Outfit itself. Of these men, Frank Laporte had the longest tenure and was generally considered the most active and involved crime leader. He was so successful that noted crime historian and writer Ovid Demaris quoted a newspaper report that described Laporte as "perhaps the biggest man in the Mafia today."[58] As such, Laporte will serve as our entrée into a discussion of the social capital that is generated by brokerage and closure. Laporte's ability to provide a bridge between the local Italian community, the Capone organization, and the networks of legitimate citizens in Chicago Heights and other neighborhood towns brought him tremendous social capital advantages and brought the Chicago Heights Outfit an unprecedented level of success.

Frank Laporte, or Frankie as he was called, was embedded in the local culture and structure of Chicago Heights. Having immigrated to America from

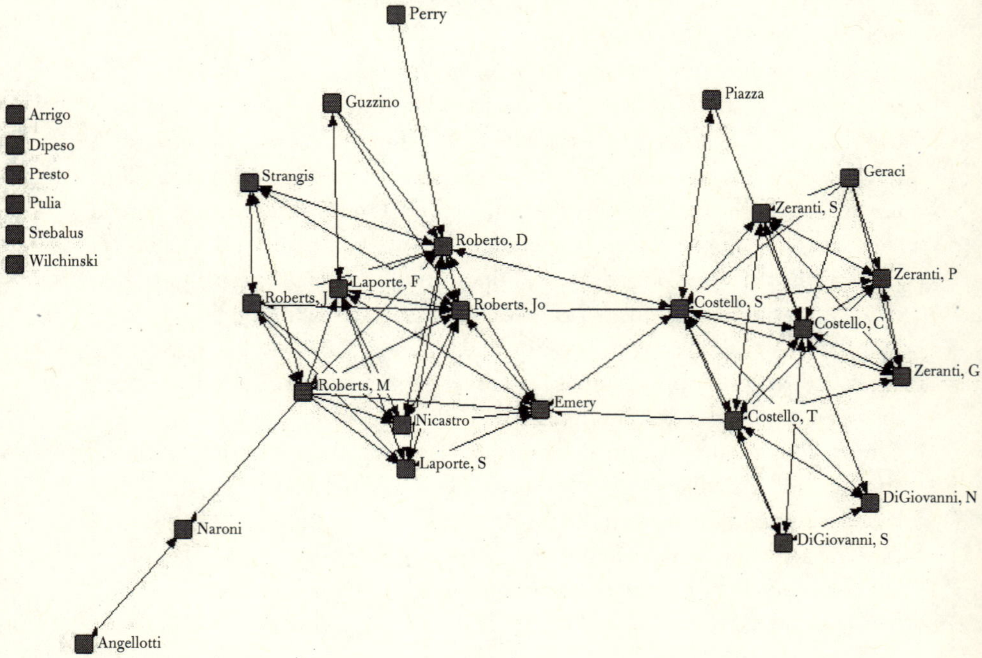

Figure 4.3. Social Networks: Boys of Chicago Heights, 1920s. Social network software courtesy of: S. P. Borgatti, M. G. Everett, and L. C. Freeman, *Ucinet for Windows: Software for Social Network Analysis* (Harvard, Mass.: Analytic Technologies, 2002).

Sambiase, Italy, in 1913, at twelve years old, Laporte acquired the right mix of cultural capital—for example, the ability to speak the Italian dialect, the East Side and Hill street savvy, the drudgery of working in the local steel mills—to solidify his identity in the closed world of the Italian neighborhood. Along with the numerous contacts he made by working in the family grocery store in the Heights, these street experiences placed Laporte within the crisscrossing network of working men, store customers, tavern owners, and street thugs. As one FBI agent concluded, Laporte's "influence appears to have been derived from his family connection and his close association with other individuals who immigrated from Sicily at the turn of the century."[59]

One of the men that Laporte formed a close association with was his cousin, Dominic Roberto. Roberto had also emigrated from Sambiase in 1913. He spent several years working in the steel mill furnace shops and scrap yards of Chicago Heights and worked alongside Laporte for a brief time in the family grocery store. Perhaps most importantly, both men were roustabouts and more than inclined to engage in violence to achieve their aims. These tendencies were enhanced when they met up with Jimmy Emery, another émigré from Calabria, who was a well-known saloonkeeper in the Heights. Together, these men were in and out of trouble with the law for the greater part of the 1920s. Thus, Roberto was arrested for robbery in 1921, Emery and Roberto charged with the intent to commit murder in 1922, and Roberto and Laporte booked for murder in 1926. For a number of reasons, not the least of which involved favorable political connections and the intimidation of witnesses, none of the charges resulted in permanent convictions, even though Roberto pleaded guilty on the robbery charge.[60]

This spate of illegal activities coincided with the more encompassing strategy of merging the Chicago Heights illegal operations with the Capone Outfit in Chicago. Previously, the Chicago Heights rackets were headed, as pointed out earlier, by Antonio Sanfilippo who provided "protection" for the local moonshiners.[61] However, because of the close, insular character of the Chicago Heights neighborhoods early in the century, Sanfilippo did not entertain the grander vision of creating a monopolistic, regional enterprise of illegal stills, gambling houses, and strip-tease joints. Indeed, in ways similar to Big Jim Colosimo in Chicago, Sanfilippo may have stood in the way of this grander scheme. As such, it was only when Roberto, Emery, and Laporte began to mesh themselves within the Capone operation in Chicago and when Capone's ties to Chicago Heights became "stronger than ever,"[62] it was only then that this collection of criminals began to forge relationships that prompted even more entrepreneurial possibilities. In Burt's terms, they began to span the structural hole.

As time and circumstances intervened, leadership in the Chicago Heights Outfit shifted. Dominic Roberto was the first to systematically marry Capone's band of killers with the illegal market and production capacities south of Chicago. Thus, he masterminded the purge of the rival Sicilian gang with help from Capone. Roberto's reign, however, was short-lived as he ran afoul of the immigration laws and was deported back to Italy in 1935. Though Roberto was no longer involved in the day-to-day operations of the Outfit, his influence remained strong through the godfather-like presence of his brother John Roberts.

With Dominic Roberto no longer in direct control, Jimmy Emery ascended to the top position, earning the sobriquet "king of the streets." Emery commanded considerable influence. He garnered such a position, in part, through fear and intimidation. But as we have pointed out, you can't shoot everyone. Thus, Emery's influence also stemmed from the fact that he was uniquely positioned on the boundary of three powerful networks—namely, the criminal operatives in Chicago Heights and the surrounding communities, the business leaders and government officials in these communities, and Capone's inner circle of friends and associates. With respect to this last grouping, Emery cemented his ties to Capone by asking Capone to serve as his daughter's godfather. Figure 1.2 shows Capone with his arm draped around Emery's daughter. And Emery was close to Louis "Little New York" Campagna, Claude Maddox (also in Figure 1.2), and "Machine Gun" Jack McGurn, among others. Emery parlayed these ties into a long-standing position of leadership in the Chicago Heights rackets. And having done so, he played a prominent role in extending the Heights operation into the prostitution houses and gambling dens in Blue Island, Hammond, and Calumet City by working with the city officials in each of these communities.

Yet as powerful as Emery may have been, ill health and a lack of interest in the daily machinations of the Outfit eventually caused him to withdraw from the operation. He came to spend more time pursuing his interests in raising and racing thoroughbreds than in attending to Outfit business. This created a vacuum at the top of the Heights rackets, an opening that John Roberts and Frank Laporte filled. Thus, Roberts became the overseer of gambling operations. As Louie Patrizi recalled, "Roberto (aka Roberts) had a hand in most every card game in the area."[63] The U.S. Treasury Department listed Roberts as one of the top Mafia members worldwide during the 1950s. He was said to be a criminal associate of Tony Accardo and "actively engaged in organized crime in Chicago for many years."[64] Roberts held a top position in the Chicago Heights Outfit until he died in 1961.

He held this top position alongside Frank Laporte. Laporte has set his sights on, and had been encouraged to pursue, a leadership position in the Outfit for a number of years. Again, Laporte's presence next to Capone in Figure 1.2 gives some indication of his early rise to prominence. At the same time, Dominic Roberto's wife, Rio Burke, recalls, "Jimmy (Emery) was grooming Frankie Laporte to take his place in the organization."[65] As such, Laporte followed Emery's path to success by developing close connections with and serving as a broker between several social capital–rich social networks in and around Chicago. One such network was the collection of Italian immigrants in Chicago Heights who in the turbulent decades of the 1930s and 1940s had become even more marginalized and distanced from legitimate chances for mobility. This network included a number of men in the closed circle that made up the Chicago Heights boys—in particular, John Perry, Charlie Costello, Joe Guzzino. It also included other Laporte friends and relatives such as Jimmy Ross, George

Montasanti, Tony Franze, "Black George" Stella, and Frankie Franze. These men provided the hard muscle, the illegal know-how, and the trusted day-to-day oversight that allowed Laporte to run his diverse illegal enterprises.

Another network consisted of more-functional ties—specifically, city officials in the neighboring towns of Chicago Heights, Calumet City, South Chicago Heights, Dixmoor, and Burnham. These ties lacked the intimacy and ensured trust of the networks previously discussed. As such, they were in most cases forged through an instrumental exchange of money, political support, and favoritism.[66] Still, such ties were extremely valuable, though less trustworthy, for they provided access to strategies, favors, and resources different and more varied from the closed networks within the Italian circle of friends. We get some sense of these ties when we examine Laporte's connections to city officials in Chicago Heights. For example, Craig Hood, a former mayor, was a Laporte associate, having represented Laporte in court on several occasions. Silvio Piacenti, at one time the city attorney and a leader of the Italian Voters' League of Chicago Heights, was deemed by FBI files to be a "close associate" of Laporte.[67] Mike Costabile, also a city attorney and a school board member, was tied to Laporte through a number of friends and political leaders. Carl McGhee, another former mayor, was subsequently hired as an attorney by Laporte. And not to be outdone, Maurino Richton, yet another former mayor, was on friendly terms with Laporte, visiting Laporte in the hospital when he was sick and attending various exclusive Laporte family functions. Exactly what these city officials gained from their relationship with Laporte is difficult to determine. Laporte's take, however, seems clear-cut. Specifically, Laporte acquired considerable political capital in these exchanges, capital in the form of public legitimacy, nonenforcement of certain city statutes, and access to otherwise clandestine information. More generally, one FBI informant said, "It is common knowledge in the Chicago Heights area (an unnamed official) is extremely close to Frank Laporte, who is considered the man who pulls strings to control the political power in the Heights."[68]

Yet a third network involved Laporte's ties to the Chicago Outfit. From Capone, to Frank Nitti, to Paul "The Waiter" Ricca, to Tony Accardo, Laporte was a confidant of the top leaders in the Outfit. Early on, State Attorney Pat Roche hinted at this when he said, "Laporte had been seen frequently loitering about the Chicago headquarters of the Capone gang."[69] Through the years, Laporte nurtured and extended these Outfit ties. Thus, once a month, Laporte met with Tony Accardo, Sam Giancanna, and Eddie Vogel in Chicago Heights to discuss Outfit business.[70] In return, Laporte was on more than one occasion a guest of Accardo at his home in River Forest, this determined by none other than a Scotland Yard detail brought in to spy on the Accardo gathering.[71] Roemer includes Laporte as one of the "connection guys," along with Murray "The Camel" Humphries and Gus Alex, who met regularly in Chicago to report on the latest developments in the Outfit.[72] Furthermore, Laporte was said to be "an admirer of Sam 'Teets' Battaglia and vice versa. Each has great respect for the other and have met secretly on a number of occasions."[73] And Laporte, though otherwise circumspect about appearing in public, was a regular attendee at the funerals of the highest-ranking Outfit leaders—a sign most likely of the strong ties that existed among these leaders.

As the leader of the Chicago Heights Outfit, the primary goal for Laporte was to generate profit. Profit not only for himself but also for the myriad friends, workers, and relatives associated with the Outfit operations.[74] And the bosses in Chicago, from Capone to Accardo, demanded a "cut of the action" and stream of revenue from the Heights rackets. This quest for profit, however, was made all the more difficult by the economic, social, and political disruptions in the 1930s, 1940s, and 1950s. Thus, the repeal of Prohibition, the Great Depression, World War II, the postwar prosperity, and the Kefauver and McLennan Committee Hearings opened up possibilities for some illegal activities and closed down others.

In this highly contingent environment, the Chicago Heights Outfit had to adapt. No longer could it rely on its premier position as a major supplier and distribution center for bootleg liquor. Laporte, with the help of others, had to avoid squandering its most valuable resource—namely, the trust, efficiencies, and coordination created by the closed networks in the local Italian culture. At the same time, he needed to move away from the stultifying and rigid practices of this network and, accordingly, take advantage of the more promising money-making ventures that were coming into focus. This Laporte did with a skill and perspective that would rival the legendary corporate leaders of the era. Specifically, Laporte charted a course for the Chicago Heights Outfit that, while frenetic, chaotic, or parasitic from an outside perspective, was from the singular goal of generating illegal profit, a widely successful decades-long run that expertly balanced innovation and preservation, vision and coordination.

A list of the illegal ventures, some successful and some not, is remarkable for its diversity and boldness. For example, in the nearby towns of Harvey and Blue Island, Laporte ran an illegal booking operation in at least seven different locations. One informant said it was "the biggest horse book in the area."[75] In Calumet City, Laporte organized a "B-girl" venture, where women would solicit customers for drinks and other favors.[76] Throughout the southern suburbs, Laporte had control of the vending machine business such that placement of a jukebox, cigarette machine, or condom dispenser in an establishment was tightly controlled by the Co-Operative Music Company, the Wilco Music and Tobacco Company, or the Regal Vending Corporation. In fact, even the cigarette machine in the Chicago Heights police department was under Laporte's control. Another source of revenue was the bonding business, where Laporte controlled "the lion's share of the bail bond business in south Cook and Will County.[77] Specifically, those charged with a crime would be steered by "friendly" police officers and lawyers to one of the offices owned by the boys. Slot machines were also a significant source of revenue. In the backrooms of a great many bars and fraternal clubs, the Outfit placed and serviced five-cent, ten-cent, twenty-five-cent, fifty-cent, and one-dollar slot machines. As one might expect, entrée into the local labor unions—especially Local 5 International Hod Carriers, Builders, and Common Laborers—provided the Outfit access to pension funds, construction jobs, and kickbacks. And to balance this out, Laporte steered the Outfit into partnerships in the Readi Mix Cement Company, the Normandy Villa Housing Corporation, the Skyline Disposal Company, as well as several real estate companies, liquor stores, motels, laundromats, insurance companies, and breweries. And in the 1950s, during the height of the teeny-bopper craze, Laporte even took a shot at capitalizing on the success of young, Italian rock-and-roll stars such as Frankie Avalon, Fabian, and Dion, by promoting the Outfit's own teenage sensation, Tommy Leonetti.[78] As a young boy, I remember being hustled along with my sisters and cousins to a performance by Leonetti at Co-Operative Music in Chicago Heights, a promotion that attracted hundreds of screaming fans. A far cry indeed from the rough-and-tumble bootleg days of Al Capone and Dominic Roberto.

These illegal operations were variously successful. There were ventures that failed. Leonetti had several top 100 hits and even appeared on the *Tonight Show* hosted by both Steve Allen and Johnny Carson (presumably these appearances were made possible by Outfit connections). However, Leonetti was generally viewed as a one-hit wonder and faded from public view fairly quickly. There were gold mines in California, uranium mines in Colorado, and tungsten mines in Nevada that, respectively, produced little gold, uranium, and tungsten. At the same time, Laporte's efforts in supporting the Chicago Outfit's own beer company, Foxhead 400, had dismal results. My father told me that the beer was so bad that even Outfit-friendly bartenders refused to sell it. "Yeah, it was a Chicago beer . . . One guy bought 100 cases the first time I asked him, the guy at the High Hat. But he used to take the labels off the bottles so the guys wouldn't know what kind of beer they were drinking. When they asked for 'a beer,' he would give them one of these."[79]

However, the successes outnumbered the failures. And beyond the success of any particular operation, the more general point is that the Chicago Heights Outfit, and Frank Laporte in particular, benefited significantly from the social capital produced by brokerage and closure. And as suggested, entrepreneurial organizations are best served when brokerage and closure work in tandem. Structural holes create the vision advantage and closed networks provide the "organizational suture that tightens coordination across the hole."[80] An example might reveal more clearly the creative tension between brokerage and closure.

We focus on the vending machine industry. As suggested previously, slot machines had long been a staple of the Chicago Heights rackets. The slot-machine trust had beguiled city officials since the early part of the century. In 1911, the *Chicago Heights Star* said there were upward of 120 machines in Chicago Heights and estimated revenues at $1,200 a week, a considerable amount for the time.[81] Even so, these gambling operations were sequestered in the predominantly immigrant enclaves in the city, especially along Twenty-sixth Street in the Hill area. As such, the *Star* appealed to the "men of repute in the community" to take a stand against the vice chieftains in the immigrant wards of the city, "the organized practitioners of immorality."[82]

This isolation of the slot machines on the Hill prevailed well into the 1930s as the Heights operation devoted its considerable expertise and resources to the production of illegal alcohol. In the meantime, the Torrio-Capone organization began expanding its operation not only to Chicago Heights but also more famously into Cicero (and Stickney, Forest View, Berwyn, and River Forest). Through a series of political maneuvers and a show of force, the Chicago Outfit settled into Cicero and filled the main streets with houses of prostitution, dance halls, and gambling dens. Most significantly, these illegal operations moved beyond the isolated immigrant enclaves and into the more respectable venues in the city—the streets, social groups, neighborhoods all across the town. As Peterson concluded, the Torrio-Capone gangsters "own Cicero—lock, stock, and barrel."[83]

In particular, Eddie Vogel, along with Jack and Sam Gusik, was one of the leading figures in the Cicero takeover. Vogel had two revealing epithets—the King of the Slot Machines and the Honorary Mayor of Cicero.[84] Apropos of both, Vogel played a key role in extending the slot-machine empire beyond the main street saloons and gambling dens of Cicero and into the myriad social clubs, fraternal organizations, and taverns throughout the town. In commenting on the proliferation of slot machines in and around Chicago, Illinois Assistant State Attorney Henry E. Ayres said, "So many machines were placed in operation that truant officers were compelled to demand that the police remove the machines from the vicinity of school buildings where school children frequently gambled on the machines."[85] Overall, Lait and Mortimer's observations of the Chicago underworld concluded that while the majority of Cicero residents were "fine family folk," Cicero was a "carnival of crime and lewdness."[86] "Here you will find," Lait and Mortimer said, "one-armed bandits everywhere except in the churches."[87]

Vogel and the Gusik brothers were long-time associates of Frank Laporte. These men, along with other "top Chicago hoodlums," were "known to participate in high-level conferences concerning the gambling situation in Cook County."[88] And these men were also mutually connected through third parties such as Babe Tuffanelli, a Blue Island racketeer; Francis Curry, the slot-machine boss of Joliet and Will County; and Chuck English, once a Cicero-based gambling operator and then a phonograph record supplier. These associations, on the other side of the hole from the Chicago Heights rackets, provided Laporte with practical, best practices advice on how to run a slot-machine business—for example, how to place the slots in "respectable" organizations, how to avoid having the slot machines hijacked by non-Outfit hoodlums, how to service and make collections on the machines, and how to spirit the slots away when an impending raid was learned about beforehand.[89] Perhaps, more importantly, Laporte was made aware of the grander, entrepreneurial vision. Laporte's association with Vogel, Gusik, and others made him more than a good manager, it promoted a wider angle regarding the expansion of the slot-machine rackets (as one of several types of illegal activities) to a number of communities south of Chicago (Harvey, Blue Island, Kankakee, Calumet City, Joliet, South Chicago Heights, Calumet Park, Willow Springs, Hammond, Steger, and Dixmoor) and within each of these communities an expansion beyond the immigrant neighborhoods per se to the more middle-class neighborhoods, where "men of repute" and their veteran organizations, country clubs, and houses of worship could enjoy these illegal ventures. In this manner, Laporte even trumped the Cicero organization by negotiating with local churches for retail outlets. As Joe Nicastro said, "St. Agnes had a garage loaded with slot machines. They got a piece of it. They split the money 50/50 after the boys took the money off the top."[90]

Laporte's associations, then, with key figures in the Chicago Outfit increased the value of the local slot-machine business. The Cicero operation, in particular, provided the blueprint, both in its successes and excesses. However, the expansion of the slot-machine trust in Chicago Heights would have been severely compromised without the social capital advantages provided by the closed social networks available to Laporte. For example, this illegal enterprise required a steady flow of customers and a reliable network of service providers. At the same time, customers had to be serviced in a circumspect manner, unlike the more blatant practices in Cicero, lest the Outfit risk unwanted attention on the part of law enforcement officials or the opprobrium of the local citizens. Thus, one FBI informant told of an incident in which Joe Barrett, an Outfit member, attempted to set up a backroom prostitution and gambling operation at a location in the center of Chicago Heights. When Laporte heard of this, he ordered the place closed immediately. Reportedly, he told Barrett that "even during the 1920s the Outfit was not brazen enough to operate openly in the downtown section of Chicago Heights."[91] More to the point, even though Chicago Heights was an "open town" and even though Laporte's ties to city officials provided nonenforcement protection, the slot-machine operations had to be coordinated in both a profitable and surreptitious manner to avoid the infamous notoriety as was the case in Cicero.

This prosaic coordination and control was achieved in large measure by embedding the slot-machine operations in the informal bonds and networks that were already in place in the community, and thereby avoiding the creation of a so-called red light district. In this respect, the fraternal organizations and clubs—for example, the Hunters Club, the Catholic War Vets, the American Legion Posts, the CIO Steel Workers Club, the Polish Democratic Club, the Loyal Order of Moose, the Fraternal Order of Eagles, the Chicago Heights Country Club, the Italian American Republican Club, the Olympia Fields Country Club, the Christopher Columbus Society, the Polish Falcons, the Military Order of the Purple Heart, to name several—were the most-favored places for the Outfit slots. The formal criteria for membership in these clubs and the strong personal ties and sanctions that developed among club members gave the boys an indigenous set of social control mechanisms and a supply of social capital to discourage "malfeasance." For example, disgruntled customers or losers were handled internally by club officials, club members, or priests. As one resident, Louie Patrizi said, "If you had a problem losing money, you took it up with other guys in the club, no one ever talked to the Outfit guys."[92] A member of the American Legion Post 131 publicly chastised a critic of the legions' slot-machine operation by wondering aloud whether this complaint stemmed from the fact that this critic had lost "a buck or two" in playing the slots.[93] In these instances, the local social networks expropriated by Laporte and his lieutenants provided cheap, secure, ready available efficiencies upon which to build a successful slot-machine empire.

These operations were undoubtedly successful for the Outfit and these local organizations and, arguably, for the community. A single slot machine generated anywhere from $5,000 to $20,000 a year, depending on its location. And most organizations housed, at minimum, three or four machines. The monies were generally split fifty/fifty between the Outfit and the local organization (though some organizations bought their slot machines from the Outfit and ran the operations themselves). For their part, these fraternal clubs also benefited immensely. Guido Markionni, a past commander of Catholic War Vets in Chicago Heights, said that the money generated by the slot machines allowed the post to purchase its own building.[94] Dominic Sesto, the founding commander of Catholic War Vets, said, "Most all of the clubs in Chicago Heights were built on slot-machine money."[95] And Wally Lueder, a civic leader in the community, responded to a citizen's complaint that the American Legion was essentially a "donation fund to five cent beers and slot machines" by arguing that charitable organizations and causes such as the Boy Scouts, Veterans Hospitals, Salvation Army, orphans, Community Fund, and leprosy hospitals had been aided immeasurably by the legion post and by implication these slot-machine "donations."[96]

Taverns posed more of a problem, since theoretically they were far less exclusive in terms of who they serviced. The networks of customers, bartenders, and owners were more open and uncontrolled. But even here, we find that the Outfit slots were placed mainly in corner bars, saloons, and liquor stores. Places where the customers were for the most part "regulars." As Haller concludes more generally, "Like other retailers in the city, some leaders of organized crime . . . were essentially neighborhood businessmen with local clientele. . . . Those providing illegal goods and services usually attempted to cultivate customer loyalty so that the same customers would return on an ongoing basis and advertise among friends."[97] Cultivating customer loyalty served the Chicago Heights Outfit well for it provided a trustworthy set of personal relations through which to run the illegal, clandestine slot-machine operation. My father, who worked for a time as a bartender at the Copa Cabana Tavern in Chicago Heights, said, "It wasn't always the case, but you pretty much had to know a guy before you let him in the backroom."[98] The backroom or the rear of the tavern was informally reserved for these regulars. Access to the slot machines in these more secluded areas generally required some acknowledgment on the part of the waitress, bartender, or owner. We get some sense of this mix of social and geographic access when charges against several tavern owners were dismissed in court because the slot machines were seized from "living quarters behind saloons"—suggesting at least both a legal and social exclusion as one moved from the front of the tavern to the rear and beyond.[99]

The variously closed systems of personal and social relations were of critical importance in running the slot-machine operation in Chicago Heights. Without the mediating social influences of fraternal club associations and neighborhood bars, the number of people willing to step into these notorious and illegal markets would have certainly been more limited. The "blue nose" factor would have been more powerful. And without the willingness on the part of club officials and tavern owners to essentially manage the slot-machine business on a daily basis for the Outfit and to take the heat when necessary—in terms of fines, public disapproval, and the vagaries of the gambling market—Laporte and his crew would have needed to spend far more of their resources on these disruptions. Force and intimidation, as significant as it was in producing the Outfit's monopoly of the slot-machine business, would have played an even more significant role in normal operating procedures. Along these lines, the gambling operation in the red light district of Cicero points to the incredible profits but also the incredible resources and exposure that the Outfit endures when it is not embedded in the local community, when violence supplants social capital. The Chicago Heights operation—in Chicago Heights and in a variety of other local communities—was built on the reservoir of mutual ties, overlapping alliances, and stock of trust that characterized these villages.

Illegal slot machines are but one example of this amalgam of brokerage and closure. The early success of the illegal alcohol trade in Chicago Heights was in large measure due to the social capital generated by structural holes and closed networks. Phil Piazza's association with the "Terrible Gennas" in Chicago provided the vision for a more aggressive, illegal empire in Chicago Heights, an alky racket that had been "controlled by a group of old-fashioned Sicilian gangsters grown complacent with age."[100] Piazza married this vision with a closed network of Sicilian racketeers in Chicago Heights. He became the undisputed "powerful boss" of these illegal operations until his reign was in fact disputed by Roberto, Emery, and Capone, and he was murdered.[101]

The infamous Owl Club in Calumet City, a multi-million-dollar moneymaker for the Outfit for over 30 years, constitutes another example of this brokerage and closure tandem. This club first began operations in 1936. At that time, most of the clubs on the "strip" had their own gambling rooms in the back. The Owl Club, spearheaded by Jack Gusik, Les "Killer Kane" Kruse, and Tony Accardo, had a different vision—in particular, a casino-type gambling operation with roulette wheels, blackjack, craps games, poker, slots machines, horse betting, and live entertainment all under one roof in "one of the best equipped and furnished gambling houses in the Chicago district."[102] With the south side political connections and muscle of Jimmy Emery, Accardo gathered the resources to put this pre-Las Vegas–style club in operation and attract big name entertainment such as Louie Armstrong, Sophie Tucker, Martha Raye, Jimmy Durante, and others. However, the size and scope of this undertaking required a phalanx of tough, trusted, and willing workers to coordinate the security, maintenance, operations, and financial ends of the business. As a protégé of Emery, Frank Laporte was given the opportunity to run the Owl Club because he had a "lot of moxie"[103] and because he spanned the structural hole between the entrepreneurial-minded Chicago Outfit and the network of eager, willing-to-make-a-fast-buck (or in the era of the Great Depression "any buck") men Laporte had encountered on the East Side and Hill areas of Chicago Heights. Men such as Al Pilotto, Joe Guzzino, "Black Mike" Costabile, Joe Barrett, Phil Bacino, Frankie Franze, John Perry, Santo Stella, John Nicastro, and Tootsie Palermo were hired at one time or another to supply Laporte with the financial skills, the intimidation, and, most importantly, a trusted set of eyes to oversee what must have been a raucous, ever-contentious gambling operation. They apparently did this quite well, at least from the vantage point of the Chicago Outfit hierarchy. For it was primarily as a result of Laporte's "excellent management of this gambling casino" that he emerged outside the shadow of Jimmy Emery.[104] Once outside, Laporte's personal abilities and social capital made him a most valuable addition to the Chicago Outfit. "When he showed promise," a newspaper reporter surmised in the vernacular, "Tony Accardo picked him up."[105]

In personal terms, therefore, Laporte stands apart from most Italian immigrants of the era. His deep involvement in organized crime led to a lifestyle that few immigrants would have recognized. And his willingness to engage in violence was certainly not typical among Italian men and women.[106] However, like many of his fellow Italians, Laporte's opportunities for success were heavily circumscribed by the strong forces of cultural, political, and economic discrimination in the Italian ethnic enclaves of Chicago Heights. This disadvantageous environment, however, supplied Laporte and his fellow Italians not only a structural motive for building an alternative path to success but also a rich source of social capital to do so. Some took this social capital and built labor unions; others invested it in mutual-aid societies; and still others set up ethnic businesses in the Italian enclave. Laporte and the boys used these social capital resources to erect a criminal organization. On a moral level, we could certainly challenge the wisdom of this leap into organized crime. And many of the methods used to sustain this criminal venture were reprehensible. However, in analytic terms, the line separating Laporte and the boys from many of their fellow Italians is not as clear. The cooperative arrangements that allowed these labor organizers, fraternal association leaders, and ethnic entrepreneurs to achieve a measure of success were mirrored in the associations of the Chicago Heights Outfit. While violence and intimidation no doubt played a role in the success of the Outfit, Laporte learned early on that these mundane associations were the backbone of the Outfit's business and long-time success. You can't shoot everyone, indeed.

CONCLUSION

The comedian Tom Dressen once joked that Chicago Heights was a town of thirty-five thousand people and five families. Everybody was related to everybody else, at least among the city's Italian residents. Even today, the dizzying connection and folk knowledge of who was married to whom or who was "actually" a Fidanzzi, a Longo, or a Narcissi before being married speaks to the rich, intimate connections that have long been a feature of the Italian community in Chicago Heights. While these ties, or at least knowledge of these ties, are fading, they nevertheless stood as a most valuable resource as Chicago Heights Italians sought to boost themselves up the social and economic ladder of success. Whether joining together to build houses in the neighborhood, or purchasing items at the local grocery store on informal credit, or, most importantly, embarking on a variety of entrepreneurial ventures, these associations provided much-needed social capital.

Alongside and at times overlapping with these ventures, a collection of Italian citizens turned these social capital resources to a darker, more nefarious set of entrepreneurial activities. They drew on boyhood friends, neighbors, in-laws, and fictive and blood ties to create a branch of the Chicago Outfit known locally as "the boys." On the basis of these associations, a highly efficient, highly profitable criminal organization was nurtured for over fifty years—running the gamut from the production of illegal alcohol, to casino gambling clubs, to prostitution rings, to a slot-machine empire, to chop shops, to union racketeering, and to a variety of other illegal enterprises.

The closed, tight-knit networks characterizing these relationships were especially valuable in the highly contingent and predatory environment of organized crime. Recruiting workers, enforcing discipline, and placing illegal operations in homes and businesses around the city would have taken far more resources, would have encountered far more resistance without the degree of certainty that closed networks provided. It was in this sense that an association with other Italians served as a social capital resource promoting stability and predictability. Ethnic identity was a signifier of a common pattern of interaction, a similarity in personal values, a presumed conscience of kind and, as such, a readily available resource for decreasing the risks of associating with other people.[1]

Still, these Italian associations were an imprecise indicator of this trust, and likewise, trust was an imprecise indicator of predictability. These closed networks could not eliminate the uncertainty and challenges in the environment. Hit men, thugs, enforcers, bombers, and the like were also on the payroll in the Chicago Heights Outfit. Tony Sanfilippo, Sam Costello, and numerous others were shot in a cold-blooded fashion because the trust did not hold, though the closed networks—through the form of insider information and rumor—in and of themselves revealed these breaches of trust.

However, if the Outfit was to survive, a resort to violence was a blunt instrument. Force and intimidation bring fear and compliance but not the wise guy solidarity and commitment to one another. Violence also brings "heat" from the outside, as law enforcement, the media, and public opinion become even more invigorated. The St. Valentine's Day Massacre and the public reaction to this carnage is the most obvious example. As such, the success of the boys also relied on a different form of social capital—precisely, "brokerage." That is, by reaching across the structural holes that traditionally divided the closed, Italian circles in Chicago Heights from the larger resources of the Chicago Outfit and by reaching again to a collection of municipal officials in the southern suburbs of Chicago, the boys were provided with the muscle, the connections to markets and suppliers, the in-roads to information (for example, upcoming raids or sweeps), and, most importantly, a larger vision on how to adapt to changing circumstances and increase the profits and monopoly of these organized crime ventures.

Ultimately, then, this study connects the decades-long "success" of the organized crime operation in Chicago Heights to the persistent balancing act between the resources of closure, violence, and brokerage. Too much or too little of one or another, broadly conceived, would be potentially damaging to this long-term success. Thus, closure brings value to the organization because it promotes a familiarity and assumed level of trust between individuals. Everybody pretty much knows the same things, knows one another (or knows where you live), and is bonded to each other through an embedded labyrinth of work, familial, neighborhood, church, or organizational ties. As I said previously, my grandfather was asked by the rival Sicilian gang in Chicago Heights to work for them and make moonshine at a substantially higher salary than Dominico Roberto, an old country *paesani*, was paying. When I innocently asked my father if my grandfather took the Sicilians up on their offer, he responded somewhat incredulously. "He came from the same hometown as Roberto. . . . The families went back a long time together. He would never do that." The bonds, set of common expectations, and sense of loyalty were strongly rooted.

Yet, closure also brings costs. When there are strong ties binding groups together, certainty and predictability triumph over variability and innovation. Individuals are unaware of or reluctant to think through or even see new opportunities because the social networks place a premium on routine beliefs and behaviors. There is ample evidence of this in the history of organized crime. At the beginning of the last century, the Mustache Petes in New York reportedly succumbed to the Young Turks because the old guard wanted to continue to exploit fellow Italians rather than expand their operations to the public at large. It took considerable bloodshed and a number of assassinations to break free of these traditional approaches.[2] Around the same time in Chicago, Big Jim Colosimo was head of a small group of tavern and brothel owners. When Johnny Torrio (and eventually Al Capone) arrived on the scene from New York, Torrio enlarged the illegal operations beyond the levee, or the Chicago vice district, to the suburbs west and south of Chicago. Over time, and especially in light of the new realities of Prohibition, Torrio chafed at Colosimo's and his followers' inability to see the advantages of moving more aggressively into these new markets. As Bilek writes, Torrio "had the vision to see what tremendous opportunities national Prohibition was going to bring."[3] As a result, Colosimo and several of his associates were eliminated. And in Chicago Heights, Tony Sanfilippo, Joe Martino, and other old timers balked at expanding their lucrative operations beyond the confines of Chicago Heights or even its Italian enclave. In the early days of the city, the close-knit, insular characteristic of this group did not open itself up to the possibilities of Chicago Heights becoming a major production and distribution center of illegal alcohol. The cohesion of this group did not fully promote an awareness that there "were farmers to supply grapes, grocers to supply sugar needed for fermentation, plumbers to construct and repair stills, and truck drivers to handle deliveries."[4] The larger vision went wanting.

From these instances, we see that an antidote to the excesses of closure is violence. New ideas and new approaches were pushed forward by force and the elimination of opposition, a quite different connotation of "knowing where someone lives." Organized crime groups distinguish themselves from most other organizations by keeping this option available both to reinforce routine and to break free of it at the same time. The judicious use of violence can therefore be a key resource for the on-going success of organized crime. Certainly, the Chicago Heights operation would have never emerged at the time without the virtual, guerrilla warfare it waged against the entrenched Sicilian gangs in the 1920s. And the strategic use of violence over the next fifty years—from hits on wayward Outfit members, to bombings of rival jukebox companies, to threats against B-girls—shored up the organization's effectiveness precisely at those points where closure was weakest. In this manner, one can understand the bluntness if not the moral character of a labor union strategy employed by the Chicago Heights operation. "It is common knowledge," said one informant, "that individuals within the union who caused problems with regards to labor practices are beating [*sic*] up."[5]

Yet violence, in turn, is a pure substitute for good ideas. That is, violence becomes a viable option only when organized crime leaders cannot think through or anticipate potential organizational problems and therefore have to resort to brute force. Thus, toward the end of the Heights Outfit's reign in the 1970s, violence triumphed over social capital and "produced more gangland murders than anything since Prohibition."[6] Arguably, what was lacking was a supply of good ideas acquired through the social capital of brokerage. As Burt suggests, "network entrepreneurs are more likely to anticipate and adapt to the problems that will inevitably arise."[7] That is, the entrepreneur's knowledge of other groups' successes and failures in similar ventures fills in what are otherwise blank spaces in the highly contentious environments of organized crime.[8] We saw some of this at work in Frank Laporte's implementation of a gambling empire in the southern suburbs, based as it was on his network ties to Chicago Outfit leaders who had previously put together a gambling monopoly in Cicero.[9] We saw this in reverse as Al Tocco's short and violent tenure as head of the Heights's operations in the 1970s brought fear and scrutiny to the Outfit rather than cooperation and support.

The Contemporary Context

In attempting to explain the success of organized crime groups, it is highly unlikely that we could specify with any certainty an optimum mix of closure, violence, and brokerage. This is for several reasons. First, one or another of these resources may be more valuable as an organized crime group develops over time. With respect to the Chicago Heights context, violence was essential early on in attaining access to criminalized markets and vanquishing rivals. However, as the organization achieved this monopoly, closure was important in consolidating and routinizing relationships so that the everyday tasks of servicing thirsty customers, installing slots machines, or hiring workers could be accomplished efficiently and with a minimum of violence. As the organization matured, brokerage assumed special importance by offering new ideas or adaptive strategies for the challenges presented by law enforcement, changing customer loyalties, and other exogenous disruptions. While closure, violence, and brokerage worked in tandem to create this entrepreneurial success, one or another of these resources may be more essential, depending on the developmental stage of the organization.

Second, each organized crime group faces different historically determined situations and opportunities. For example, the timing of the Italian immigration to the United States, the massive size of this immigrant population, and the vicissitudes of the Great Depression all conspired, along with a host of other local factors, to create an ethnic enclave and a rich source of social capital for Chicago Heights's Italians at the beginning of the twentieth century. Under different historical circumstances, the closed networks may not have been as readily available and Italians may have had to resort to force and violence in a more-consistent manner to prosper in their illegal activities. These are conjectures. However, they should alert us to the fact that different historical situations may call for a different mix of closure, violence, and brokerage.

Let me illustrate this point with a brief look at organized crime in Chicago Heights today. As we have noted before, the Italian presence has diminished significantly. The Chicago Heights crew has been absorbed into the South Side crew and the Chicago Outfit as a whole has been dealt a critical, though not fatal, blow by the Family Secrets trial and subsequent prosecutions. At the same time, the Chicago Outfit and the Chicago Heights boys have been seriously undermined because of the changing ethnic neighborhoods. Robert Lombardo argues, "An important reason why the outfit is faltering today is because it doesn't have any neighborhoods to recruit from."[10] This point is well taken. It is one feature of a broader explanation that places the blame for the decline of the Italian involvement in organized crime on the more-general decline in social capital resources available to Italian criminals. Specifically, as Italians in Chicago Heights moved outside the East Side and the Hill, indeed, outside the city, a valuable component—specifically, an assumed trust and closure—has been lost. Whatever the complex of reasons, the Chicago Heights boys are now largely defunct. Thus, upon hearing that the Chicago Heights crew had basically ceased operations and was no longer included among the crews in the Chicago Outfit, retired Internal Revenue Service investigator Robert Fuesel said, "It's hard for me to believe they still don't have six crews. At the very least, it's hard for me to believe the Heights isn't part of one of these crews."[11]

Though the Italian organized crime presence in Chicago Heights has significantly diminished, organized crime in Chicago Heights persists. African Americans and Latinos have largely taken over the vice operations. And like their Italian counterparts nearly a century before, most of the illegal operations are organized into street gangs on the East Side and the Hill. Thus, the Almighty Latin Kings claim the general area from Twenty-second to Twenty-sixth Streets along Wentworth and State Streets; the Gangster Disciples control the area around Twelfth and Wentworth; and the Latin Counts are found around Fourteenth Street and Park Avenue. Other prominent groups include the Black Disciples, the Conservative Vice Lords, and the Four Corner Hustlers. Among these groups, there appears to be a constant verbal, and at times violent, jockeying for supremacy between the African American and Mexican gangs. Thus, one observer wrote, "Kings and Counts hell alot of Mexicans out there now, used to be more blacks. Gds and Vice Lords."[12] Another commented, "Chi Heights is where da count and ALKN beef go da hardest. yea u best off avoding that area, and dem 4's be on it out there I heard. and u already know how da g's numbers go, if u see 10, only half got heart."[13]

As one might suspect, the primary moneymaking activity of these groups is based on the sale and distribution of drugs. Cocaine, heroin, and marijuana are the major products. For example, in 2006, a drug bust in the Heights resulted in the breakup of a crack cocaine ring that produced a nearly $20,000 a day profit for the local gangs.[14] In 2008, police arrested ninety-five dealers and customers, mostly Four Corner Hustlers and Gangster Disciples members, in another roundup of crack cocaine pushers and addicts.[15] And in 2010, 11 *tons* of marijuana, waiting to be shipped to a warehouse in the Heights, were seized aboard six railroad freight cars in a Chicago Heights switching terminal. All told, the amount of illegal drugs that passes its way through the local street gangs in Chicago Heights rivals in many ways the 1920s characterization of Chicago Heights as "the pickup depot for most of the illicit alcohol trade in the entire Middle West."[16] While the drugs of choice have changed, Chicago Heights is still a prime location for these illicit operations.

As suggested, African American and Latino residents are the principal entrepreneurs in these illicit businesses. In Chicago Heights as a whole, African Americans make up over 41 percent of city residents (out of a total city population of 30,276 in 2010) and Latinos close to 34 percent (with Mexicans 31 percent of the total).[17] The East Side is almost exclusively African American; the Hill area is primarily Mexican. Like their Italian counterparts in the previous century, both of these groups find themselves in extremely disadvantageous situations along cultural, political, and economic lines. Though cultural discrimination does not find its way into the public sphere as blatantly as in the past, prejudices against the African American and Mexican groups are still strong. For example, in 1993, the City of Chicago Heights was sued based on a complaint that during the 1980s, city officials falsified documents and actively engaged in criminal activities because of the fear that too many African Americans and Mexicans were moving into the west side of Chicago Heights.[18] More recently, one Latina woman from Chicago Heights wrote, "Now days, racism is still alive in some areas of the city. Even as an American citizen just for the fact that I can speak Spanish, I have felt rejection and discrimination from some people."[19] Politically, many black residents felt disenfranchised because of the nearly century-old at-large commission form of government, which hindered their ability to participate effectively in the Chicago Heights political process. As such, a lawsuit was filed in 1987 on behalf of black residents of the city on grounds that the at-large system violated the federal Voting Rights Act of 1965. After a number of challenges and rulings, a federal judge ruled largely in favor of the black residents and a new aldermanic structure and redistricting were implemented.[20]

Along economic lines, we also find a good deal of discrimination against African Americans and Latinos. In 1998, Ford Motor Company paid $1.5 million to settle a lawsuit in its local plant, a suit that alleged racial slurs and discriminatory behavior against African American and Hispanic workers.[21] In 2010, a federal judge found in favor of black employees in a Chicago Heights trucking firm that had a history of bias and discrimination against black workers. Not only did the court rule that these workers were subject to harsher discipline, but evidence was available that these black employees "had been exposed to hangman's nooses and racist graffiti, cartoons and comments."[22] And in 2012, Chicago Heights was the hardest hit suburb in the discriminatory lending practices of Wells Fargo & Co., which illegally steered African American and Hispanic borrowers into high-cost, subprime mortgage loans. Illinois Attorney General Lisa Madigan commented, "When you look at what's taken place, it's horrendous. It's not an understatement at all to say that there's an entire generation of wealth in minority communities that's been taken away."[23]

That is not to say that the parallels between the early 1900s and 2000s in Chicago Heights are the same on all points along the line. Discrimination in the early part of the last century was more wide-opened and raw; today it is generally more subtle, yet more insidious, and hemmed in by legal and cultural bounds. The economic well-being of the community has also changed. At the beginning of the last century, low-skilled (and mainly low pay) factory jobs were plentiful in Chicago Heights; at the beginning of this century, the city is engaged in an all-out effort to attract most any industrial or low-skilled employment.[24] Previously, the national and ethnic composition of the city was divided among a number of groups with Italians the most prominent; now, two ethnic groups—African Americans and Mexicans—make up the clear majority. This dominance has translated into more political power for the Mexican residents, as Alex Lopez was appointed to the office of mayor in 2008 and David Gonzales became the first elected Latino mayor of Chicago Heights in 2011. One thing that has been consistent, however, is the menacing presence of crime and illegal substances. Thus, on election night in 2011, Gonzales sounded a theme that could have been taken from one of any number of mayors over the last century. "We're going to go ahead and start tackling the problems," Gonzales said. "The number one priority is crime and drugs in the city of Chicago Heights."[25]

With these similarities and differences in mind, we can turn to a brief comparison between the Italian organized crime groups of the past and the contemporary street gangs in the present. We begin with an assumption of a common set of motives—that both then and now individuals seek to better themselves in terms of their economic and social life chances. This is a broad assumption that conflates a range of experiences and motives to a baseline common denominator. There are no doubt exceptions. Schatzberg and Kelly's examination of African American organized crime reveals the variety of motives and underlying causes for organized crime even within the African American community.[26] However, we do not assume a de facto criminal motive for Italians, African Americans, or Mexicans. Organized criminal activity is more properly viewed in its wider historical and social context, especially as a way out of and up from a disadvantaged environment.

Also, we have made various assumptions and inferences about the human capital skills of the various groups. Thus, we have some indication that Italians at the beginning of the last century were hampered, at least initially, by their low levels of literacy skills and ability to speak English. This may have prompted, along with the heavy doses of discrimination outlined previously, the movement into the entrepreneurship of crime. By comparison, most Mexican residents of Chicago Heights today, especially the younger generation, have capable reading and writing abilities and fluency with the English language.[27] However, as Perlmann points out more generally, the educational credentials and individual level skills required for success in the present economic structure are considerably higher than they were at the beginning of the last century.[28] As such, many Mexican residents of Chicago Heights still find themselves in a highly disadvantageous situation regarding their immediate prospects for social mobility—much like their Italian counterparts in the 1930s.

At the same time, the social and economic chances for African Americans remain bleak. The base human capital skills of reading and writing pose a serious obstacle for many African American residents of Chicago Heights. Thus, the reading test scores for students who attend East Side elementary schools rank near the very bottom compared to those of other students in Illinois.[29] And the Prairie State Achievement Exam, which measures foundational skills related to college and "real world" occupational skills, found that only 20 percent of high school juniors in Chicago Heights met even the lowest benchmark indicators of these baseline skills.[30] When these deficiencies are coupled with the persistent, and at times virulent, discrimination we just discussed, African Americans' chances for social mobility are indeed problematic.

In taking a step back, then, one could conclude, at least in the Chicago Heights context, that Italians, Mexicans, and Blacks have had much in common in the pursuit of mobility. Economic and cultural discrimination, neighborhood geographies, and low human capital skills, at least in a relative sense, made it difficult for each of these groups to climb the economic and social ladder to success—for the Italians in the first half of the last century, for the Mexicans and African Americans during this same period but continuing on throughout the century.

In response, each ethnic group generated a collective effort focused on illegal activities. However, these organized crime ventures were distinctive due to the unique set of historical circumstances that accompanied each group's ascent up the "crooked ladder."[31] A useful way of understanding this distinctiveness is to center on the social capital resources available to each of these groups. We have detailed these resources for Chicago Heights Italians throughout this study. To summarize, the Italian organized crime operations were built on a bedrock of close, overlapping, long-standing ties and networks in the Italian East Side and Hill neighborhoods. There was an institutional completeness, a denseness to these neighborhoods that produced an incredibly thick set of relationships and social capital resources. As such, after its bloody entrance onto the Chicago Heights scene, the Heights Outfit was spared an overreliance on violence, at least in a comparative sense. Deals were made, illegal operations were set up and maintained, and law enforcement was nullified on the basis of an extensive web of obligations and trust.[32]

The Mexican presence in Chicago Heights has also been characterized by a considerable allotment of social capital. Beyond the extensive neighborhood and family ties on the Hill and other areas of the city, the Mexican community is dotted by a collection of voluntary dance halls and clubs, political organizations (for example, the Southland Hispanic Democratic Organization, Hispanic Empowerment Chicago Heights, Southland Hispanic Leadership Council, the Alex Lopez Ray of Light Foundation), and community church groups. These church groups are especially important in bringing Mexican residents together and cementing community ties. "Although Chicago Heights Hispanics aren't visible in citywide Hispanic parades or festivals, they gather in great numbers at St. Agnes and St. Paul Catholic Churches for Hispanic services."[33] These social capital resources have helped produce a large number of entrepreneurial ventures, in particular Mexican restaurants and groceries, as well as construction companies, bakeries, bars, and laundromats.

They have also contributed to the success of the local Mexican street gangs. In ways much like their Italian counterparts years before, these street gangs benefit from the familial ties and friendships in terms of recruiting gang members, finding locales to carry out their drug production and sales, and completing the complicated and highly volatile interactions with suppliers. Thus, just as Italians used ethnicity as a filter in terms of who to trust in these illegal activities, the Mexican cartels do the same. An undercover narcotics officer suggested that while the street-peddler may sell to just about anyone, the higher up you go in the cartels, the more likely you will be dealing with "Spanish-speaking smugglers."[34] Again, ethnicity, while certainly offering no guarantees, offers important elements of trust and familiarity and reduces the risks of working with people who could intentionally or not undermine the secrecy of the organization.

However, it is doubtful as to whether the social capital resources and sense of common identity within the Mexican neighborhoods of Chicago Heights are as strong or as uniform as in the Italian neighborhoods in the past. Thus, some of the most vociferous disparagements of street gangs come from the Mexican residents themselves—comments more critical and more public than the Italian community's reaction to the boys years earlier. For example, one local resident expressed her displeasure at a Chicago Heights council meeting when she spoke of her "concern with the decline of her neighborhood because of drug dealers and gang bangers."[35] And the economic plight and dislocations of the Hill itself have made for a far less viable and fully formed community from which to draw down these resources. At the same time, as the Mexican population has been able to spread itself out to various parts of

Chicago Heights the geographies do not favor as much the development of these ties and social capital resources. As such, these street gangs cannot as readily count on closed social networks to carry out their operations. In turn, violence, primarily against rival street gangs and as an internal method of social control, becomes a more prominent feature of the organization. Thus, partly in response to the botched drug deal in Chicago Heights where federal officials seized eleven tons of marijuana, one narcotics officer predicted, "You will see people getting shot, being beheaded back in Mexico because of this." And in a more general comparison, Jack Riley, head of the U.S. Drug Enforcement Administration's office in Chicago, also held that the Mexican cartels in the area are far more lethal than their Italian predecessors were. If a confrontation with the old-line Italian mob of the previous era were to have taken place, Riley concluded that he would put his money on the Mexican cartels and gangs. The Italians would not have stood a chance; the Mexican cartels "would eat them alive."[36]

African American street gangs in Chicago Heights are also lacking strong social capital resources in the community and as a consequence are more reliant on violence to promote their illegal ventures. These social capital deficits have occurred despite the valiant attempts of many local community pastors and organizers to enhance community solidarity in the interests of economic and social justice. However, these efforts are thwarted by the overwhelming obstacles of poverty and social isolation and a lack of community participation. The standard indicators of social capital in the community—for example, group memberships, attendance at town meetings, volunteerism, informal socializing in each other's homes—reveal little social capital. Even an attempt at collecting data on these measures has proven difficult given the distressed character of these neighborhoods. The East Side district, in particular, is increasingly deserted as houses are torn down and most commercial places boarded up. Those residents who are left must struggle with school closings, few employment opportunities, and the lack of adequate city services. For example, a common complaint among East Side residents is the unkempt, overgrown appearance of yards and lawns because as Second Ward Alderman states, "no one is around to tend to the landscaping."[37] The Harold Jones Community center still stands as a viable social service agency and gathering place, but it faces serious funding problems. Broken windows are the least of its problems. A roof that is in danger of collapsing threatens to close this last remaining service agency in the area and serves unfortunately as a daily reminder of the uncertain future for the children and adults on the East Side.

Most significantly, there appears to be a disconnection, an uncoupling between the street gangs and the local community. For better or worse, the Italian crime groups in Chicago Heights were a part of their community. This seems not to be the case with respect to the African American street gangs in Chicago Heights. Thus, one East Side resident who grew up in the neighborhood gave some indication of this lack of trust by suggesting that people "don't feel like they have anyone to turn to and they don't have confidence in the police department."[38] Unable to rely on a ready supply of trust and a series of ties and associations in the community, the black street gangs in Chicago Heights have increasingly turned to violence to maintain their illicit operations. "We're out there to make a better community," said Chicago Heights police chief, Michael Camilli. "We cannot convert every person. There are some people we have to remove from the street. That trust level has gone down, with police, pastors, teachers. We have to bridge that gap."[39]

Lessons from The Italian Experience

Obviously, there is much more to the story regarding these contemporary manifestations of organized crime in Chicago Heights. A more thorough, systematic investigation of both the Mexican and African American street gangs would add greatly to our understanding on a number of levels. First, it would provide a comparative base for explaining the emergence of organized crime groups. Ethnic succession theory tells one side of this story—that is, how criminal groups who achieve a certain social mobility move up in the larger society and leave a vacancy to be filled by another disadvantaged group further down on the ladder. However, what we do not clearly understand is why some disadvantaged groups rather than others fill these structural holes and come to dominate organized crime—why the Italians achieved such success when there were other disadvantaged groups (for example, the Poles, the Czechs, the Lithuanians) also down on the ladder. Or why the Mexican and African American street gangs control most of the drug market today and not the Puerto Ricans, poor whites, or other ethnic groups. Being disadvantaged is apparently not sufficient to becoming successful at organized crime. As such, a more in-depth understanding of the social capital resources available to the Mexican and African American street gangs in Chicago Heights is in order—specifically an examination of the processes of discrimination, the consequent social and geographic isolation, and the mix of closed and brokered ties available to each group. As difficult as this study may be, it would provide a unique opportunity to conduct a historical and comparative study of organized crime in a singular setting and add a necessary horizontal dimension to the otherwise linear theory of ethnic succession.

Second, additional research may provide insights into the practicalities of controlling organized crime. As suggested, the success of organized crime rests on a judicious mix of closure, violence, and brokerage. If this is in fact the case, then the most effective long-term strategy for control would be to attack all three in a coordinated fashion. Thus, if closure provides trust and efficiencies, then undermining closure in the form of undercover agents, informers, and snitches would eventually eat away at the ease of making profits and would increase the transaction costs of doing business. However, under such circumstances, violence may increase as an organizational necessity to reestablish control. Thus, law enforcement efforts must be focused and "heat" placed on organized crime groups in the form of grand jury investigations, public prosecutions, and increased police presence. In so doing, the goal is to once again raise the costs of doing business and make violence an extremely risky organizational adjustment. As they have done in the past, the most successful organized crime groups would most likely respond to these measures by appealing to their brokered relationships and alliances in the police department, city hall, or elected officials to call off these efforts. To combat this, public officials would need to be held accountable in a more transparent manner to limit collusion between organized crime and the networks of public officials.[40]

This takes in a lot. However, within the theoretical framework outlined, it may be possible to evaluate the success of efforts to control organized crime in Chicago Heights over the last several decades. Specifically, each of the control strategies presented—the use of informants, public prosecutions, and media exposés—has been employed to combat the drug networks in Chicago Heights. Each has achieved a measure of success in terms of arrests and increased public awareness of these criminal activities. Yet, we might ask if these somewhat separate strategies would have been more effective if they had been coordinated in an intentional manner and directed more consciously at undermining the social capital resources of the Mexican and African American street gangs in the Heights. The boys of Chicago Heights, for example, prospered for decades because attempts at controlling the organization—despite wholesale raids, numerous arrests, public denunciations and Eliot Ness—could not undermine the vast social capital resources of closure and brokerage. It is not clear whether the current street gangs with their more transnational linkages and reliance on violent methods of social control are as heavily dependent on such social capital resources as were their Italian predecessors. Still, an investigation into the social capital processes used by street gangs today would tell us a great deal about the role of these processes in the success of organized crime ventures and a great deal about the underlying premises of this study.

Finally, additional research would most likely further discredit the cultural essentialism that still pervades our understanding of organized crime. I began this study with a concern that the general public, law enforcement, and, more subtly, academic circles have long regarded Italians as somehow inclined toward criminal behavior in an endemic fashion. What began as genetic dispositions have shifted in large measures to less poignant but more subtly pervasive cultural dispositions.[41] There are still strong undercurrents of anti-Italian prejudice and links to crime in American society.[42] What I have tried to do in this study is to show that this supposed "inner relationship" between Italians and crime was historically contingent. An Italian identity and the social networks that flowed out of it were social capital resources to promote a variety of collective goals. Italians were no more culturally programmed to engage in crime than they were to become tailors, barbers, or *contadini*.

But if Italians, with their significant gains in social mobility, still struggle with these essentialist perceptions, Mexicans and African Americans face even greater criminal definitions. This stems from the historically more repressive and severe forms of exclusion both groups have experienced in mainstream American society and Chicago Heights. This strikes at Mexicans in a number of ways. In particular, there exists a generalized belief that drugs and violence are so pervasive among Mexicans that both are a way of life, a cultural component rather than criminal behavior per se, let alone resources for achieving social mobility in society. For young African American men in places like the East Side of Chicago Heights, labels such as urban criminals, gangsters, predators are so ingrained, it is exceedingly difficult to find a place for them or carry on a discourse relative to the family, school, or work. Even social theory has found it difficult to overcome these seemingly innate criminal tendencies of the black street gang member. Thus, while the "queer ladder of mobility" theory tends to recast organized crime, in part, as a question of social inequality, it does so most successfully for the Irish, the Jews, the Italians, and, presumably, the Mexicans sometime in the future. Muhammad argues that the perceived exceptionality of the black criminal did not allow for this reinterpretation of the black experience. "At no point did any of the scholarship suggest that African-Americans shared the same notions of success or that their crime could be similarly understood in these terms."[43] As with the ideological and institutional biases against Italians at the beginning of the last century, these contemporary blind spots divert us from a more clear-headed, genuine understanding of the no doubt destructive character of organized crime but also the largely unfavorable structural realities that make organized crime an avenue for advancement. In some small part, I have tried to address a number of these issues in this study. New directions, new research, new theoretical developments on top of the already established discussions of organized crime would tell us even more about crime, ethnicity, and the society that generates both.

NOTES

Introduction

1. Estes Kefauver, foreword to *Barbarians in Our Midst, by* Virgil Peterson (Boston: Little, Brown, and Company, 1952), ix.

2. Giovanni Schiavo, *The Truth about the Mafia and Organized Crime in America* (New York: Vigo Press, 1962), 189.

3. Ronald Farrell and Carole Case, *The Black Book and the Mob* (Madison: University of Wisconsin Press, 1995), 228.

4. For example, see Richard Mayo-Smith, *Emigration and Immigration* (New York: Scribner's, 1908); Edward Ross, *The Old World in the New* (New York: Century Company, 1914); Henry Zorbaugh, *The Gold Coast and the Slum* (Chicago: University of Chicago Press, 1929).

5. For example, see Daniel Bell, "Crime as an American Way of Life: A Queer Ladder of Social Mobility," in *The End of Ideology* (New York: Free Press, 1960); Francis Ianni, *Black Mafia: Ethnic Succession in Organized Crime* (New York: Simon & Schuster, 1974); Alan Block and William Chambliss, *Organizing Crime* (New York: Elsevier, 1981).

6. Peter Reuter, "Research on American Organized Crime," in *Handbook of Organized Crime in the United States*, ed. Robert Kelly, Ko-lin Chin, and Rufus Schatzberg (Westport, Conn: Greenwood Press, 1994), 109.

7. James Coleman, "Social Capital in the Creation of Human Capital," *American Journal of Sociology* 94 (Supplement 1988), S95-S120.

8. Robert Putnam, *Bowling Alone: The Collapse and Revival of American Community* (New York: Simon & Schuster, 2000), 350–363.

9. Quoted in Donald Cressey, *Theft of a Nation: The Structure and Operations of Organized Crime in America* (New York: Harper & Row, 1969), 11–12.

10. Personal interview, Joe Nicastro, August 5, 1995.

11. Virgil Peterson, *A Report on Chicago Crime for 1967* (Chicago: Chicago Crime Commission, 1968), 128.

12. Thus, only recording the percentage of "foreign born" at the beginning of the century left out the children of these Italian immigrants, who, though born in the United States, still contributed significantly to the Italian "presence" in Chicago Heights over the next several decades. Along these lines, one Chicago Heights resident suggested, "We have a very mixed community. We have a great many Italians. At one time they must have been about 60 percent of the community." See Charles Seymour Liebman, "Some Political Effects of the Functional Differentiation of Suburbs" (PhD diss., University of Illinois, 1960), 165. The data for 1960 and 1970 does include these first- and second-generation Italians. But even here, Candeloro estimates that if one were to include third- and fourth-generation Italians in Chicago Heights, the number of "Italians" in the city would "easily double." See Dominic Candeloro, "Suburban Italians: Chicago Heights, 1890–1975," in *Ethnic Chicago: A Multicultural Portrait,* ed. Melvin G. Holli and Peter d'A. Jones (Grand Rapids, Mich.: W. B. Eerdmans, 1994), 241. Conversely, identifying the "ancestry" of Chicago Heights residents at the end of the century may overrepresent the Italian influence in the city. Though the percentages suggest a relatively large number of people who claim an ethnic identification with Italians, the degree of attachment or identification remains uncertain given, in most cases, the number of generations removed from a viable Italian culture or subculture.

13. Eliot Ness with Oscar Fraley, *The Untouchables* (New York: Messner, 1957), 61.

14. Robert Schoenberg, *Mr. Capone* (New York: Morrow, 1992), 232.

15. John O'Brien, "Investigators in Chicago Heights Seek to Break 'Unholy Alliance,'" *Chicago Tribune*, August 4, 1992.

16. Laurence Bergreen, *Capone: The Man and the Era* (New York: Simon & Schuster, 1994), 366.

17. Matt Luzi, *The Boys in Chicago Heights* (Charleston, S.C.: The History Press, 2012).

18. The most detailed studies on the Chicago Heights Outfit include: Luzi, *The Boys in Chicago Heights*; and Matthew Luzi, "From the Boys in Chicago Heights" (unpublished manuscript, 2003). Other useful works are: Robert Lombardo, "Recruitment into Organized Crime: A Study of Social Structural Support of Deviance" (PhD diss., University of Illinois, Chicago, 1994); Lombardo, "The Organized Crime Neighborhoods of Chicago," in *Handbook of Organized Crime in the United States,* 169–187; and Laurence Bergreen, *Capone: the Man and the Era.*

Studies on the Chicago Outfit that make more than a passing reference to Outfit activities in Chicago Heights include: Robert Schoenberg, *Mr. Capone*; John Kobler, *Capone: the Life and World of Al Capone* (New York: Putnam, 1971); John Binder, *The Chicago Outfit* (Charleston, S.C.: Arcadia, 2003); Robert Lombardo, *Organized Crime in Chicago: Beyond the Mafia* (Urbana: University of Illinois Press, 2013).

And the following histories of Chicago Heights include at least some mention of the Italian presence and organized crime: Rudolph Vecoli, "Chicago's Italians Prior to World War I: A Study of Their Social and Economic Adjustment" (PhD diss., University of Wisconsin, 1963); Liebman, *Some Political Effects*; Dominic Candeloro and Barbara Paul, *Chicago Heights: At the Crossroads of the Nation* (Charleston, S.C.: Arcadia, 2004); and Marian LaFranchi, "A Political History of Chicago Heights" (MA thesis, Governors State University, 1960).

19. Reuter, "Research on American Organized Crime," 116.

20. Bell, "Crime as an American Way of Life: A Queer Ladder of Social Mobility," 127.

21. Oscar Handlin, *Race and Nationality in American Life* (Boston: Little, Brown, and Company, 1948), 107.

22. U.S. Immigration Commission (1907–1910), *Statements and Recommendations Submitted by Societies and Organizations Interested in Immigration* (Washington, D.C.: Government Printing Office, 1911), vol. 41, 29.

23. U.S. Immigration Commission (1907–1910), *Emigration Conditions in Europe* (Washington, D.C.: Government Printing Office, 1911), vol. 4, 209.

24. Ibid., 209.

25. National Commission on Law Observance and Enforcement, *Report on Crime and the Foreign Born,* report 10 (Washington, D.C.: Government Printing Office, 1931), 58.

26. Dwight Smith, "Wickersham to Sutherland to Katzenbach: Evolving an 'Official' Definition of Organized Crime," *Crime, Law, and Social Change* 16 (September 1991), 2.

27. Michael Woodiwiss, *Organized Crime and American Power: A History* (Toronto: University of Toronto Press, 2001), 236.

28. Dwight Smith, *The Mafia Mystique* (New York: Basic Books, 1975), 309; Joseph Albini, "Donald Cressey's Contributions to the Study of Organized Crime: An Evaluation," in *Understanding Organized Crime in Global Perspective*, ed. Patrick Ryan and George Rush (Thousand Oaks, Calif.: Sage Publications, 1997), 16–25.

29. Thomas Guglielmo's work on the immigration of Italians to Chicago in the first half of the twentieth century provides a nuanced discussion of the prejudice toward Italians in terms of race and color. In particular, his chapters "The White Peril of Europe" and "Race, Color, and Crime" show the depth of anti-Italian, anti-immigrant sentiments during this period. See his *White on Arrival: Italians, Race, Color and Power in Chicago, 1890–1945* (New York: Oxford University Press, 2003).

30. The Repplier characterization can be found in Rita Simon, *Public Opinion and the Immigrant* (Lexington, Mass.: Lexington Books, 1985), 143; Arthur Sweeny, "Mental Tests for Immigrants," *North American Review* 215 (May 1922), 600–612; Henry Pratt Fairchild, *The Melting-Pot Mistake* (Boston: Little, Brown, and Company, 1926), 214.

31. Gay Talese, *Unto Thy Sons* (New York: Ballantine Books, 1993), 462.

32. "The Distribution of Ethnic Group Attachments and Hostilities," *Fortune* magazine, Roper Center, University of Connecticut, Storrs, August 1939.

33. Richard Capozzola, *Five Centuries of Italian American History* (New Orleans: American Italian Renaissance Foundation, 1992).

34. Commission for Social Justice, Order Sons of Italy in America, Response Analysis Corporation, Princeton, N.J., January 1991.

35. National Italian American Foundation, Zogby International, New York, 2001.

36. Lee Bernstein, *The Greatest Menace: Organized Crime in Cold War America* (Amherst: University of Massachusetts Press, 2002), 23.

37. Marylee Reynolds, *From Gangs to Gangsters: How American Sociology Organized Crime, 1918–1994* (Guilderland, N.Y.: Harrow and Heston, 1995), 151.

38. For a discussion of the various collective strategies used by Italians to pursue social mobility, see Mark Haller, "Organized Crime in Urban Society: Chicago in the Twentieth Century," *Journal of Social History* 4 (Winter 1971), 210–234.

39. The general framework for this study owes a great deal to the "interaction theory" of ethnic entrepreneurship elaborated by Roger Waldinger and Howard Aldrich. In particular, see Roger Waldinger, Howard Aldrich, and Robin Ward, *Ethnic Entrepreneurs: Immigrant Business in Industrial Societies* (Newbury Park, Calif.: Sage Publications, 1990).

Chapter 1. Chicago Heights and Organized Crime

1. See Edward Caldwell, "First Landowners in Chicago Heights 1838," 1926 (Chicago Heights Public Library Pamphlet File). Also, Caldwell, "Some Notes on the Founding of the Presbyterian Church and the Other Pioneers of Thorn Grove," 1923 (Chicago Heights Public Library File).

2. Geraldine Baader and Robert Newgard, "Brief History of Chicago Heights: 1882–1992," *Centennial Book* (Chicago: Chicago Heights Centennial Committee, 1992), 14.

3. Alfred Theodore Andreas, *History of Cook County* (Chicago: A. T. Andreas, 1884), 887.

4. Andreas, *History of Cook County*, 887.

5. Quoted in Chris Devatenos (Gregory), "Chicago Heights History" (working paper, University of Chicago, 1924), 10.

6. "Suddenly, the Town Grew into an Industrial Giant," *Chicago Heights Star*, September 23, 1982. In 1913, upon dedication of San Rocco Church in Chicago Heights, the *New World* could report that the church "commands a panoramic view of the whole village and a beautiful expanse of country to the south and east" (June 7, 1913). The view to the north and west, however, would have been considerably less panoramic and expansive.

7. Dominic Candeloro and Barbara Paul, *Chicago Heights: At the Crossroads of the Nation* (Charleston, S.C.: Arcadia, 2004), 39.

8. Ann Durkin Keating, *Building Chicago: Suburban Developers & the Creation of a Divided Metropolis* (Columbus: Ohio State University Press, 1988), 75.

9. See Dorothy Culp, "The Radical Labor Movement, 1873–1895," *Papers in Illinois History* 44 (1937), 92–99.

10. U.S. Industrial Commission (vol. 8, 415) quoted in David Gordon, "Capitalist Development and the History of American Cities," in *Marxism and the Metropolis: New Perspectives in Urban Political Economy*, ed. William Taub and Larry Sawers (New York: Oxford University Press, 1984), 41.

11. "Suddenly, the Town Grew into an Industrial Giant," *Chicago Heights Star*, September 23, 1982.

12. Dominic Candeloro and Barbara Paul, *Chicago Heights* (Charleston, S.C.: Arcadia Publishing, 1998), 14.

13. Candeloro and Paul, *Chicago Heights: At the Crossroads*, 41.

14. Weson Goodspeed and Daniel Healy, ed. *History of Cook County*, vol. 2 (Chicago: Goodspeed Historical Association), 347–348; Louise Michalek, "Back Then, Settlement Was Called Thorn Grove," *Chicago Heights Star*, September 23, 1982.

15. Conceivably, a small number of these workers may have come from towns other than Chicago Heights. Still, if we assume that the vast majority of these workers actually resided in the city, then in 1910 over 30 percent of the city's population worked in the industrial sector (and many more people were directly impacted by these industrial jobs when we take into account the families of these workers). This percentage gave Chicago Heights the highest proportion of industrial workers to city population of any city in Illinois—greater than Chicago, Peoria, and Joliet, among others. And within the nation as a whole, only twenty-five cities with a population greater than 10,000 people had a higher percentage of workers engaged in industrial production, many of these primarily single industry towns (e.g., Winston, North Carolina, or South Bethlehem, Pennsylvania) or long-established industrial centers (e.g., Lynn, Massachusetts, or Manchester, New Hampshire). The data here is compiled from an examination of "persons engaged in industry" by city population for cities of 10,000 or more in the Department of Commerce and Labor, Bureau of the Census, *Thirteenth Census of the United States: 1910, Volume 9, Manufacturers: Reports by States with Statistics for Principal Cities, Illinois* (Washington, D.C.: United States Census Bureau).

16. Chris Devatenos (Gregory), "Chicago Heights History," 27.

17. Department of Commerce, Bureau of the Census, *Thirteenth Census of the United States 1910, Volume 2, Population: Reports by States, with Statistics for Counties, Cities, and other Civil Divisions, Illinois* (Washington, D.C.: United States Census Bureau).

18. See Dominic Candeloro's analysis of applications for citizenship filed by Italians in Chicago Heights between 1907 and 1954 in Candeloro, "Suburban Italians: Chicago Heights, 1890–1975," in *Ethnic Chicago*, ed. Melvin G. Holli and Peter d'A. Jones (Grand Rapids, Mich.: W. B. Eerdmans, 1981), 108–209.

19. Candeloro and Paul, *Chicago Heights: At the Crossroads*, 49.

20. The numbers and percentages were based on data from the Department of Commerce, Bureau of the Census, *Thirteenth Census of the United States 1910, Volume 2, Population: Reports by States, with Statistics for Counties, Cities, and other Civil Divisions, Illinois.*

21. Richard Kozdras, "The Hill: The History of an Ethnic Neighborhood" (Chicago Heights: City of Chicago Heights, 1977), 10.

22. Though the opportunities for Italians to live in other parts of the city were certainly restricted, the opportunities for African Americans were virtually nonexistent. According to long-time resident Genevieve Ford Reed, the Italians and Polish people living on the

East Side rented out rooms or apartments to Blacks, for "there was no other place for the Blacks to live. . . . No Blacks lived on the West Side of town." See Genevieve Ford Reed, *Looking over Our Shoulders* (n.d.), 1, Chicago Heights History 1900–1930, Chicago Heights Public Library Pamphlet File.

23. Candeloro and Paul, *Chicago Heights: At the Crossroads,* 55.

24. Goodspeed and Healy, *History of Cook County,* 348–349.

25. Rudolph Vecoli, "Chicago's Italians Prior to World War I: A Study of Their Social and Economic Adjustment" (PhD diss., University of Wisconsin, 1962), 205; Candeloro, "Suburban Italians," 182; Kozdras, "The Hill," 10.

26. Kozdras, "The Hill," 10.

27. Vecoli, "Chicago's Italians," 205.

28. Kozdras, "The Hill," 7.

29. The numbers and percentages were drawn from a comparison between U.S. Bureau of the Census, *Thirteenth Census of the United States 1910, Volume 2* and U.S. Bureau of the Census, *Fourteenth Census of the United States 1920, Volume 1, Population: Number and Distribution of Inhabitants, Illinois* (Washington, D.C.: United States Census Bureau), and the Department of Commerce and Labor, Bureau of the Census, *Thirteenth Census of the United States: 1910, Volume 9, Manufacturers* and Department of Commerce and Labor, Bureau of the Census, *Fourteenth Census of the United States, 1920, Volume 9, Manufacturers: Report for States with Statistics for Principal Cities, Illinois* (Washington, D.C.: United States Census Bureau).

30. Candeloro and Paul, *Chicago Heights: At the Crossroads,* 48.

31. "Chicago Heights Prepares for Rapid Growth," *Chicago Tribune*, December 13, 1925. In a speech before the newly formed Chicago Heights Chamber of Commerce, Charles Wacker argued, "throughout the country Chicago Heights stands second to no city of its size . . . the potentialities of this city were great." "Chamber of Commerce Is Properly Launched," *Chicago Heights Star,* June 19, 1919.

32. Evelyn Kitagawa and Karl Taeuber, *Local Community Fact Book Chicago Metropolitan Area 1960* (Chicago: University of Chicago, 1963), 176.

33. U.S. Department of Commerce, *Fifteenth Census of the United States: 1930: Volume 1, Unemployment: Unemployment Returns by Classes for States and Counties, for Urban and Rural Areas, and for Cities with a Population of 10,000 or More, Illinois* (Washington, D.C.: United States Census Bureau).

34. Kitagawa and Taeuber, *Local Community Fact Book,* 176.

35. Fred DeLuca, "Our Neighbors in Heights—The Italian-Americans," *Chicago Heights Star*, May 1, 1936.

36. Robert Heinsen, "The Economic and Industrial History of Chicago Heights" (MA thesis, University of Iowa, 1937).

37. Heinsen, "The Economic and Industrial History," 32.

38. Personal interview, Dominic Sesto, April 15, 2007.

39. Arthur Longini, *Chicago—Chicago Heights Industrial Economic Blueprint* (Chicago: Chicago and Eastern Illinois Railroad, 1957), 330.

40. Chicago Heights Mayor's Housing Committee, "Report of the Mayor's Housing Committee of the City of Chicago Heights, Illinois," August 17, 1949.

41. Chicago Fact Book Consortium, *Local Community Fact Book, Chicago Metropolitan Area 1990* (Chicago: University of Illinois at Chicago, 1995), 238.

42. Matt O'Connor, "U.S. Jury Rules Against Chicago Heights," *Chicago Tribune,* June 19, 1992.

43. U.S. Department of Commerce, *1963 Census of Manufacturers: Volume III, Area Statistics* (Washington, D.C.: United States Census Bureau).

44. U.S. Department of Commerce, *1977 County and City Data Book: A Statistical Abstract Supplement* (Washington, D.C.: United States Department of Commerce), 650.

45. For example, in 1997, Chicago Heights had the less than favorable distinction of having the second highest violent crime rate in the state, with neighboring Ford Heights the highest. See John Carpenter, "Poverty Plagues High-Crime Towns," *Chicago Sun-Times,* April 27, 1997. A great deal of this violent crime can be attributed to the on-going organized crime activities found within segments of the African American and Hispanic populations. See Olivia Wu, "Prostitution Ring Nets 127 in Suburb," *Chicago Sun Times,* September 22, 1997; Phat X Chiem, "71 Arrested in 3-Day Narcotics Sweep in Suburbs," *Chicago Tribune,* December 12, 1997; "Cops Sting More Than 100," *Chicago Sun Times,* August 23, 1998; "Police Cameras Keep Eye on Street," *Chicago Tribune*, April 11, 2004. In 2003, federal authorities broke up a powerful, "well-defined hierarchy" of drug dealers in the city, whose profit was estimated at $20,000 a day. See Chris Hack, "Are the Mobsters Gone from the Southland?," *Chicago Heights Star,* May 8, 2005.

46. Matt O'Connor, "A New Ugly Stain for Chicago Heights," *Chicago Tribune*, June 22, 1992.

47. Lloyd Went, "Suburb Erases Blot of Capone Wide Open Days," *Chicago Tribune*, April 26, 1936.

48. Rosalind Rossi, "Mob Image Backdrop to Chicago Hts. Trial," *Chicago Sun-Times*, January 25, 1993.

49. "One Reason Why the 'Star' Opposes Mayor J. C. Mote," *Chicago Heights Star*, March 30, 1911.

50. "City's Candidates before the Women," *Chicago Heights Star*, April 8, 1915.

51. "Council Stirred by Open Letter of Vice Situation," *Chicago Heights Star*, July 22, 1920.

52. "McSwiggen Death Story to Jury: Raid Nets Guns," *Chicago Tribune*, June 3, 1926; "Heights Crime Reputation Is World By-Word," *Chicago Heights Star*, February 15, 1929.

53. "Heights Crime Reputation Is World By-Word," *Chicago Heights Star*, February 15, 1929.

54. Tom McNamee, "Tocco Trial Fuels Chicago Hts. Mob Image," *Chicago Sun Times,* December 3, 1989.

55. Marin Lanfranchi, "A Political History of Chicago Heights" (MA thesis, Governors State University, 1960), 30.

56. "City Huge Distillery," *Chicago Heights Star*, August 10, 1928.

57. John Kobler, *Capone: The Life and World of Al Capone* (New York: Putnam, 1971), 76.

58. "Juliano Seized as Member of Bomb Syndicate," *Chicago Tribune*, April 10, 1929.

59. Laurence Bergreen, *Capone: The Man and the Era* (New York: Simon & Schuster, 1994), 200.

60. Federal Bureau of Investigation, "Frank Laporte," Freedom of Information Act, file 92-5793-130, United States Department of Justice, 6.

61. "Sanfilippo Killer Produces Mystery," *Chicago Heights Star*, April 24, 1924.

62. In this regard, see "Murder Reveals Terror Reign in Chicago Heights," *Chicago Tribune*, December 8, 1928; "Assassins Kill Alky Chief in Chicago Heights," *Chicago Tribune*, December 1, 1928; and Eliot Ness with Oscar Fraley, *The Untouchables* (New York: Messner, 1957), 47–57.

63. Ness, *The Untouchables,* 50.

64. See Robert Schoenberg, *Mr. Capone* (New York: Morrow, 1992), 72–73; Matthew Luzi, "From the Boys in Chicago Heights," 14.

65. Bergreen, *Capone: The Man and the Era,* 200.

66. The *Chicago Tribune* estimated that Piazza had controlled several hundred alcohol cookers before his untimely death and that he was the "biggest man" in the south side rackets. See "Feudists Slay Booze King," *Chicago Tribune,* July 23, 1926; "Shotgun Murder of Man and Woman Traced to Booze War," *Chicago Tribune,* June 3, 1926.

67. Federal authorities speculated on the correlation between the on-going slayings in Chicago and Chicago Heights. See "Capone To Testify in Heights Case," *Chicago Heights Star*, March 19, 1929. At the same time, several Chicago Heights sources contended that the Chicago Heights gangsters played a more prominent role in the Saint Valentine's Day Massacre than the still largely unsubstantiated, conventional accounts have led us to believe. For the most detailed and well-researched review of these accounts, see William Helmer and Arthur Bilek, *The Saint Valentine's Day Massacre: The Untold Story of the Gangland Bloodbath that Brought Down Al Capone* (Nashville, Tenn.: Cumberland House, 2004).

68. Schoenberg speculates that it was not the Weiss-Moran-Drucci gang that took revenge on the Gennas, but the Torrio-Capone organization that seized this opportunity to eliminate the unpredictable and challenging west side operation posed by the Gennas. See Robert Schoenberg, *Mr. Capone,* 128–136.

69. "Assassins Unknown, Is Jury Report," *Chicago Herald and Examiner,* July 24, 1926.

70. Personal interview, Andy Corsino, March 13, 1993.

71. Federal Bureau of Investigation, "Frank Laporte," Freedom of Information Act, file 92-5793-155, United States Department of Justice; "U.S. Digs up Old Murder Case in Trial of Roberts," *Chicago Heights Star*, March 4, 1932.

72. Luzi, "From the Boys in Chicago Heights," 14.

73. Schoenberg, *Mr. Capone*, 133.

74. "Rope Murder Called 8th in Cavalier Feud," *Chicago Tribune*, September 3, 1926.

75. "Three Killings Spur County Police to War on Alky Ring," *Chicago Tribune,* January 19, 1928.

76. John Binder and Matthew Luzi, "Al Capone and Friends" (Chicago: Unpublished [Copyrighted], September 25, 1995); see also Bergreen, *Capone: The Man and the Era,* 202.

77. "Inside Story of Capone Gang's Downfall Told," *Chicago Daily News*, February, 24, 1936.

78. See, Schoenberg, *Mr. Capone*, 232; and "Ellis Indicted in Heights Slot Machine Inquiry," *Chicago Tribune*, January 9, 1929; "Chicago Wearies Capone, But He Has To Remain," *Chicago Tribune*, March 22, 1929.

79. Alan Block, *East Side-West Side: Organizing Crime in New York, 1930–1950* (New Brunswick, N.J.: Transaction Books, 1983), 13.

80. Rossi, "Mob Image Backdrop to Chicago Hts. Trial."

81. Bergreen, *Capone: The Man and the Era*, 366.

82. "Mayor Invites Gaming Critics to Reveal All," *Chicago Heights Star*, February 4, 1938.

83. "1 Slain, 3 Shot; Guard against Reprisal War," *Chicago Tribune*, February 10, 1938.

84. "The Heat's on! Slot Machines Are Shut Down," *Chicago Tribune*, June 1, 1939.

85. "Whir of Gaming Tables Stilled by Roving Police," *Chicago Tribune,* September 3, 1937.

86. Personal interview, Louie Patrizi, August 11, 1998.

87. John Binder, *The Chicago Outfit* (Charleston, S.C.: Arcadia, 2003), 61; Chicago Crime Commission, "Memorandum: Re: John Roberts, alias Roberto," January 12, 1960.

88. Personal interview, anonymous source, February 8, 1997.

89. Federal Bureau of Investigation, "Frank Laporte," Freedom of Information Act, file 92-5793-155, United States Department of Justice, 115.

90. *Life* magazine, January 20, 1941, 75.

91. Personal interview, Andy Corsino, July 10, 1995.

92. "Pilotto's Role with Hod Union Proves Puzzle," *Chicago Tribune*, May 13, 1963.

93. "U.S. Probes Hood Terror Tactics on Strippers Here," *Chicago Tribune*, November 19, 1961.

94. Kerry Segrave, *Jukeboxes: An American Social History* (Jefferson, N.C.: McFarland & Company, 2002).

95. Personal interview, anonymous source, February 8, 1997.

96. For example, on one occasion, my sister was asked to drive one of the boys home from our house. To avoid detection, he sprawled on the floor of the car in the back seat and instructed my sister to simply slow down so as to let him roll out the back and scurry into his house.

97. During the trial, Tocco's wife testified that Tocco had been one of the persons who buried Tony "The Ant" Spilotro, a case portrayed in the Martin Scorsese film *Casino.*

98. Robert Lombardo, "Recruitment into Organized Crime: A Study of Social Structural Support of Deviance" (PhD diss., University of Illinois at Chicago, 1994), 164.

99. Chris Hack, "Where Have All the Mobsters Gone?," *Chicago Heights Star,* May 8, 2005; Lombardo, "Recruitment into Organized Crime," 164.

Chapter 2. Were They Pushed?

1. Diego Gambetta, *Were They Pushed or Did They Jump? Individual Decision Mechanisms in Education* (Cambridge: Cambridge University Press, 1987).

2. Robert Merton, *Social Theory and Social Structure* (New York: The Free Press, 1968), 73–139. See James O'Kane, *The Crooked Ladder: Gangsters, Ethnicity and the American Dream* (New Brunswick, N.J.: Transaction Publishers, 1992); Daniel Bell, "Crime as an American Way of Life: A Queer Ladder of Social Mobility," in Daniel Bell, *The End of Ideology* (New York: Free Press, 1960); Robert Lombardo, *The Black Hand: Terror by Letter in Chicago* (Urbana: University of Illinois Press, 2009).

3. Merton, *Social Theory and Social Structure,* 132.

4. In his later formulations, Merton came to see this link between structural strain and social capital. See Robert Merton, "Opportunity Structure: The Emergence, Diffusion, and Differentiation of a Sociological Concept, 1930s-1950s," in *Advances in Criminological Theory,* vol. 6, ed. Freda Adler and William Laufer (New Brunswick, N.J.: Transaction, 1987). Also see John Hagan and Bill McCarthy, "Anomie, Social Capital, and Street Criminology," in *The Future of Anomie,* ed. Nikos Passas and Robert Agnew (Boston: Northeastern University Press, 1997).

5. Chris Devatenos (Gregory), "Chicago Heights History" (working paper, University of Chicago, 1924), 31.

6. Interview with Dominic Pandolfi, box 36, folder 449, Italian American Collection Records (IACR), (1979–1980), Italians in Chicago, Department of History, University of Illinois-Chicago Circle Campus.

7. Interview with Aldo DeAngelis, courtesy of Dominic Candeloro, Casa Italia Cultural Center, March 1, 1997.

8. Interview with Dominic Pandolfi, IACR.

9. Interview with Nick Tieri, box 48, folder 621, IACR.

10. Interview with Theresa Giannetti, box 21, folder 239, IACR.

11. Interview with Nick Tieri, IACR.

12. Interview with Oliva Kowalski, box 24, folder 282, IACR.

13. Interview with Nick Zaranti, box 52, folder 668, IACR.

14. Rudolph Vecoli, "Prelates and Peasants: Italian Immigrants and the Catholic Church," *Journal of Social History* 2 (1969), 230. Also, see Peter D'Agostino, *Rome in America: Transnational Catholic Ideology from the Risorgimento to Fascism* (Chapel Hill: University of North Carolina Press, 2004).

15. Harold Colbert Jones Memorial Community Center, accessed November 10, 2011, www.jonescenter.org/.

16. Ibid.

17. Interview with Zeranti, IACR.

18. Collen Newquest, "The Hill Boasts a 'Rich' Tradition," *Chicago Heights Star,* September 8, 1988.

19. Interview with Mario Bruno, box 7, folder 71, IACR.

20. For example, in the 1909 city elections, the total number of votes cast in the fifth ward aldermanic race far surpassed the voting totals in any other ward. And for the five citywide positions up for election (mayor, clerk, attorney, treasurer, and police magistrate), the third, fourth, and fifth wards contributed 45 percent of the votes cast. See "Official Figures of City Election," *Chicago Heights Star,* April 29, 1909.

21. Dominic Candeloro and Barbara Paul, *Chicago Heights: At the Crossroads of the Nation* (Charleston, S.C.: Arcadia, 2004), 50.

22. "First Forum Meet Proves Successful," *Chicago Heights Star,* January 10, 1921.

23. "Patriotism Feature of Industrial Club," *Chicago Heights Star,* April 19, 1917.

24. Interview with Dominic Pandolfi, IACR.

25. "Italians Organize League of Voters," *Chicago Heights Star,* January 12, 1934.

26. "Both Sides Report Gains in Commission vs. Ward Fight," *Chicago Heights Star,* November 29, 1938.

27. Ibid.

28. John Wozny, *Growing Up Polish: History of Polish Pioneers in Chicago Heights Volume II* (Chicago Heights: Growing up Polish Publishers, 1993), 105.

29. Candeloro and Paul, *Chicago Heights: At the Crossroads of the Nation,* 103.

30. Letter, Albert La Morticella to Nino La Morticella, courtesy of Dominic Candeloro, Casa Italia Cultural Center files, October 11, 1979.

31. Vecoli, Rudolph, "Chicago's Italians Prior to World War I: A Study of Their Social and Economic Adjustment," (PhD diss., University of Wisconsin, 1963), 209.

32. *La Parola dei Socialisti,* March 12, 1908.

33. Giovanni Schiavo, *The Italians in Chicago: A Study in Americanization* (Chicago: Italian American Publishing Company, 1928), 22.

34. Joel Perlmann, *Ethnic Differences: Schooling and Social Structure among the Irish, Italians, Jews and Blacks in an American City, 1880–1935* (Cambridge: Cambridge University Press, 1988), 87.

35. John Logan, "White Ethnics in a New York Economy, 1920–1960," Russell Sage Foundation Working Paper 112 (n.p., 1997).

36. Stephan Thernstrom, *The Other Bostonians: Poverty and Progress in the American Metropolis, 1880–1970* (Cambridge: Harvard University Press, 1973), 144.

37. For the sake of comparison, we analyzed the occupational standing of Poles in Chicago Heights using the 1930 census manuscripts. Not too surprisingly, we found that Polish adult males (n = 517) also resided disproportionately at the lower ends of the occupational rankings. Thus, 55 percent self-identified as laborers, 12 percent as semi-skilled workers. In this sense, the economic standing of Poles was quite similar to that of the Italian population. Perhaps, one moderating difference was the relative proportion of adult females in the labor force. Thus, only 7 percent of Italian females were employed

outside the home, compared to 19 percent of Polish females. In this sense, Polish families may have mitigated some of the distressing aspects of the Great Depression. "As the fathers started losing their jobs because of factory closings, the mothers were the ones who tried to find work of one kind or another" (Wozny, *Growing Up Polish,* 31).

38. Along these lines see Robert Higgs, "Race, Skill and Earnings: American Immigrants in 1909," *Journal of Economic History* 31 (1971), 424–425; Paul McGouldrick and Michael Tannen, "Did Manufacturers Discriminate against Immigrants before 1914?," *Journal of Economic History* 77 (1977), 726.

39. Higgs, "Race, Skill and Earnings," 427.

40. Gary Becker, *The Economics of Discrimination* (Chicago: University of Chicago Press, 1957), 19.

41. Fred DeLuca, "Our Neighbors in the Heights—The Italian Americans," *Chicago Heights Star,* April 24, 1936.

42. Becker, *The Economics of Discrimination*, 13.

43. Interview with Nick Tieri, IACR.

44. Interview with Oliva Kowalski, IACR.

45. Interview with Dominic Pandolfi, IACR.

46. Interview with Jerry Colangelo by Dominic Candeloro, Casa Italia, Italian Cultural Center, n.p:n.p., n. d.

47. Interview with Carlo Pulcini, box 41, folder 511, IACR.

48. Juan Ramon Garcia, *A History of the Mexican American People in the Chicago Heights, Illinois Area* (Chicago Heights: Prairie State College, 1976), 14.

49. Stanley Lieberson, *Ethnic Patterns in American Cities* (Glencoe, Ill.: Free Press, 1962), 206–218; Stanley Lieberson, *A Piece of the Pie: Black and White Immigrants since 1880* (Berkeley: University of California Press, 1980), 253–291.

50. Douglas Massey and Nancy Denton, *American Apartheid: Segregation and the Making of the Underclass* (Cambridge: Harvard University Press, 1993), 33; David Cutler, Edmund Glaeser, and Jacob Vigdor, "Ghettos and the Transmission of Ethnic Capital," in *Ethnicity, Social Mobility, and Public Policy: Comparing USA and UK,* ed. Glen Loury, Tariq Modoud, and Seven Teles (Cambridge: Cambridge University Press, 2005), 204–221.

51. Again, we also analyzed the residential patterns for Poles in Chicago Heights based on the data available in the 1930 census manuscripts. Like their Italian counterparts, Poles were heavily concentrated in Wards 3, 4, and 5. Eighty-six percent were to be found in one or another of these three wards. And the dissimilarity index for Poles over against native whites of native parentage was 0.71. These data, along with the data on the occupational rankings of Poles provided earlier, suggest that the social and economic standing for Poles were quite similar to that of Chicago Heights Italians. Theoretically, one might argue that the Poles, as a group, would be inclined to engage in a variety of collective mobilizations to enhance their social mobility—specifically, labor organizing, mutual-aid societies, ethnic businesses, and organized crime. There is evidence that in the first part

of the last century, Chicago Heights Poles did pursue each of these mobilization strategies. However, the relatively small number of Poles in Chicago Heights, as least compared to Italians, inhibited the potential for success in each of these venues. For example, Polish organized crime tended to be more sporadic and less centralized than in the Italian enclaves. The social capital resources upon which to build an on-going structure, while present, were never as deep or as prolific as in the larger Italian community. The critical mass necessary to centralize criminal activities and create the economies favoring the costs of organized crime were not readily available. Along these lines, see Thomas Schelling, *Choice and Consequences* (Cambridge: Harvard University Press, 1984). In part, we see these processes at work in Michael Rizzo's study of organized crime in Buffalo, New York. His description of the Polish "gangsters" highlights the episodic, predatory character of their criminal activities. On the other hand, his description of Italian "organized crime" reveals a criminal organization that is embedded in the local neighborhoods of Buffalo. See Michael Rizzo, *Gangsters and Organized Crime in Buffalo: History, Hits, and Headquarters* (Charleston, S.C.: The History Press, 2012). For a more detailed look at the Polish experience in Chicago Heights, see Wozny, *Growing Up Polish.*

52. Richard Kozdras, *The Hill: The History of an Ethnic Neighborhood* (Chicago Heights: City of Chicago Heights, 1977), 24.

53. Interview with Zeranti, IACR.

54. Lieberson, *A Piece of the Pie,* 278–279.

55. Paul Cressey, "The Succession of Cultural Groups in the City of Chicago" (PhD diss., University of Chicago, Chicago, 1930), 256.

56. Interview with Mario Bruno, IACR.

57. "I Don't Want Votes Gained by Such Methods," *Chicago Heights Star,* April 2, 1935.

58. Dominic Candeloro, "Suburban Italians: Chicago Heights, 1890–1975," in *Ethnic Chicago,* ed. Melvin G. Holli and Peter d'A. Jones (Grand Rapids, Mich.: W. B. Eerdmans, 1981), 240.

59. Interview with Theresa Giannetti, box 21, folder 239, IACR.

60. William Julius Wilson, *The Truly Disadvantaged: The Inner City, the Underclass, and Public Policy* (Chicago: University of Chicago Press, 1987), 60.

61. Devatenos (Gregory), "Chicago Heights History," 20.

62. Fred DeLuca, "Our Neighbors in Heights—The Italian-Americans," *Chicago Heights Star,* April 21, 1936.

63. Devatenos (Gregory), "Chicago Heights History," 20.

64. Kozdras, *The Hill,* 14.

65. Richard Alba, *Italian-Americans: Into the Twilight of Ethnicity* (Englewood Cliffs, N.J.: Prentice Hall, 1985), 141.

66. See Massey and Denton, *American Apartheid,* 149–185.

67. Kozdras, *The Hill,* 14.

68. Candeloro and Paul, *Chicago Heights: At the Crossroads,* 114.

69. Personal interview, Joe Nicastro, August 5, 1995.

70. Interview with Dominic Prancrazio, courtesy of Dominic Candeloro, Casa Italia Cultural Center, n.p.: n.p., n.d.

71. James Coleman, *Foundations of Social Theory* (Cambridge: Harvard University Press, 1990), 310–311.

72. Newquest, "The Hill Boasts a 'Rich' Tradition."

73. Ibid.

74. Candeloro and Paul, *Chicago Heights: At the Crossroads,* 104.

75. Edward Banfield, *The Moral Basis of a Backward Society* (Glencoe, Ill.: Free Press, 1958).

76. Nathan Glazer and Daniel Patrick Moynihan, *Beyond the Melting Pot* (Cambridge: MIT Press, 1970), 190, 205. Also, see Andrew Greeley, *Ethnicity in the United States* (New York: Wiley, 1974).

77. David Ward, *Poverty, Ethnicity and the American City, 1840–1925* (Cambridge: Cambridge University Press, 1989), 177. There is a rich literature on the reactive, emergent qualities of ethnicity in the early decades of the last century. A sample of these works would include: David Roediger, *The Wages of Whiteness: Race and the Making of the American Working Class* (New York: Verso, 1999); Matthew Fyre Jacobson, *Whiteness of a Different Color: European Immigrants and the Alchemy of Race* (Cambridge: Harvard University Press, 1999); Robert Orsi, *Gods of the City: Religion and the American Urban Landscape* (Bloomington: Indiana University Press, 1999); Joseph Cosco, *Imagining Italians: The Clash of Romance and Race in American Perceptions, 1880–1910* (Albany: State University of New York Press, 2003); Jennifer Guglielmo, *Are Italians White? How Race Is Made in America* (New York: Routledge, 2003); Thomas Guglielmo, *White on Arrival: Italians, Race, Color, and Power in Chicago, 1890–1945* (New York: Oxford University Press, 2004).

78. Alejandro Portes and Julia Sensenbrenner, "Embeddedness and Immigration: Notes on the Determinants of Economic Action," *American Journal of Sociology* 98 (1993), 1331.

Chapter 3. Did They Jump?

1. Interview with Frank Corradetti, box 13, folder 146, Italian American Collection Records (IACR), (1979–1980), *Italians in Chicago*, Department of History, University of Illinois–Chicago Circle Campus.

2. "Riot in Downtown Street," *Chicago Heights Star*, September 23, 1908.

3. "Matteson," *Chicago Heights Star*, July 13, 1911.

4. Rudolph Vecoli, "Chicago's Italians prior to World War I: A Study of Their Social and Economic Adjustment," (PhD diss., University of Wisconsin, 1963), 205.

5. Letter, Albert La Morticella to Nino La Morticella, courtesy Dominic Candeloro, Casa Italia Cultural Center files, October 11, 1979.

6. *La Cooperativa Italiana di Consumo di Chicago Heights, Ill.*, Casa Italia Cultural Center files, n.p.:n.p., n. d.

7. Interview with Nick Zaranti, box 52, folder 668, IACR.

8. *La Parola dei Socialisti*, March 12, 1908; also, see *Il Proletario*, August 11, 1909.

9. Joseph Thompson, *Diamond Jubilee of the Archdiocese of Chicago, Antecedents and Developments* (Des Plaines, Ill: St. Mary's Training School Press, 1920), 604.

10. *New World*, February 29, 1908.

11. "Assassins after a Chicago Priest," *Chicago Tribune*, February 27, 1908. The "reasonableness" of this fear was fueled by an incident in Denver, Colorado, where an Italian immigrant had taken the life of a Catholic priest.

12. "Assassins after a Chicago Priest."

13. "Priests in Dread; Uneasy at Altar," *Chicago Tribune*, March 2, 1908.

14. Interview with Nick Zaranti, box 52, folder 668, IACR.

15. Kenan Helse, "Joe Giganti, 81, Economist," *Chicago Tribune,* September 17, 1986; Interview with Joseph Giganti, box 92, Tamiment Library/Robert F. Wagner Labor Archives, Elmer Holmes Bobst Library (1983).

16. Youngsoo Bae, *Labor in Retreat: Class and Community among Men's Clothing Workers of Chicago, 1871–1929* (Albany: State University of New York Press, 2001), 212.

17. Letter, Albert La Morticella to Nino La Morticella, Casa Italia Cultural Center.

18. "I.W.W. Meeting Nipped in the Bud," *Chicago Heights Star*, June 20, 1918.

19. Ibid.

20. Letter, Albert La Morticella to Nino La Morticella, Casa Italia Cultural Center.

21. "Mfrs. Association Annual Banquet," *Chicago Heights Star*, December 21, 1922.

22. Lizabeth Cohen, *Making a New Deal: Industrial Workers in Chicago, 1919–1939* (Cambridge: Cambridge University Press, 1990), 163.

23. "Mfrs. Association Annual Banquet."

24. "Socialists Bested by Loyal Italians," *Chicago Heights Star*, November 28, 1917.

25. Jack Morris, *Inland Steel at 100: Beginning a Second Century of Progress* (Chicago: Inland Steel Industries, 1993), 23.

26. Interview with Dominic Pandolfi, box 36, folder 449, IACR.

27. Letter, Albert La Morticella to Nino La Morticella, Casa Italia Cultural Center Files.

28. "Inland Strike Officially Denied," *Gary Evening News Times,* August 9, 1922.

29. William Kornblum, *Blue Collar Community* (Chicago: University of Chicago Press, Chicago, 1974), 95.

30. Dominic Candeloro, "Suburban Italians: Chicago Heights, 1890–1975," in *Ethnic Chicago,* ed. Melvin G. Holli and Peter d'A. Jones (Grand Rapids, Mich.: W. B. Eerdmans, 1981), 195.

31. Interview with Nick Tieri, box 48, folder 621, IACR.

32. Interview with Oliva Kowalski, box 24, folder 282, IACR.

33. Interview with Corradetti, IACR.

34. Personal interview with Dominic Sesto, April 15, 2007.

35. Interview with Alphonse Leone, box 27, folder 305, IACR.

36. Interview with Nick Zaranti, IACR.

37. For example, the Calabrese Social Club claimed 115 members in 1935 (see "Calabrese Society Enrolls New Members," *Chicago Heights Star,* March 19, 1935), the Marchegianni Society put its membership at 272 in 1934 (see "New Italian Union to Sponsor Picnic," *Chicago Heights Star*, July 17, 1934), the Italian Consumer Co-operative of Chicago Heights had 101 members when it began in 1911 (see *La Cooperativa Italiana di Consumo di Chicago Heights, Ill.*, Casa Italia Cultural Center files, n.p.: n.p., n. d.).

38. Personal interview with Dominic Sesto, August 19, 2010.

39. Xavier de Souza Briggs, "Social Capital and the Cities: Advice to Change Agents," presented at an International Workshop on Community Building, The Rockefeller Foundation, Bellagio, Italy, October 1997, 2.

40. Ibid.

41. Dominic Candeloro, "Mostly Melted/Still Connected: The Marchigiani in Chicago Heights 1893–1997," H-Net Humanities and Social Science On-line, accessed February 19, 2002, h-net.msu.edu/cgi-bin/logbrowse.pl?trx=vx&list.

42. Ibid.

43. Jean Guarino, "Chicago Hts. Still Caring for Its Own," *Chicago Tribune*, July 20, 1984.

44. "Good Food and Fun at Dante Banquet," *Chicago Heights Star*, January 29, 1929.

45. "Civic Leaders Predict Prosperity for Heights," *Chicago Heights Star*, May 10, 1929.

46. Dominic Candeloro, "Suburban Italians," 197.

47. "New Italian Union to Sponsor Picnic."

48. Interview with Mario Bruno, box 7, folder 71, IACR.

49. "Italo Union Plans Anniversary Picnic," *Chicago Heights Star*, June 4, 1935; also, "Anniversary Fete of Italo Union is Successful Event," *Chicago Heights Star*, June 14, 1935.

50. Rudolph Vecoli, "Contadini in Chicago: A Critique of the Uprooted," *Journal of American History* 51 (1964), 413.

51. Cohen, "Making a New Deal," 228.

52. Exemption Affidavit Form 1025, Treasury Department, March 12, 1945, Marchegianna Society, Casa Italia Cultural Center Files.

53. John Bodnar, *The Transplanted: A History of Immigrants in Urban America* (Bloomington: Indiana University Press, 1985), 120.

54. A sampling of this literature would include: Roger Waldinger, Howard Aldrich, and Robin Ward, *Ethnic Entrepreneurs: Immigrant Business in Industrial Societies* (Newbury Park, Calif.: Sage Publications, 1990); Leo-Paul Dana (ed.), *Handbook of Research on Ethnic Minority Entrepreneurship: A Co-Evolutionary View on Resource Management* (Northampton, Mass.: Edward Elgar Publishing, 2007); Alejandro Portes (ed.), *The Economic Sociology of Immigration: Essays on Networks Ethnicity, and Entrepreneurship* (New York: Russell Sage Foundation, 1995); Ivan Light and Carolyn Rosenstein, *Race, Ethnicity and Entrepreneurship in Urban America* (New York: Walter de Gruyter, 1995).

55. Ivan Light, "The Ethnic Economy," in *Handbook of Economic Economy*, ed. Neil Smelser and Richard Swedberg (New York: Russell Sage Foundation, 2004).

56. Personal interview, Vito Chementi, July 15, 1996.

57. Personal interview, Pat Pancrazio, March 8, 1997.

58. Letter, Albert La Morticella to Nino La Morticella, Casa Italia Cultural Center.

59. Collen Newquest, "The Hill Boasts a 'Rich' Tradition," *Chicago Heights Star*, September 8, 1988.

60. Lizabeth Cohen, "Encountering Mass Culture at the Grassroots: The Experience of Chicago Workers in the 1920s," *American Quarterly* 41 (1989), 12.

61. "Santi Cipriani," *Chicago Tribune*, February 27, 2000.

62. The Department of Commerce and Labor, Bureau of the Census, *Thirteenth Census of the United States: 1910 Population* (Washington, D.C.: United States Census Bureau) and *Fifteenth Census of the United States: 1930 Population* (Washington, D.C.: United States Census Bureau), Chicago Heights manuscripts. The self-employment rates for Italian adult males in Chicago Heights are similar to the rates in other smaller cities. For example, Pascucci finds a 5.9 percent self-employment rate for Schenectady, New York, in 1905 (see Robert Pascucci, "Electric City Immigrants: Italians and Poles of Schenectady, N.Y., 1880–1930" [PhD diss., State University of New York at Albany, 1984]). Andreozzi's state census manuscript data for Italians in Lacawanna, New York, reports only a handful of small retailers and peddlers for the years 1905, 1915, and 1925 (see John Andreozzi, "Italians in a Mill Town: Lackawanna, New York," in *Italian Americans: The Search for a Usable Past: Proceedings of the 19th Conference of the American Italian Historical Association,* ed. Richard Juliani and Philip Cannistraro, [New York: American Italian Historical Association, 1989]). Bogan and Darity put the overall United States self-employment rate for white immigrants at 7.9 percent in 1910 and 7.7 percent in 1920 (see Vicki Bogan and William Darity, "Culture and Entrepreneurship? African-American and Immigration Self-Employment in the United States," *Journal of Socio-Economics* 37 (2008), 2011).

63. Ron Rothbart, "The Ethnic Saloon as a Form of Immigrant Enterprise," *International Migration Review* 27 (1993), 341.

64. Interview with Dominic Prancrazio, courtesy of Dominic Candeloro, Casa Italia Cultural Center, n.p.: n.p., n.d.

65. Chris Devatenos (Gregory), "Chicago Heights History" (working paper, University of Chicago, 1924), 19.

66. Dominic Candeloro and Barbara Paul, *Chicago Heights: At the Crossroads of the Nation* (Charleston, S.C.: Arcadia, 2004), 49.

67. Jeremy Boissevain, Jochen Blacken, Hanneke Rotenberg, Isaac Joseph, Ivan Light, Marlene Sway, Roger Waldinger, and Pnina Werner, "Ethnic Entrepreneurs and Ethnic Strategies," in *Ethnic Entrepreneurs*, ed. Roger Waldinger, Howard Aldrich, and Robin Ward (Beverly Hills: Sage Publications, 1990), 146.

68. Michael Laborite, "Occupations of Italian Immigrants in Turn-of-The-Century America," in *The Italian American Experience: An Encyclopedia*, ed. Salvatore J.

LaGumina, Frank Gumino, Salvatore Primeggio, and Joseph Varracalli (New York: Garland Publishing, 1999), 421.

69. Howard Abadinsky, *Organized Crime* (Belmont, Calif.: Thomson Wadsworth, 2007), 45–48.

70. Perry Duis, *The Saloon: Public Drinking in Chicago and Boston 1880–1920* (Urbana: University of Illinois Press, 1983), 147.

71. Ibid., 170.

72. "Beer Garden Excites Anger," *Chicago Heights Star*, August 22, 1897.

73. "In Aid of Reform," *Chicago Heights Signal*, August 1, 1907.

74. Chicago Heights City Directory, 1914.

75. In an attempt to prevent soft drink parlors from turning into illegal taverns, the Chicago Heights city council passed an ordinance that made it illegal for parlors to place curtains or screens on their premises and, thus, "inhibit a full view of such parlors or rooms." See "No Secrets in Parlors," *Chicago Heights Star*, February 13, 1924.

76. Gus Russo, *The Outfit: The Role of Chicago's Underworld in the Shaping of Modern America* (New York: Bloomsbury, 2001), 19.

77. Duis, *The Saloon,* 164.

78. In this regard, saloon owners were often called on for their advice and support in obtaining naturalization and citizenship status. For example, Chicago Heights saloon owner Pasquale Luongo served as a witness for twenty-two Italian citizens; Pete Cassaza for another twelve; and other Italian saloon owners also served in this capacity.

79. Duis, *The Saloon,* 147.

80. Laurence Bergreen, *Capone: The Man and the Era* (New York: Simon & Schuster, 1994), 200.

81. Nancy Foner and Richard Alba, "The Second Generation from the Last Great Wave of Immigration: Setting the Record Straight," *Migration Information Source* (October 2006), accessed July 13, 2012, http://www.migrationpolicy.org/article/second-generation-last-great-wave-immigration-setting-record-straight.

82. Mark Haller, "Organized Crime in Urban Society: Chicago in the Twentieth Century," *Journal of Social History* 4 (1971), 214.

83. Letter, Albert La Morticella to Nino La Morticella, Casa Italia Cultural Center.

Chapter 4. You Can't Shoot Everyone

1. For example, Sonny Talamonti achieved local fame as a racecar driver; Dr. Hugo Long became a prominent physician and community leader; and somewhat later, Jerry Colangelo achieved recognition as an innovative and highly successful owner of the NBA Phoenix Suns and MLB Arizona Diamondbacks.

2. Dominic Candeloro, "Suburban Italians: Chicago Heights, 1890–1975," in *Ethnic Chicago: A Multicultural Portrait,* ed. Melvin G. Holli and Peter d'A. Jones (Grand Rapids, Mich.: W. B. Eerdmans, 1981), 204.

3. Pierre Bourdieu, *Algeria 1960* (Cambridge: Cambridge University Press, 1979), 4.

4. U.S. Department of Justice, Federal Bureau of Investigation, March 3, 1967, Subject: Frank La Porte, bureau file 92-5793, 51.

5. "Barber's Mom Could Not Refuse Capone's Offer," *Chicago Sun Times,* February 29, 2004.

6. Alan Block, *East Side-West Side: Organizing Crime in New York, 1930–1950* (New Brunswick, N.J.: Transaction, 1983), 13.

7. "Bloom Township Italian Republican Club," *Chicago Heights Signal,* July 21, 1925.

8. Matthew Luzi, "From the Boys in Chicago Heights" (unpublished manuscript, 2003).

9. Luzi, "From the Boys."

10. Luzi's identifications were based on the accounts of two people included in the picture and a third individual who was closely associated with one of the principal figures, Jimmy Emery. Additional confirmations were based on a comparison of the photo with other pictures in which individuals had been clearly identified. Newspaper reports and naturalization records provided collaborating evidence. I also undertook my own identifications based on conversations with three individuals who were friends, relatives, or associates of many of the men pictured. Naturalization records, newspaper accounts, obituaries, and FBI files were also useful.

11. The exceptions here are Anthony Scibi, a stable boy who helped Neroni on his farm, and J. Pulia, who was a mystery man that few people in Chicago Heights could identify further.

12. "Burned to Death with Own Alky," *Chicago Heights Star,* January 10, 1930.

13. "1 Slain, 3 Shot; Guard against Reprisal War," *Chicago Tribune,* February 10, 1938.

14. "Chicago Heights Raided by U.S.," *Chicago Tribune,* January 7, 1929.

15. Chicago Crime Commission, "John Roberto," file A-5 113 860, January 12, 1960, 4.

16. "Chicago Heights Raided by U.S.," *Chicago Tribune,* January 7, 1929.

17. Virgil Peterson, *A Report on Chicago Crime for 1960* (Chicago: Chicago Crime Commission, 1961), 43.

18. U.S. Department of Justice, Federal Bureau of Investigation, March 24, 1966, Subject: Frank La Porte, bureau file 92-5793, 5.

19. "Chicago Officers Raid Roadhouse," *Chicago Heights Star,* May 31, 1923.

20. U.S. District Court, Northern District of Illinois, Eastern Division, United States v. Thomas D'Amico et al. Indictment, no. 19444, May 3, 1929.

21. "Anti-Gambling Drive Revived by Juror's Activity," *Chicago Tribune,* July 25, 1942.

22. John Wozny, *Growing Up Polish: History of Polish Pioneers in Chicago Heights Volume II* (Chicago Heights: Growing up Polish Publishers, 1993), 101.

23. Most recently, the so-called Last Supper picture was used in the Family Secrets trial of the Chicago Outfit. Prosecutors argued that the picture provided tangible evidence for the existence of organized crime under the RICO statutes, for it showed the leading members of the Chicago Outfit gathered together at one time, one place. Indeed, when Joey Lombardo, a senior member of the Outfit, argued that he had simply wandered into the restaurant to get a beef sandwich and just happened to have his picture taken with friends, the jury found his testimony less than credible. See Jeff Coen, *Family Secrets: The Case that Crippled the Chicago Mob* (Chicago: Chicago River View Press), 2009.

24. Luzi, "From the Boys." Also see John Binder and Matthew Luzi, "Al Capone and Friends," *Criminal Organizations* 10 (1996), 16–22.

25. Personal interview, Andy Corsino, July 6, 1992.

26. U.S. District Court, Northern District of Illinois, Eastern Division, United States v. Thomas D'Amico, 3.

27. Personal interview, Joe Nicastro, August 5, 1995.

28. U.S. Department of Justice, Federal Bureau of Investigation, January 16, 1963, Subject: Frank La Porte, bureau file 92-5793, 2.

29. Personal interview, Louie Patrizi, June 17, 2000.

30. Department of Commerce, U.S. Bureau of the Census, *Census of Manufacturers, 1919, Illinois* (Washington, D.C.: United States Census Bureau).

31. Chicago Heights Chamber of Commerce, "Industrial Survey," n.p., section IV, 1927, 7.

32. Ibid., section IV, 1.

33. "For Chicago Heights," *Chicago Heights Star,* November 25, 1927.

34. *Chicago Heights Star,* August 28, 1924.

35. "Oral History Collection: Frank Thompson," The Cable Center, May 23, 1989, accessed July 10, 2006, http://www.cablecenter.org/barco-library-hauser-oral-history/item/thompson-frank.html.

36. "A 'Business' That Is Out of Its Place," *Chicago Heights Star,* November 25, 1927.

37. Ibid.

38. With respect to the use of nicknames, Bernard argues that they "verify and constantly remind their bearers of their own socially unacceptable characteristics. By making such things as stinginess, rumor mongering, the persistent use of vulgar language and other anti-social characteristics the butt of constant joking, society continuously reminds itself of what it considers good and bad behavioural traits." (R. H. Bernard Paratsoukli, "Institutionalized Nicknaming in Rural Greece," *Ethnologia Europaea* 2 (1969), 74.) As Gambetta points out on the use of nicknames in the criminal underworld, there are most likely multiple motives for using nicknames though most explanations focus on the attempt to manage one's criminal identity. (Diego Gambetta, *How Criminals Communicate* [Princeton University Press, Princeton, 2009], 230–250.)

39. Editorial, *Chicago Heights Star,* May 4, 1929.

40. Candeloro, "Suburban Italians," 204.

41. Laurence Bergreen, *Capone: The Man and the Era* (New York: Simon & Schuster, 1994), 202.

42. Max Weber, *Economy and Society: An Outline of Interpretive Sociology*, ed. Guenther Roth and Claus Wittich (Berkeley: University of California Press, 1978), 941–956.

43. Ibid., 72.

44. This point is argued more generally by Coleman who states, "The public goods quality of most social capital means that it is in a fundamentally different position with respect to purposive action than are most other forms of capital. . . . Because the benefits of actions that bring social capital into being are largely experienced by persons other

than the actor, it is often not in his or her interest to bring it into being. The result is that most forms of social capital are created or destroyed as by-products of other activities." (James Coleman, "Social Capital in the Creation of Human Capital," *American Journal of Sociology* 94 [Supplement 1988]: S118.)

45. Ronald Burt, *Brokerage and Closure* (Oxford: Oxford University Press, 2005).

46. Ronald Burt, "The Contingent Value of Social Capital," *Administrative Science Quarterly* 42 (1997), 340.

47. Burt, *Brokerage and Closure,* 139–141.

48. Ibid., 97.

49. The eighth man is John Nicastro who, though born in the United States, had a large extended family in Nicastro, Italy—the town adjacent to Sambiase.

50. The eighth man here was Joe Guzzino whose mother and father were born in Caccamo.

51. Alejandro Portes, "Social Capital: Its Origins and Applications in Modern Sociology," *Annual Review of Sociology* 24 (1998), 7.

52. Miller McPherson, Lynn Smith-Lovin, and James Cook, "Birds of a Feather: Homophily in Social Networks," *Annual Review of Sociology* 27 (2001), 415.

53. This "15-minute walk" criteria is a rough indicator of local friendship networks. See Robert J. Sampson and W. Byron Groves, "Community Structure and Crime: Testing Social-Disorganization Theory," *American Journal of Sociology* 94 (1989), 783–784. Also, see Peter Lupsha, "Networks versus Networking: An Analysis of an Organized Crime Group," in *Career Criminal,* ed. Gordon Waldo (Beverly Hills: Sage, 1983), 59–87.

54. The connections between these men were derived from an analysis of a variety of sources, including U.S. Immigration and Naturalization Service Department; U.S. Bureau of the Census, Population and Housing manuscripts; World War I Draft Registration records, newspaper accounts, FBI files, and personal communications. In each instance, I searched for information connecting the men to one another previous to their association with the Chicago Heights boys (roughly, previous to 1927) and apart from their associations related to their criminal activities (for example, as boyhood friends, in-laws, workmates, and the like). Given the difficulties in reconstructing and certifying personal ties that may go back decades, it is quite conceivable that the social ties in figure 4.3 underestimate the actual ties that may have existed among these men. In developing this network matrix, I was guided by the rubrics set out by Renee C. vander Hulst in his "Introduction to Social Network Analysis (SNA) as an Investigative Tool," *Trends in Organized Crime* 12 (2009), 101–121.

55. Burt, *Brokerage and Closure,* 95.

56. U.S. Department of Justice, Federal Bureau of Investigation, November 30, 1961, Subject: Frank La Porte, bureau file 92-5793, 90.

57. Ronald Burt, "The Social Capital of Structural Holes," in *The New Economic Sociology: Developments in an Emerging Field,* ed. Mauro F. Guillen, Randall Collins, Paula England, and Marshall Meyer (New York: Russell Sage Foundation, 2002), 211.

58. Ovid Demaris, *The Last Mafioso: The Treacherous World of Jimmy Fratianno* (New York: Times Books, 1981), 177.

59. U.S. Department of Justice, Federal Bureau of Investigation, June 4, 1964, Subject: Frank La Porte, bureau file 92–5793, 17.

60. Chicago Crime Commission, "Domenico Roberto," file A-5 113 860, January 12, 1960, 5.

61. Bergreen, *Capone: The Man and the Era,* 200.

62. Ibid., 199.

63. Personal interview Louie Patrizi, June 17, 2000.

64. U.S. Treasury Department, Bureau of Narcotics, *Mafia: The Government's Secret File on Organized Crime* (New York: HarperCollins Publishers, 2007), 833.

65. Bergreen, *Capone: The Man and the Era,* 198–199.

66. William Roemer, *Man against the Mob* (New York: Ivy Books, 1989), 81–84.

67. U.S. Department of Justice, Federal Bureau of Investigation, January 16, 1963, Subject: Frank La Porte, bureau file 92-5793, 35.

68. U.S. Department of Justice, Federal Bureau of Investigation, September 17, 1964, Subject: Frank La Porte, bureau file 92-5793, 14.

69. "Roche Seizes 8; Suburb Courts Set Them Free," *Chicago Tribune,* October 6, 1930.

70. U.S. Department of Justice, Federal Bureau of Investigation, December 15, 1964, Subject: Frank La Porte, bureau file 92-5793, 5.

71. U.S. Department of Justice, Federal Bureau of Investigation, July 10, 1962, Subject: Frank La Porte, bureau file 92-5793, 49.

72. Roemer, *Man against the Mob*, 81.

73. U.S. Department of Justice, Federal Bureau of Investigation, November 20, 1962, Subject: Frank La Porte, bureau file 92-5793, 3.

74. Along these lines, an informant alleged that he heard Laporte state that he employed most of his relatives, realizing, however, that they often cut into his profits by stealing from him. Nevertheless, Laporte was seemingly aware of the advantages of closure for he philosophized "better by my relatives than by a stranger." U.S. Department of Justice, Federal Bureau of Investigation, November 20, 1962, Subject: Frank La Porte, bureau file 92-5793, 18.

75. U.S. Department of Justice, Federal Bureau of Investigation, June 4, 1964, Subject: Frank La Porte, bureau file 92-5793, 18.

76. For a general discussion of the "girlie" show trade and Calumet City, in particular, see Rachel Shteir, *Striptease: The Untold History of the Girlie Show* (Oxford: Oxford University Press, 2004), especially 274–275; also see "Saturday Night in Calumet City, the Barbary Coast of the Booming Midwest," *Life* magazine, January 20, 1941, 74–77.

77. "Vice, Handbook Go Full Blast in Will County," *Chicago Tribune,* November 17, 1961.

78. "The Jukebox Tune," *Time* magazine, March 2, 1959.

79. Personal interview, Andy Corsino, March 13, 1993.

80. Burt, *Brokerage and Closure,* 164.

81. "One Reason Why the 'Star' Opposes Mayor J. C. Mote," *Chicago Heights Star,* March 30, 1911.

82. "Council Stirred by Open Letter on Vice Situation," *Chicago Heights Star,* July 22, 1920.

83. Virgil Peterson, *Barbarians in Our Midst* (Boston, Little, Brown and Company, 1952), 125.

84. See Mark Haller, "Illegal Enterprise: A Theoretical and Historical Interpretation," *Criminology* 28 (1990), 207–235, especially 217–223.

85. John Bollinger, "I'm Walking, Yes, Indeed, But Not Talking: The Great 1929 Slot Machine Scandal," Rick Porrello's AmericanMafia.com, April 2006, accessed June 22, 2012, http://www.americanmafia.com/Feature_Articles_348.html.

86. Jack Lait and Lee Mortimer, *Chicago Confidential* (New York: Crown Publishers, 1950), 95.

87. Lait and Mortimer, *Chicago Confidential*, 96. Also see Kenneth Allsop, *The Bootleggers and Their Era* (Garden City, N.Y.: Doubleday, 1961), 61–66.

88. U. S. Department of Justice, Federal Bureau of Investigation, July 10, 1962, Subject: Frank La Porte, bureau file 92-5793, 51.

89. Along these lines, see "Legion, Clubs Band to Repel Slot Bandits," *Chicago Tribune,* March 18, 1950.

90. Personal interview, Joe Nicastro, August 5, 1995.

91. U.S. Department of Justice, Federal Bureau of Investigation, March 20, 1968, Subject: Frank La Porte, bureau file 92-5793, 5.

92. Personal interview, Louie Patrizi, June 17, 2000.

93. Letters from the Readers, *Chicago Heights Star*, February 4, 1949.

94. Casey Toner, "Catholic Veterans Group Marches On," *Southtown Star*, November 19, 2010.

95. Personal interview, Dominic Sesto, November 10, 2008.

96. Letter from the Readers, *Chicago Heights Star,* February 4, 1949.

97. Mark Haller, "Organized Crime in Urban Society: Chicago in the Twentieth Century," *Journal of Social History* 5 (1971), 226.

98. Personal interview, Andy Corsino, April 2, 1991.

99. "No Warrants; Dismiss 3 on Gaming Charges," *Chicago Tribune,* October 20, 1949.

100. Bergreen, *Capone: The Man and the Era,* 199.

101. "Phil Piazza Is Murdered in Mafia Manner," *Chicago Heights Star*, July 23, 1926.

102. "Courtney Runs Calumet City Gamblers Out," *Hammond Times,* September 9, 1937.

103. U.S. Department of Justice, Federal Bureau of Investigation, March 20, 1968, Subject: Frank La Porte, bureau file 92-5793, 9.

104. U.S. Department of Justice, Federal Bureau of Investigation, October 5, 1962, Subject: Frank La Porte, bureau file 92-5793, 8.

105. Jack Levin, "County Gaming Thrives," *Chicago Daily News,* April 9, 1960.

106. An FBI informant said Laporte "was born to be a leader" but also observed that Laporte was "mean and violent." See U.S. Department of Justice, Federal Bureau of Investigation, November 20, 1962, Subject: Frank La Porte, bureau file 92-5793, 2.

Conclusion

1. Hence, Fredo's ultimate betrayal of Michael Corleone in *The Godfather II* was about a violation of trust. When Michael tells Fredo, "you're nothing to me now," this is a severing of a relationship premised upon kinship and ethnicity.

2. Alan Block, *East Side-West Side: Organizing Crime in New York, 1930–1950* (New Brunswick, N.J.: Transaction Books, 1983).

3. Arthur Bilek, *The First Vice-Lord: Big Jim Colosimo and the Ladies of the Levee* (Nashville, Tenn.: Cumberland House, 2008), 250.

4. Laurence Bergreen, *Capone: The Man and the Era* (New York: Simon & Schuster, 1994), 201–202.

5. U.S. Department of Justice, Federal Bureau of Investigation, November 19, 1973, Subject: Al Pilotto, bureau file 92–7815, 2.

6. Matt Luzi, *The Boys in Chicago Heights* (Charleston, S.C.: The History Press, 2012), 107.

7. Ronald Burt, *Brokerage and Closure* (Oxford: Oxford University Press, 2005), 86–87.

8. For a detailed look at the role of brokerage in criminal organizations and the flexibility brokerage provides in dealing with organizational challenges, see Carlo Morselli and Julie Roy, "Brokerage Qualifications in Ringing Operations," *Criminology* 46 (2008), 71–98. Also see Carlo Morselli, *Crime and Networks* (New York: Routledge, 2013).

9. One of the "good ideas" Laporte learned was to build on the close ties and networks in the various cities in the southern suburbs rather than taking over a city in a violent confrontation as happened in Cicero. See Kenneth Alsop, "When You Smell Gun Powder, You're in Cicero," in *The Bootleggers and Their Era* (Garden City, N.Y.: Doubleday & Company, 1961), 61–66.

10. Robert Herguth and Steve Warmbir, "Report Shows Mobs Alive and Well in Suburbs," *Daily Herald,* September 21, 1998.

11. Chris Hack, "Where Have All the Mobsters Gone?," *Chicago Heights Star,* May 8, 2005.

12. BigBoyHarlem, "Who Run Chicago Heights?" TheHoodup.com message board, July 3, 2011, accessed August 1, 2012, http://thehoodup.com/board/viewtopic.php?f=24&t=52920#.UCQXKKBE6Iw.

13. Kensingtons Finest, "Who Run Chicago Heights?" TheHoodup.com message board, June 29, 2011, accessed August 1, 2012, http://thehoodup.com/board/viewtopic.php?f=24&t=52920#.UCQXKKBE6Iw.

14. "Drug Kingpin Gets Life Plus 30 Years," *Chicago Tribune,* June 15, 2006.

15. Patrick Rehkamp, "South Suburban Crack Sting Nabs 95," *Chicago Sun-Times,* March 31, 2008.

16. Eliot Ness with Oscar Fraley, *The Untouchables* (New York: Messner, 1957), 61.

17. U.S. Census Bureau, 2010 Census, "Profile of General Population and Housing Characteristics 2010: Chicago Heights, Illinois," American FactFinder, accessed July 8, 2012, http://factfinder2.census.gov/faces/tableservices/jsf/pages/productview.xhtml?pid=DEC_10_DP_DPDP1.

18. See Wolf v. City of Chicago Heights, United States District Court, N.D. Illinois, E.D., No. 92 CV 8317, June 16, 1993.

19. "Chicago Heights, Illinois: A Striving Community," OccidentalView, February 14, 2012, accessed August 14, 2012, http://occidentalview.wordpress.com/2012/02/14/chicago-heights-illinois-a-striving-community/.

20. Lolly Bowern, "Chicago Heights Overhall Ordered," *Chicago Tribune,* February 10, 2006.

21. Nancy Millman, "Ford Pays $1.5 Million in Area Harassment Suit," *Chicago Tribune,* January 30, 1998.

22. Lisa Donovan, "Racist Antics Cost Trucking Firm $11 Million," *Chicago Sun-Times,* August 15, 2010.

23. Mary Podmolik, "Wells Settles Fair-lending Case," *Chicago Tribune,* July 13, 2012.

24. For example, in 1997, the city put in a bid to attract two correctional institutions to Chicago Heights in an effort to create local jobs. See T. Shawn Taylor, "Chicago Heights To Bid for Two Prisons," *Chicago Tribune,* March 29, 1997.

25. Christopher Paicely, "David Gonzales Will Be the Next Mayor of Chicago Heights," *Chicago Heights Patch,* April 5, 2011, accessed July 18, 2012, http://chicagoheights.patch.com/articles/david-gonzalez-will-be-the-next-mayor-of-chicago-heights. For comparison, on election night in 1913, the newly elected mayor, Lee Hook, announced that the first order of business was to "require saloons to close up promptly a one o'clock every morning.... The second to stop the mechanical music boxes and to remove them entirely from the saloons. ... The third was to station policeman in the vicinity of the bawdy houses and to prevent that traffic" ("Mayor Tackles Clean-up Problem in City Morals," *Chicago Heights Signal,* May 28, 1913).

26. Rufus Schatzberg and Robert Kelly, *African American Organized Crime: A Social History* (New Brunswick, N.J.: Rutgers University Press, 1997).

27. For example, the Illinois Standards Achievement Test (ISAT) scores show that on average 61 percent of students at the predominantly Latino school on the Hill (Garfield Elementary/Middle School) meet the statewide average for reading in the eighth grade. See Illinois State Board of Education, "Student Assessment, Illinois Report Card," accessed August 22, 2012, http://www.isbe.state.il.us/assessment/reading.htm.

28. Joel Perlmann, *Italians Then, Mexicans Now: Immigrant Origins and Second Generation Progress, 1890–2000* (New York: Russell Sage Foundation, 2005), 123–125.

29. For example, the ten-year (2002–2012) average ISAT scores for reading and math in the eighth grade places the predominantly African American, East Side Lincoln Elementary/Middle School near the very bottom of all middle schools in Illinois. See Illinois State Board of Education, "Student Assessment, Illinois Report Card," accessed August 22, 2012, http://www.isbe.state.il.us/assessment/reading.htm.

30. "2012 Illinois School Report Card," *Chicago Tribune,* accessed July 30, 2012, http://schools.chicagotribune.com/city/chicago-heights.

31. James O'Kane, *The Crooked Ladder* (New Brunswick, N.J.: Transaction Publishers, 1992).

32. This should not imply that Outfit muscle and intimidation was absent from the day-to-day operation of the business. As Lutz writes, "A resistant club owner might have been paid a visit by some tough guys that might trash the place or harm the owner physically." See Matthew Luzi, *The Boys in Chicago Heights* (Charleston, S.C.: History Press, 2012), 53. However, these reluctant owners were the exception, for most businesses were only too glad to accept the efficiencies and profits offered by the Outfit's gambling and vending machine operations.

33. Melita Maria Garza and Constanza Montana, "Hispanic Areas on the Grow Dreams of Owning Homes; Businesses Helping These Communities To Flourish," *Chicago Tribune,* September 11, 1991.

34. Frank Main, "Vicious, Violent Drug Cartels Put Chicago Area on Mexican Border," *The Courier News,* November 1, 2011.

35. City Council Meeting, City of Chicago Heights, July 2, 2012, accessed August 11, 2012, http://chicagoheights.net/www/minutes.php?fn_mode=fullnews&fn_id=23.

36. Main, "Vicious, Violent Drug Cartels Put Chicago Area on Mexican Border."

37. "Chicago Heights Officials Try To Keep Up with Unkempt Lawns," City of Chicago Heights, June 26, 2008, accessed June 30, 2012, http://www.chicagoheights.net/www/newsarchive.php?fn_mode=fullnews&fn_id=19.

38. "Murders Plague Chicago Heights," *Southtown Star,* January 26, 2011.

39. "Chicago Heights Summit Aims To Halt Violence," *Southtown Star,* June 5, 2011.

40. For examples of what this might entail, see David Sterrett, Melissa Mouritsen Zmuda, Thomas J. Gradel, and Dick Simpson, *Green Grass and Graft: Corruption in the Suburbs,* Anti-Corruption Report 6 (Chicago: University of Illinois at Chicago, Department of Political Science, 2012).

41. For example, an elected official in New York laid bare once again this underlying conception that there was "something" about Italians that was unsettling, if not hinged to a criminal inclination. Thus, in commenting on the question as to whether New York Governor Andrew Cuomo would be a viable candidate for president in 2016, State Senator Greg Ball said, "I think he is going to have a tough time running for president, first let's be honest he is an Italian American." "Sen. Ball on Andrew Cuomo for President?" *Antico Reports,* July 4, 2011, accessed May 15, 2012, http://www.italystl.com/ra/5131.

42. For a more detailed discussion of the various ways this anti-Italianism has played itself out in American society, see William Connell and Fred Gardaphe (eds.), *Anti-Italianism: Essays of Prejudice* (New York: Palgrave-MacMillan, 2010).

43. Khalil Gibran Muhammad, *The Condemnation of Blackness: Race, Crime, and the Making of Modern Urban America* (Cambridge: Harvard University Press, 2010), 275.

INDEX

LOUIS CORSINO is a professor of sociology at North Central College.

The University of Illinois Press
is a founding member of the
Association of American University Presses.

University of Illinois Press
1325 South Oak Street
Champaign, IL 61820-6903
www.press.uillinois.edu